PHILOSOPHY
AND
FREEDOM

STUDIES IN CONTINENTAL THOUGHT

JOHN SALLIS, GENERAL EDITOR

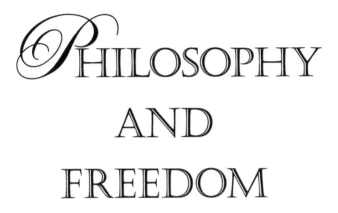

PHILOSOPHY AND FREEDOM

Derrida, Rorty, Habermas, Foucault

John McCumber

INDIANA UNIVERSITY PRESS   BLOOMINGTON & INDIANAPOLIS

THIS BOOK IS A PUBLICATION OF

INDIANA UNIVERSITY PRESS
601 NORTH MORTON STREET
BLOOMINGTON, IN 47404-3797 USA

HTTP://WWW.INDIANA.EDU/~IUPRESS

Telephone orders 800-842-6796
Fax orders 812-855-7931
Orders by e-mail IUPORDER@INDIANA.EDU

THE PAPER USED IN THIS PUBLICATION MEETS THE MINIMUM REQUIRE-
MENTS OF AMERICAN NATIONAL STANDARD FOR INFORMATION SCIENCES—
PERMANENCE OF PAPER FOR PRINTED LIBRARY MATERIALS, ANSI
Z39.48-1984.

MANUFACTURED IN THE UNITED STATES OF AMERICA

LIBRARY OF CONGRESS CATALOGING-IN-PUBLICATION DATA

MCCUMBER, JOHN.
PHILOSOPHY AND FREEDOM: DERRIDA, RORTY, HABERMAS, FOUCAULT /
JOHN MCCUMBER.
P.   CM. — (STUDIES IN CONTINENTAL THOUGHT)
INCLUDES BIBLIOGRAPHICAL REFERENCES AND INDEX.
ISBN 0-253-33697-X (CLOTH : ALK. PAPER) — ISBN 0-253-21363-0
(PBK. : ALK. PAPER)
1. LIBERTY. 2. PHILOSOPHY, MODERN.   I. TITLE.   II. SERIES.

B824.4 .M37 2000
123'.5 21—DC21
99-043396

1 2 3 4 5   05 04 03 02 01 00

TO JONATHAN AND DANIELLE MCCUMBER,
WHO HAVE RAISED ME WELL

AND TO PETER NICHOLAS MCCUMBER

$\mathscr{C}$ONTENTS

ACKNOWLEDGMENTS

I would like to thank the people at Indiana University Press, especially Janet Rabinowitch and Dee Mortensen, for their rare combination of professional excellence and human understanding; my chair, Géza von Molnár, and my former chair, Kenneth Seeskin, for helping me find the time for this book (and others); and John Sallis.

Also to be thanked for general encouragement over the years are Jürgen Habermas, Richard Rorty, and especially Jacques Derrida. I dare to hope that each of them will approve of what I say, at least about the other two.

Parts of chapters 3 and 4 first appeared in "Reconnecting Rorty: The Situation of Discourse in Richard Rorty's *Contingency, Irony, and Solidarity,*" *diacritics* 20 (1990): 2–19.

Parts of chapters 5 and 6 first appeared in "Philosophy as the Heteronomous Center of Modern Discourse: Jürgen Habermas," in Hugh Silverman, ed., *Continental Philosophy I* (London: Routledge & Kegan Paul, 1987), pp. 211–231.

ABBREVIATIONS

AS	Michel Foucault, *L'archéologie du savoir*
CIS	Richard Rorty, *Contingency, Irony, and Solidarity*
CP	Rorty, *Consequences of Pragmatism*
Diss.	Jacques Derrida, *La dissémination*
ED	Derrida, *L'écriture et la différence*
Gramm.	Derrida, *De la grammatologie*
Marges	Derrida, *Marges de la philosophie*
PDM	Jürgen Habermas, *Der philosophische Diskurs der Moderne*
Pos.	Derrida, *Positions*
SP	Foucault, *Surveiller et punir*
TKH	Habermas, *Theorie des kommunikativen Handelns*
VP	Derrida, *La voix et le phénomène*
VS	Foucault, *La volonté de savoir*

References to English translations follow a slash.

PHILOSOPHY
AND
FREEDOM

INTRODUCTION: THE GREAT DEMARCATION

Describing something he called *die große Loslösung,* the Great Getting-Loose, Nietzsche wrote this (I translate):

> One may suspect that a person in whom the genus "free spirit" might at some point sweeten and ripen to perfection has had her decisive event in the form of a *Great Getting-Loose,* prior to which she was all the more a spirit tied down, shackled forever in the corner and to her post. But what binds most securely? Which cords are almost indestructible? . . . The Great Getting-Loose comes suddenly to those thus bound, like a tremor in the earth: the young soul is all at once shaken, ripped free, ripped away: it understands nothing of what is happening. A drive, a force takes over and becomes the soul's master, like a command. A will and wish awakens, a will to go forth, anywhere, at any price: an impassioned, dangerous curiosity about an undiscovered world ignites and flames in all its senses.[1]

A little later he wrote (I translate again):

> "Better to die than live here"—so sounds the masterful voice and seduction: and this "here," this "at my house" is everything that the soul has loved up to now! A sudden horror and rage against what it had loved, a bolt of contempt for what had been its duty, an insurgent, willful, volcanic demand for wandering, for foreign places; for becoming foreign, for grow-

ing cold, growing sober, for glaciation, a hatred for love, perhaps a sacrilegious grip and glance backward, back to what it had until then worshiped and loved, perhaps a blaze of shame for what it has been doing, and simultaneously a jubilation that it has done it, an intoxicated, internal, exuberant shudder, in which a victory betrays itself—A victory? Over what? Over whom? Riddlesome, suggestive, questionable victory, but for all that —the first victory: This sort of unfortunate and painful thing belongs to the story of the Great Getting-Loose.

Still later, he wrote (and I . . .):

In the background of this bustling and roaming—for the freed spirit is restless and underway, without goal, as if wandering in a desert—stands the question mark of an ever more dangerous curiosity: "Can we not overturn all values? And is good not perhaps evil? And God just a discovery and refinement of the devil? Is everything perhaps false in its final ground? And if we are deceived, are we not—precisely because of that—also deceivers? *Must* we not also be deceivers?" Such questions guide and entice the freed spirit, leading it ever farther forth, ever farther off. Solitude encircles and encoils it, ever more threatening, ever more suffocating, ever more heart stifling, choking—solitude, fearsome goddess and *mater saeva cupidinum*, fierce mother of the passions.—But who today knows what *solitude* is?

And then later . . . :

There is an intermediate condition . . . which a person so fated later remembers not without emotion: a pallid, delicate happiness in light and sun, a feeling of birdlike freedom, birdlike panorama, birdlike frolicsomeness, a third condition in which curiosity and tender contempt have bound themselves together. A "free spirit"—this cool phrase does good in that condition, it virtually warms. . . . One lives, no longer in the shackles of love and hate, without yes or no, voluntarily near, voluntarily far, most happily slipping away, turning aside, fluttering forth, off again, again flying upward; one is pampered, as is everyone who has seen a monstrous great variety *beneath* her—and one becomes a counterpart to those who concern themselves with things that do not concern them. Indeed: by this time sheer things concern her—and how many things!—which no longer *trouble* her!

And . . . :

Another step forward in healing and the free spirit approaches life again, slowly to be sure, almost recalcitrantly, almost distrustfully. It grows warmer around her, as if more yellow; feeling and sympathy gain depth, mild winds of all kinds pass over her. It seems to her almost as if her eyes, for the first time, were opening up to what is nearby. She is amazed, and sits still: *where* has she been, then? These near and nearest things: how they seem transformed! What fluff and magic they have acquired in the meantime! She looks back thankfully: back to her wanderings, her hardships and self-alienation, her views from afar and winged flights into cold heavens. How wonderful that she did not remain, like a loving, stolid loafer, always "in my house," always "self-contained." For that she *was* beside herself, there is no doubt. Only now does she see herself, and what surprises she finds! What unsuspected shudders! What happiness still lies in fatigue, in the old illness, in the relapses of recovery! Convalescent! How it pleases her to sit still in her affliction, to spin forth patience, to lie in the sun! Who is as expert as she at happiness in winter, in spots of sun on the wall?

These are the most grateful animals in the world, and the most unassuming, these convalescents and lizards who have turned themselves halfway back toward life.

1. THE GREAT GETTING-LOOSE

Stretched between oppositions it neither resolves nor subverts, Nietzsche's story of the Great Getting-Loose presents contemporary philosophy with a momentous double challenge: to place itself at the disposal not of truth but of freedom; and to construe freedom in terms of situations, not of subjects.

The story conceives the formation of a "free spirit" as getting loose of the house, escape from domesticity. The escape progresses through four stages: rejecting everything that once was loved; wandering in radical solitude; viewing from distant heights; and, finally, returning to a renewed world— renewed precisely because it once furnished the start of this new, and most disjointed, story.

The story is emancipatory in part just because it is disjointed, and in part because it is imaginative rather than literally true. Its imaginative dimension, crudely sketched, works as follows. The protagonist, the "free spirit," is not identified or defined except as someone who goes through the process narrated in the story. As the reader follows that process out, she too of course goes through it—in her imagination. As she does, she imagines herself into the position of such a "free spirit," so that the story becomes her story and the liberation it presents becomes her own. That this liberation takes place "only" in the reader's imagination is not an objection to it but part of how it works. For what imprisons the free spirit at the beginning of the story is, precisely, an incapacity to imagine: her inability to conceive of anything different from what she already knows. Simply knowing that Nietzsche's story is possible frees her from that, and places her on the road of the Great Getting-Loose.

Reading the story is thus the kind of aesthetic liberation envisioned by Heidegger in "The Origin of the Work of Art." In experiencing a work of great art, Heidegger writes,

> ... the extraordinary is thrust to the surface and what seems to be the long-familiar thrust down or overthrown. . . . [the work transports] us out of the

realm of the ordinary.... What went before is refuted in its exclusive reality by the work.[2]

The discontinuities in the story of the Great Getting-Loose are, like its imaginative structure, part of the way it works. For it emancipates its reader by presenting her with—indeed, forcing her imaginatively into—a succession of discontinuities and ruptures. As she goes through it, each of its stages "refutes" old stories, by presenting alternatives to them—to "everything the soul has loved up to now." The story's discontinuity also means that each of its phases similarly "refutes" earlier phases of the story itself. For the overall development shows each stage to be merely part of a larger, looser process, and so deprives it of any claim to absolute self-enclosure.

Nietzsche's story of the Great Getting-Loose thus *situates* the reader: for to be situated, as I have suggested elsewhere,[3] is to be surrounded and defined, not by a set of particular limits, but by the lifting of such limits. In accomplishing this, the Great Getting-Loose opens up a double future, for in telling it Nietzsche sets himself a double goal: on the one hand to unveil or decipher (*entschleiern*, p. 10 ¶ 6) the process of liberation, and on the other hand to generalize it: "How it went with me is how it must go for *everyone*" (p. 11 ¶ 7). This "must" is, presumably, *ethical* in nature. Nietzsche is not predicting what will, by some historical or biological necessity, happen to everyone. His liberation is not a natural process but a task, something that everyone ought to undertake. And so it is not he, Nietzsche, who accomplishes the generalization: that task is for everyone, including ourselves. Nietzsche himself can at most accomplish the first goal: unveiling or deciphering—or, as we might say, "imagining"—the process of liberation.

This is the "first" goal because the two goals which Nietzsche himself sets must be fulfilled in a certain order, which is first to unveil and only then to generalize. For how can we generalize Nietzsche's tale, apply it to our own lives, unless we understand it first? And how can we understand it unless Nietzsche himself, who created it, explains it to us?

At this point, we encounter a pair of suspensions. For Nietzsche's unveilings are, paradoxically, more than a bit dissatisfying. He writes,

> . . . You were to become the master (*Herr*) over yourself; master also, however, over your own virtues. Earlier they were your masters; but now they are to be merely your tools, among other tools. You were to attain authority over your own For and Against, to learn how to bring them out and put them away, always according to your own higher purposes.[4]

This portrayal of the *terminus ad quem* of liberation plays on a contrast—or is suspended—between two types of mastery. One is mastery over oneself *in the name of* virtue; the other is self-mastery, which includes mastery *over* one's own virtues and duties themselves—mastery over morality. The latter form of mastery, of course, is Nietzsche's own invention, deeply opposed to the traditions of Western moral thought. In fact, however, this concept of mastery is a *re*invention; for it is anything but new. Socrates might with pride have found himself addressed by the quote above, for his own style of self-mastery included the placing of all virtues in the service of wisdom. And wisdom was not *a* virtue, but the condition of all virtues: it is Socrates's own true nature, what the oracle at Delphi claimed distinguished him from all other men, his own "determination" (*Bestimmung*).

In a quite traditional sense, indeed, we humans have, for Nietzsche, our *Bestimmung*. It is what "disposes us; even when we are not yet acquainted with it: it is the future, which gives the rule to our Today."[5] Our determination, then, not only makes us different from others; it disposes us even when we are not (yet) acquainted with it. It is, as our future, the *telos* of our lives, which makes us what we are right now. If Nietzsche advances from the Socratic picture, then, the advance is in one respect only to Aristotle. For the free spirit has a fate, and that fate is to be herself. Whatever ruptures and discontinuities the free spirit's life exhibits, it is still the unfolding of what one will turn out to have been all along. The difference with Aristotle, for whom happiness was the telos of human life and rational activity was its determination, is, of course, that for Nietzsche the goal is unknown as long as we are working toward it. As unknown as it was, to give just one ancient example, for Oedipus.

Nietzsche's story of the Great Getting-Loose thus works with both the traditional moral concept of mastery over oneself in the name of virtue, and with Nietzsche's new conception of mastery over one's virtues: it is positioned between Nietzsche's own "new" thought and the tradition which it seeks to engage and subvert. This "new" concept of mastery itself turns out itself to be articulated in quite traditional ways. On both levels, Nietzsche hovers between new ideas and old, between the traditional conceptuality and its subversion. And this holds throughout the story of the Great Getting-Loose. Together with its radical newness, running along through its stages like wolves among the caribou, we find such traditional notions as Determination and Duty and Reverence and Authority, Will and Freedom of the Will, Health, Self-Control, Inner Abundance, Higher Purpose, and others—all incited, of course, by the most lupine of Nietzsche's couplets: the Will to Power.

What ancient words these are; what unquestioned power they dispense! Is any Western conceptuality more traditional than this? In spite of the efforts of many to read Nietzsche as an implacable critic of the Western metaphysical tradition—and in spite of the fact that in important respects he was just that—he clearly remains, in other important respects, its captive. As Heidegger, who is the inspiration for many contemporary readings of Nietzsche, puts it,

> Maintaining the level of power of willing consists in this: that the will surrounds itself with a circle (*Umkreis*) of things to which it can always and reliably resort . . . This circle bounds the reserve (*Bestand*) of present

beings which is immediately disposable for the will (*Ousia* in the everyday meaning of the word among the Greeks). What is reserved (*das Beständige*) is however stabilized (*wird jedoch zu einem Ständigen*), i.e., rendered something which constantly stands at [one's] disposal, in that it is brought to a stand through a positing. . . . Despite all [his] overturnings and revaluings of metaphysics, Nietzsche remains within the unbroken course of its inheritances.[6]

Heidegger's identification of the residual domesticity (*ousia*) in Nietzsche's thought amounts to an accusation that the "free spirit" does not fully break out of its house, but brings it along: that its freedom is merely the freedom of the snail.

Nietzsche's use of a traditional vocabulary to articulate his new thoughts suggests that one form that his residual domesticity takes—one "circle of fixed possessions" which remains reliably at his disposal—consists in the very words in which he tells his story, and the traditional thematics which those words introduce. It seems that while Nietzsche *shows* us liberation as demarcation, as the escape from "everything the soul has loved up to now," he *conceives* and *articulates* it in the terms of his beloved German language, with all its ancient inheritances. It would follow that radical liberation is impossible for him: his language fends it off even as his story depicts it. It is as if the whole process of liberation—the enraged destruction of house and temple, the solitary escape through the forests, the climb and birdlike flight past the highest mountains, and finally the reptilian return to warmth —were not "unveiled" but merely glimpsed—and from a single kitchen corner.

We can save Nietzsche from Heidegger's critique, if we can, only by claiming that his words are not reliable tools at his disposal, but independent proliferators of meaning: new wine fermenting within old skins. And this is, of course, generally quite accurate. From it follows the inexhaustible polyvalence of Nietzsche for contemporary thought. From which, in turn, it follows that Nietzsche's thought (like Hegel's) has always already become what it is not, so that it cannot be overcome. But however accurate this general view of Nietzsche's language may be, it will not quite apply to the present case. For how could words which proliferate their own meanings be "generalizable"? How could Nietzsche claim that "how it went for me is how it must go for everyone" unless his words can be reliably applied to the lives of others? How can they be so applied unless they have stable, universal meanings? What could those meanings be except what they seem to be: the standard meanings, inflected with the metaphysical heritage of the West?

In short: if Nietzsche's account of the Great Getting-Loose can be generalized—as he himself claims—then he is a prisoner of his language and Heidegger's criticism of him holds. And generalization is not merely Nietzsche's own claim or authorial intention. The process of generalizing Nietzsche's story has in fact proceeded apace in contemporary philosophy. For

6

without fully understanding what Nietzsche was writing about—certainly without understanding it any better than Nietzsche himself did—recent Euro-American culture seems not only to have heard his words, but to have taken them to heart.

2. THINKERS OF THE GREAT DEMARCATION

So, at least, I will argue in this book, which seeks to show that the four stages of Nietzsche's Great Getting-Loose are represented by four of the most important philosophers of the late twentieth century: Jacques Derrida, Richard Rorty, Jürgen Habermas, and Michel Foucault, respectively. If I am right, Derrida's explosive displacements of the binaries of metaphysics, Rorty's solitary rambles through "enclaves of freedom," Habermas's ascent to the cold counterfactual heaven of communicative action, and Foucault's serpentine microstudies of power are stages in a process which Nietzsche recounted but did not conceptually unveil. I will call this process, generalized from the Great Getting-Loose, the "Great Demarcation."

That these four thinkers should be located in Nietzsche's narrative in this way is surprising, because they do not at first seem to be localizable in *any* determinate intellectual space, to say nothing of a single story. What do they have to do with each other, and why should they be interconnected via something so different from any of them—a riddlesome story told a century before their time?

If we look at them *in* their time, in the historical period where they live and work, Derrida, Foucault, Habermas, and Rorty are not necessarily so very different from one another. All belong to a single generation, born at a time when history was becoming global enough to produce world wars. Two of them grew up in a Europe dominated by Nazism. Another, an Algerian Jew, grew up in an Africa dominated by Europe. The fourth came of age in an intellectually colonized America. All developed their characteristic insights in a postwar world frozen by ideological truth-claims. It need not be surprising, then, that their thought should challenge powerful hegemonies. In that respect, they are all not only enemies of Hitler but heirs of Nietzsche. Even Habermas.

As such, they make the great step which, too obvious perhaps to be easily recognized, sets them apart from traditional philosophy and together in the Great Demarcation: they advance their various discourses not merely as "true," but as emancipatory. In so doing, they challenge the hegemony of truth over philosophy. Just what sorts of "emancipation" this can bring remains to be seen; but that they claim to be emancipatory in *some* sense is not open to much doubt. Hence, Nietzsche's story of the Great Getting-Loose can be generalized to them: they can enter into the Great Demarcation.

But Nietzsche's problem, alas, can also be generalized. We saw that Nietzsche, wedded to his linguistic heritage, was unable to articulate and state what he so clearly presented: a radically new concept of liberation-through-discontinuity. I will argue in this book that something similar holds for Derrida, Rorty, Habermas, and Foucault. What we will find in them will not be a reasoned account of the overall process, but a set of gestures—unthematized, incomplete, sporadic, and inconsistent—which in effect serve to carry that process forward. I call these gestures "challenges."

Understanding the nature of such challenges would require understanding three sorts of thing. First, we should understand what is being challenged and how. But, since challenge is incomplete, sporadic, and inconsistent, we should also understand why it is that way; which means understanding the *failure* of reflection common to all four thinkers. For, as I will seek to show in this book, their practice, a rich set of challenging gestures, is in fact richer than the reflective accounts they can give of it. Why cannot those who engage in the challenges I have suggested thematize them, complete them, or render them consistent? Finally, it follows from the two-sided nature of this task that we cannot understand challenge as challenge without surpassing it: we must carry out the very reflection which eludes the thinkers of the Great Demarcation. Because it is that failure which relegates their thought to merely "challenging" status, overcoming it will overcome challenge itself. The ground would thus be prepared for an emancipatory thought that is complete, constant, and consistent. I call such emancipatory thought "situating reason." It will not be the task of this book to discuss it in detail,[7] but merely to show how the Great Demarcation, reflectively understood, leads to it. The clue to both the other issues is to be found in the quote from Heidegger above: in his use of the term *ousia* to indicate the residual domesticity in Nietzsche's thought.

3. PRESENCE AND OUSIA

The common Greek meaning of *ousia* was, as Heidegger points out, the household, with its possessions and people (women, children, slaves). Heidegger's analysis of the Will to Power claims, as I have suggested, that in spite of appearances Nietzsche's "free spirit" carries its house along with it.

But Heidegger's quote misses an important point. Being "brought to a stand," rendered dependably present, is necessary for ownership, but hardly sufficient. In order to be subject to my will, a thing must not merely be stable; it must also belong to me and no one else. Domesticity is grounded not merely in the stability of the bounded circle of possessions (an aspect which I call "boundary") but in the fact that everything within that circle is at my disposition—I can order it without resistance, moving my furniture or commanding my slaves (and wife, and children) as I will. And it requires, thirdly, that whatever they produce is as if I produced it myself: I profit from its sale or benefit from its use, and they do so only at my behest. These two traits—my ordering "disposition" over what I own and my "initiative" with respect to its use—are features of the *metaphysical* concept of ousia: the one articulated by Aristotle. The three traits of boundary, disposition, and initiative constitute what I call "ousiodic" structure.

It is, I will argue in this book, ousiodic structure—or, as I will also call it, ousia itself—which the Great Demarcation most deeply contests. Ousia, the "at my house" in the full sense of boundary, disposition, and initiative, is the domesticity which the free spirit seeks to escape but only brings with it. That Heidegger misses this, concentrating his critique on the stability of the owned object and in this reducing ousia to mere presence, is of crucial importance for the thinkers of the Great Demarcation. For when they follow Heidegger in keying their thought to issues concerning presence, they give themselves over to modern philosophy's distinctive obsession with "epistemological" issues: issues of whether and how the mind can have access to what is outside it. Such access is truth, the excellence of presence. In allowing their understanding of themselves to be dominated by the issue of presence and truth—pro and con—the thinkers of the Great Demarcation not only remain in the grip of modernity, but also remain unable to conceptualize the emancipatory character of their own thought.

As long as we remain focused on such issues as the nature of presence and the possibility of truth, we cannot get clear on the Great Demarcation: we cannot see how these thinkers belong together or why. Their mutual encounter will be presented in the usual, obvious, and entirely correct configuration: Rorty and Habermas accept presence, while Derrida and Foucault question it. Rorty and Derrida take as the preferred objects of their acceptance or questioning of presence selected texts which they approach with the aid of their own philosophical imaginations, while Foucault and Habermas turn to more detailed examinations of history and social science.

The main problem with this, and with the philosophical situation it bequeaths us, is that the resulting intellectual grid cannot be philosophically mediated. As a single example of failure at such mediation by two thinkers of the Great Demarcation themselves, I adduce Derrida's famous reaction to Habermas: ". . . Habermas goes on to intervene in, interpret, arbitrate, conclude my debate with Searle without making the slightest reference to my text."[8] The complaint is justified, but where has Derrida ever discussed Habermas in the detail he deserves? If we do not accept presence, it seems, no argument is possible: acceptance vs. questioning cannot be argued out. And whether we make use of imagination or of historical investigation to flesh out the abstract rigors of philosophy is a matter of temperament and abilities, not of reasoned argument.

4. A SHORT HISTORY OF OUSIA

We cannot get clear on the Great Demarcation, then, without seeing it as challenging ousiodic structure, rather than as affirming or questioning presence. In order to do that, and to gauge the scope and power of the challenges presented, we must understand the nature of ousia and the role it has played in Western culture. I began to tell that story in a previous volume, *Metaphysics and Oppression: Heidegger's Challenge to Western Philosophy*.[9] The "history of ousia" contained in that volume is thus a necessary preliminary to the present work. Its relevant portions can be summarized as follows.

4.1. Aristotle's Classical Articulation of Ousia

The story of ousia began, on my telling, with the hylomorphic ontology of Aristotle's *Metaphysics*. There, the idea was advanced that to be a "being," something had to have a structure in which one part or aspect—Aristotle called it the "form" or "essence" of the thing—generated and/or ordered everything within the thing's boundaries, and governed its effects on the world beyond those boundaries. In addition to its definite *boundaries,* then, an ousia exhibited the *disposition* of its form over the rest of it and form's *initiative* with respect to the outside world. The form or essence of a thing was very special, then; every other aspect of the cosmos was either (a) excluded externally, i.e., posited to be beyond the boundaries of the thing; (b) excluded internally, as a part or attribute of the thing but not part of its identity; or (c) disposed by the form or essence, i.e., generated and/or ordered by it.

Aristotle's account is multiply confusing, not least because he also uses "form" to refer, more broadly, to any determinate property of a thing. Moreover, as he well knew, not everything exhibits boundary, disposition, and initiative in plenary form. Beings may have porous boundaries; their parts may relate to each other, not as its central unity disposes, but on their own initiative or randomly; and they may also interact freely with the world outside. A contemporary example, writ large, of such a non-ousiodic entity is the United States, in contrast, for example, to the lamented aspirations of the European nation-state or to the excesses of boundary, disposition, and initiative exhibited by totalitarian regimes. America's boundaries, for example, are notoriously porous—in part because they are designed to be: foreigners can become American in ways they cannot become French, German, or Russian. Similarly, the country is not ordered by a single sovereign body, but has a bewildering plurality of governmental bodies designed to be at odds with one another; and its actions on the world outside its borders are hardly initiated by some single authority.

Aristotle thus arrives at a concept of "being" which does not apply to all beings, and he resolves this problem in two ways. Theoretically, he instates ousiodic structure as the model for intelligibility: since form is what is intelligible, things can be understood only to the degree that they coincide with their forms—to the degree that their forms alone account for their internal order and their effects on the outside world. Hence the unintelligibility of the sublunary realm, where matters are many and obstreperous.

But that realm is where we live; and with respect to the human world, the concept of ousia becomes practical, i.e., acquires normative status. This is most evident in Aristotle's moral hierarchy, which is keyed to the power of reason. On its highest level, that of the *phronimos,* reason orders desire without resistance, and from it proceed all the person's acts. The reason of the *phronimos* thus has dispositive and initiatory power over his moral self. On the lowest level, reason in the *akolastos* is pushed around by desires emanating from his matter, and acts according to them: the form is controlled by the matter. The same sort of thing, I have argued, holds in the other two domains of Aristotle's version of the human realm: the household and the polis.

The normative status of ousia in the human world is grounded for Aristotle in nature itself. As he puts it in the *Politics,* defining the West at its outset:

> in all things which are composed out of several other things, and which come to be some single common thing . . . in all of them there turns out to be a distinction between that which rules, and that which is ruled; and this holds for all ensouled things by virtue of the whole of nature. . . .[10]

It is *philosophy,* of course, which enables Aristotle to say this. For it is philosophy which first, as metaphysics, establishes ousiodic structure as the nature of Being—and then draws the consequences for ethics, economics, and politics. Thus, for Aristotle ousia is the middle term between philosophy and social and political issues. It remains so for the thinkers of the Great Demarcation; but since they cannot see ousia, the connection is difficult to fathom, as in Derrida and Foucault, and easy to deny, as in Rorty. Only Habermas even seems to retain it—but, as we will see, he does so at the price an attempted divorce from the substantive philosophical tradition, reinterpreting the discipline into the position of "place holder" and "interpreter."

The Middle Ages—represented in my narrative by Thomas Aquinas—innovated significantly on Aristotle's original conception. For one thing, Aquinas clearly distinguishes between a weak form of being, in which to be is to be the subject of a true proposition (even a negative one: the subject of "the golden mountain does not exist" has being in this sense), and a stronger sense which has to do with substantial forms. For another, the boundaries of a thing are no longer established by the thing's form, as they were for Aristotle. Rather it is God who shapes matter up into the discrete clumps we call "bodies," which are then fit to receive forms, substantial and otherwise. This process is called the "designation" of matter. But the ancient pattern of legitimation continues: ousia, its new format decreed by God, justifies ethical stances and social relationships.

4.2. Modern Retentions of Ousia

This overall pattern of legitimation ran into problems in the modern era. For ousiodic structure, under such names as "final causes" and "substantial forms," was found not to exist in nature, which became merely the field of interplay of matter and force. This rendered suspect the normative status of ousia in the human realm. But ousia could not be dispensed with as the basic norm for the human world. For then, presumably, that world itself would become a mere chaos of material forces—a possibility sketched with persuasive repugnance in Hobbes's account of the state of nature.

Faced with this impasse, modern philosophy reacted with two different strategies. Those who are called "Rationalists" relocated ousiodic structure from nature to a divine or "supersensible" realm: Spinoza's account of "substance" and Leibniz's of the "Kingdom of Grace" are prime examples. The Empiricists were more radical. They did not relocate ousia to a supersensible world but simply reinstated it, unargued and unacknowledged, as the supreme evaluative standard for the human world. Hobbes's Leviathan and Locke's property owner, for example, exhibit boundary, disposition, and initiative in ways that are never explicitly recognized or justified—and which function all the more absolutely for that. Thus we get the modern subject: an ousia existing in a "de-ousiafied" nature of matter in motion.

Modernity, then, hardly dispenses with ousia. But it occludes it, and in two main ways. First, the very fact that ousia had been driven from nature was covered over by modern philosophy's concern with a somewhat different issue: that of what I call "substance," the substrate or bearer of properties. This concern has its historical warrant: ousia was first articulated by Aristotle, in his *Categories*, as such a substrate, or "primary substance"; his hylomorphic modifications of that doctrine begin in his *Physics*. In modern philosophy, the existence and nature of substrates becomes a difficult obsession, as is shown by the problems with Descartes's *res corporea*, Locke's "x I know not what," and Kant's noumenon. But this entire problematic covers over a more basic question, which is that of why the existence and nature of such substrates became important in the first place. In fact, the whole issue presupposes the nonexistence, in nature, of final causes and substantial forms.

The substrate as a bearer of sensible properties eventually had to go, for it was incompatible with the absolute boundaries of the modern subject. In more Berkeleyan language (for it was Berkeley who established this), the material substrate was incompatible with the *generic* difference between ideas and matter. When Kant rearticulated the idea of the substrate as something immanent to the mind—as a characteristic of ideas, or "representations," themselves, rather than as something supporting them from outside the mind—he did so in terms of his own category of substance, which was defined in terms of its permanence and independence with respect to other representations.

This brought substance into overt connection with presence. For being permanent meant that a substance could persist unchanged: an intellectual "snapshot" of it (a true sentence in the present tense) taken (or asserted) at one time would look just like snapshots of it taken at other times. And because it was independent, such snapshots could be taken of it alone. Such a Kantian substance, as Derrida would put it, could then be "summed up (*résumée*) in some absolute simultaneity or instantaneity."[11] This quality is what Derrida, like others, calls "presence." In becoming obsessed with substrates, then, modern philosophy became obsessed with presence.

The modern subject, when it looks outward, finds only more or less stable and independent ideas: it finds a domain of the merely present. Looking inward, it finds—but does not name, and therefore occludes—all the structures of traditional ousia. The Hobbesian state and the Lockean property owner, for example, exhibit the features of boundary, disposition, and initiative, which are "reinstated" to structure them unargued, undiscussed, and indeed unmentioned. In the individual Cartesian, Hobbesian, or Kantian mind, disposition over ideas—their right ordering—is achieved by intellect or reason, i.e., by philosophy. Initiative with respect to the external world is exercised by the will—which for Kant at least is explicitly the same thing as reason.

4.3. Modern Challenges to Ousia

Deprived of their metaphysical justification, however, these structures seem to hang in the air, and are increasingly subject to challenge (the more so after the Rationalist relocation of them to a divine realm independent of the mind lost plausibility). The traditional hierarchy in the human mind, for example, is upended in Hume's famous statement that "reason is, and ought to be, the slave of the passions."[12] The structures of state sovereignty are challenged in thought by Locke, and in practice by the Americans: governors derive their just powers from the consent of the governed. As the centuries roll on, challenges multiply: Freud, Marx, and Nietzsche all seek to overturn or modify relations of ousiodic dominance on the human world, and their various writings are taken as battle cries by multitudes.

Two of the many discourses of challenge in recent philosophy, however, operate somewhat differently from the above examples: they concern philosophy itself. "Philosophy," as I use the term here, is not merely what it seems to be (not accidentally) to so many: an arcane and fruitless discipline dedicated to arguing about the unprovable. For philosophy has had, since Aristotle, a peculiarly intimate, and important, relationship with ousia. For Aristotle, philosophy was the argued importation of ousiodic structure from nature into the human realm: a grand train of thought that began in metaphysics and ended in ethics, economics, and politics. Whatever we may think of the arguments, Aristotle's whole enterprise is keyed to ousia from first to last.

When ousiodic structure was dismissed from nature, it is noteworthy that philosophy went as well: the study of nature was reassigned to natural science. Philosophy for its part concentrated mainly on the human realm. It no longer imported ousiodic structures into that realm from nature, but sought to establish them there in their own right. In this effort, philosophy did not merely *employ* ousiodic structure as a norm for the human world; it *enforced* it as well. It was by means of philosophy, for such modern thinkers as Descartes, Hobbes, Hume, and Spinoza, that the intellect ordered its ideas, thus establishing the disposition of reason over the mind.[13] It is metaphysical reflection and discussion, in the view of Kant's "Transcendental Doctrine of Method" at the end of the *Critique of Pure Reason,* which consolidate the hegemony of the rational will. The complicities of philosophy with ousiodic structure are so deep, indeed, that when they came to be challenged—first by Hegel and Heidegger—the challenges themselves were not understood.

Freud and Marx, like Hume and Locke before them, had challenged ousiodic structure outside philosophy, and to do so had used the standard philosophical toolbox: argument in the service of true assertions. But the paramount status of assertional truth as the single goal of philosophy is itself, as will be argued in more detail later, an artifact of ousiodic structure. It presupposes a bounded domain, "philosophy," which is distinct from such other discursive pursuits as poetry, rhetoric, and, later, natural science. It accords to that domain an initiative, for the true assertions it produces will find their way into other minds and perhaps the social order. And it disposes the production of such assertions in accordance with the laws and rules of logical argumentation. Hence, the traditional philosophical toolbox, tailored to ousiodic structure, was inadequate to contest that structure in the case of philosophy itself. Hegel and Heidegger thus found themselves required to enlarge that toolbox, but their new tools, I have argued elsewhere, have not been understood. That does not keep them from being employed by the thinkers of the Great Demarcation.

4.4. Heidegger and the Play of Diakena

Metaphysics and Oppression did not deal with Hegel in detail, and I will follow that policy here. Heidegger, for his part, adopts Aristotle's model of a being as something which comes to be via a sort of gathering, as when a form gathers matter to itself. But what does the gathering, for Heidegger, is not an intelligible determinate plenitude—not a form—but an active nothing, or what I have called a diakenon. Diakenic unification as Heidegger presents it is characterized by three traits:

A. None of the components so unified is adequately understood apart from the others.

B. None is the ground of the others, i.e., explains them.

C. No yet more basic phenomenon can ground, i.e., explain, all of them together.

With an emptiness at its core, a diakenon—or, as Heidegger himself calls it in his later writings, a "thing" (*Ding*)—cannot be closed within its boundaries the way an ousia is.[14] For emptiness is emptiness: the gathering center of a Heideggerean diakenon is not distinguishable from those at the centers of other such things. By the principle of the identity of indiscernibles, all such centers are identical: a diakenically constituted thing is open to the outside world not at its boundaries, but at its core. Similarly, a nothing cannot order or generate the components of the thing it unifies; those components are independent beings which engage in a gathering interplay in their own right. And finally, a thing so unified cannot exercise determinate initiative: all it can do is open up emptinesses in other things.

Diakenic interplays cannot, in the final analysis, be described: they cannot be captured in a set of true sentences which leave them as they were. For there is, in the case of diakena, no "as they were." A diakenon is defined by the nothing at its core, which—since it is nothing—cannot be described. The interplay which it sets in motion is unpredictable and unstable, and is an interplay with us: any activity of ours, such as describing it, affects it. The purpose of such Heideggerean writings as "The Thing" is to put diakena into play, allowing them to operate, first by clearing away the "metaphysical" views that kept readers from recognizing their possibility and then by actually carrying on their interplay.[15]

But Heidegger, like Hegel, never adequately clarifies just what he is up to. In *Being and Time,* for example, he is unable to describe the Nothing at the core of world, and is forced instead—since he is committed to describing *something*—to describe the structures of Dasein's inherence in world, from which world's structures could somehow be read off. Dissatisfied with this "unconditional inherence" of Dasein in world, Heidegger later changes his ways. But his explanations of the procedures of those later writings are so terse and cryptic that many readers, including Habermas,[16] see no "procedures" there at all—only dogmatic ranting. Heidegger is not only unclear about the concerns and gestures of his own thought, but commits a *protê hamartia* which keeps him from such clarity: as we saw in the criticism of Nietzsche adduced earlier, he mistakes the nature of what he is challenging. He considers it to be stable presence (the substrate), rather than the structures of domination peculiar to ousia. In this respect, the founder of "postmodernity" continues modernity's obsession with presence.

5. CHALLENGE IN THE GREAT DEMARCATION

It is clear that, when the ousiodic structures of philosophy itself become challenged, it is a momentous occasion. For it means that ousiodic structure in general is about to be deprived of its own final legitimacy, and that a new age is (once again) at hand: an age in which ousiodic structure is at best an occasional unfortunate (but perhaps necessary) feature of the human realm, rather than its single most basic norm. This, and nothing less, is the promise of the Great Demarcation when it raises—however surreptitiously—the problematic of philosophy and freedom.

As will be seen, there are many ways in which philosophy can exhibit ousiodic structure. It can, as Aristotle did, take such structure as its basic model and apply it to various domains. But it can also constitute itself according to such structure, and this too in several ways. It can take itself as a discourse which has a single ordering form—traditionally, logic as a means to the telos of truth.[17] Or it can constitute a community of philosophers which itself is structured according to ousiodic norms: as a closed community with certain goals and structured by certain principles. All these ways, and others, will be challenged by the thinkers of the Great Demarcation.

The ways in which ousiodic structure in general is challenged can also, as will be seen, take a variety of forms. Something may be criticized for exhibiting ousiodic structure, though without that fact being stated. Various ousiai may be redescribed in terms which turn out, upon investigation, to be non-ousiodic. Alternatives to ousiodic structure may be advanced, though under other names. And what escapes ousiodic structure completely may be invoked in various ways. The thinkers of the Great Demarcation, I will seek to show, engage constantly in this sort of thing. But they are unable to carry out their challenges reflectively—to convert them from mere, almost instinctual, gestures into fully explicit, consistent critiques. The reason for this can now also be sketched: it is because Derrida, Rorty, Habermas, and Foucault retain two salient features of the modern occlusion of ousia.

One of these, attributable primarily to Derrida and Foucault, is the occlusion of ousia by substrates, or with the issue of what is or can be independent and permanent in experience. Since independence and permanence, as noted above, are traits of presence, antipathy to presence easily translates to a continuance of the modern "obsession" with substance; the thought of Derrida and Foucault, I will argue, is (mis)directed against presence itself, rather than against its (ousiodic) dominance over philosophy. And since presence is the condition of discourse—nothing can be spoken of that is not to some degree permanent and independent of other things—Derrida and Foucault find themselves at an impasse: they must either become unintelligible or disown their own critique.

The other continuation of modernity, attributable primarily to Habermas and Rorty, is to reinstate, unacknowledged, the structures of ousia within one's own discourse itself, while contesting versions of them elsewhere in philosophy. Thus exhibiting ousiodic structure, such discourse faces an alternative: either to remain within its own distinct "enclave" (Rorty), or to seek to expand its sway by introducing its own structures into other realms, such as political debate (Habermas).

Like Nietzsche, then, none of these thinkers gets beyond the philosophical tradition they seek to criticize. "Postmodernity" remains in their hands an impossible project, for it remains bound to the modernity it rejects— much as Hegel's ascetic consciousness remains famously bound to the body it continually mortifies. If I am right, "postmodernity" understood rigor- ously is impossible because we cannot get beyond "modernity" without also getting beyond the more ancient structures of which it is merely the latest manifestation, those of ousia itself. This, I think, is a key point. We can never get "beyond modernity" by rejecting such concepts as clarity, truth, rigor, and intelligibility, for *modernity never adhered to them in the first place*. Its oc- clusion of ousia as the structuring principle of the human realm worked in the service of ousia and rendered modernity a giant adventure in obfusca- tion, falsification, prattle, and incomprehension. The real problem today is to articulate forms of thought that would be, not "postmodern," but "post- ousiodic." Until we do, we are still trying to think through liberation from within Nietzsche's kitchen corner.

6. BEYOND THE GREAT DEMARCATION

It is thus no timid reinstatement of modern categories of reflection to say that the failure of the Great Demarcation is its failure to understand it- self. The Great Demarcation's failure of lucidity is its failure to get beyond modernity, which made such lack of self-understanding into a principle too basic to be expressed. The success of the Great Demarcation lies in the rich repertory of anti-ousiodic gestures by which it seeks, and to some extent achieves, the emancipation of philosophy from ousiodic structure. When we see philosophy this way, as this book will seek to show, its thinkers come into productive confrontation with one another. Can such confrontation yield a new (or perhaps, yet again, very old) conception of thought as no longer challenging ousiodic structure, but as operating beyond it—as genu- inely "postousiodic"?

I will merely adumbrate this issue, in the concluding chapter of this book; even to do that, however, will require an external framework. The thinkers of the Great Demarcation, I have suggested and will argue, cannot under- stand themselves on their own terms. An external framework, that of ousia and its history, is required for this. Such an external framework is also re- quired to go beyond them: the new "paradigm" for which their thought calls cannot be simply developed, as Hegel would have tried to do, out of their thought itself. I began to explore such a framework in my *Poetic Interaction*.[18] The results of that investigation, like my history of ousia, will be appealed to at various points in this book, though not with the same urgency.

I argued in that book that freedom is intrinsic to language itself, even its most ordinary varieties. In this it is unlike truth, which is only indirectly related to language. For a language-game or discourse is never intrinsically true; its truth is not guaranteed by it alone but must be established by such other means as the rigor of its argumentation or its adequacy to the facts. Speech, however, can be intrinsically emancipatory, in that simply to engage in certain types of language-game *is* to achieve a sort of freedom. Such speech is "poetic interaction."

There are, most basically, four types of such interaction. All begin with an utterance that cannot be understood, in the traditional sense of having a single meaning assigned to it, because it has either more than one meaning or fewer; it is either ambiguous or senseless. In poetic interaction, the speaker cannot be appealed to as the decisive instance for her own words: it is up to the hearer to "make" a meaning for them, a demand for which I adapted the original Greek sense of *poiêsis*. Senseless or ambiguous utterances can be responded to poetically either with an utterance that is itself senseless or ambiguous, and thus continues the encounter as poetic, which I called "non-terminating" poetic interaction; or with one which creates a single meaning for the utterance and thus "terminates" the encounter as poetic. The four types of poetic interaction, which I argued corresponded to meanings of "freedom" which have been developed (and in some cases forgotten) by the philosophical tradition, were then as follows:

(1) *Terminating normal poetic interaction:* an utterance is ambiguous and the hearer chooses, from the possibilities resident in the language, a meaning for it.

(2) *Nonterminating normal poetic interaction:* an utterance is ambiguous, and the hearer responds with another utterance which is likewise ambiguous.

(3) *Terminating abnormal poetic interaction:* an utterance has no meaning at all, but appears to be a senseless combination of known words; the hearer responds by inventing a meaning for it.

(4) *Nonterminating abnormal poetic interaction:* an utterance has no meaning at all, and the hearer responds with a similarly meaningless utterance.

Though types of poetic interaction are "normal," none of them is "normed": *Poetic Interaction* offered no account of what distinguished a "good" case of, say, terminating normal poetic interaction from a "bad" or defective one. I suggested, however, that norms could be formulated to make such distinctions. When that had been done, poetic interaction—so long ignored and occluded in political thought and philosophy of language—would become criticizable, or "rational"; it would become what I called "situating reason."

The four thinkers of the Great Demarcation, I will argue, in fact present us with versions of the four types of poetic interaction. The alignment will be as follows:

(1) Terminating normal poetic interaction: Foucault

(2) Nonterminating normal poetic interaction: Habermas

(3) Terminating abnormal poetic interaction: Rorty

(4) Nonterminating abnormal poetic interaction: Derrida

It is thus the account of poetic interaction which will provide the basis, alien to all four thinkers, for understanding and going beyond their work.

That the thinkers of the Great Demarcation contest ousiodic structure in philosophy itself is what makes them different from earlier challengers of such structure; it is what places them into the wake of Hegel and Heidegger. But focusing on it makes them seem arcane, for the nature of philosophy itself is widely held to be, today, both a closed and a trivial matter. Hence, my discussions here will tend to focus not on what are usually taken to be the central topics of the central texts of the thinkers of the Great Demarcation, but on a series of subthemes to which those thinkers themselves rarely attend.

I hope to show that, however abstruse they seem, the challenges to philosophy in the Great Demarcation are momentous. To be momentous does not mean to be public or decisive; something can be momentous without being acknowledged or even understood. To be momentous is to have a certain relation to time: it means to be the point of departure for a wide variety of new kinds of thing.

But ground must be prepared for such departures. If they are reflective, as philosophy must be, this means that "new sorts of thing" must already be going on, requiring only to be reflectively formulated to trigger changes. So it is with the challenges of the Great Demarcation: they are already going on, and their momentousness requires only—but oh, how profoundly—to be understood.

CHALLENGES TO OUSIA IN THE WORK OF
JACQUES DERRIDA

*"Better to die than live here"—so sounds the masterful voice
and seduction: and this "here," this "at my house" is everything
that the soul has loved up to now! A sudden horror and rage
against what it had loved, a bolt of contempt for what had been
its duty, an insurgent, willful, volcanic demand for wandering,
for foreign places; for becoming foreign . . . perhaps a sacrilegious grip and glance backward, back to what it had until then
worshiped and loved, perhaps a blaze of shame for what it has
been doing, and simultaneously a jubilation that it has done it,
an intoxicated, internal, exuberant shudder, in which a victory
betrays itself—A victory? Over what? Over whom? Riddlesome,
suggestive, questionable victory, but for all that—the first
victory: this sort of unfortunate and painful thing belongs
to the story of the Great Demarcation.*

Martin Heidegger ("the masterful voice and seduction") committed many
sins, both personally and philosophically; but in his philosophical life, at
least, he also avoided a few. It will prove useful, in assessing the thinkers of
the Great Demarcation, to begin by noting the specific sins that each attributes to Heidegger.

For the Derrida of "The Ends of Man," Heidegger's sin emerges from his
concept of authenticity. This, in turn, is held to be predicated upon a concept of proximity: world for Heidegger is structured so that some things are
nearer to Dasein than other things. Nearest of all to Dasein is its "ownmost
possibility": death. The pejorative language in which *Being and Time* famously presents inauthenticity[1] thus manifests not merely the valorizing of authenticity over inauthenticity, but more deeply the valorizing of what is
"near," "own," and "proper." Inauthenticity is bad in Heidegger's view, according to Derrida, because it assumes a distance from what is our own.
Heidegger's presentation of it, in Derrida's view, manifests what he calls

> ... the *dominance*, in the discourse of Heidegger, of a whole metaphoric of
> proximity, of simple and immediate presence, associating to the nearness

of Being the values of neighboring, shelter, *house,* service, guard, voice, and listening.[2]

There is a curious sense in which this criticism echoes Heidegger's own criticism of Nietzsche, which I discussed in the introduction: both target a residual "domesticity" in the thinker criticized. For Heidegger, that domesticity was defined as the heritage of metaphysics; for Derrida, it is a "whole metaphoric of . . . simple and immediate presence." Until we understand how Derrida's "metaphoric" relates to Heidegger's "metaphysics," we cannot know whether Derrida's criticism of Heidegger does not rather betoken a secret alignment with him.

I will follow Rodolphe Gasché in largely limiting myself to Derrida's works up to *Glas.*[3] This is not because the later Derrida does not contain important challenge to ousia, but because my ultimate concern is not with those gestures. I seek, rather, to bring out a certain lack—indeed, a defining empty space—in Derrida's thought. For the manifold challenges to ousia that are found in that thought (as in that of the other thinkers of the Great Demarcation) are never identified as such. In this regard, the later works prolong the earlier ones: no discussion of ousia, as I have defined it, is to be found in any of them.

1. THE PROMISE OF DECONSTRUCTION

It is clear from the above quote that the early, openly "deconstructive" work of Derrida challenges, among other things, domesticity. If Heidegger, in spite of his criticism of Nietzsche, ultimately remains within the "House of Being," Derrida seems to want out of the house altogether.[4] What sort of "house" does Derrida seek to escape? Is the object of Derrida's challenge an unnamed version of ousia? If so, does that version share Heidegger's fateful reduction of ousia to presence? (*"Better to die than live here"—so sounds the masterful voice and seduction: and this "here," this "at my house" is everything that the soul has loved up to now!*)

In this chapter, I will argue that Derrida's earlier works in fact contain a set of diverse and fecund challenges to ousiodic structure. In the next, I will claim that Derrida sometimes misidentifies the object of his challenges as "presence." This misidentification is neither overt nor fatal, for it is incomplete: "presence" itself has a variety of meanings for Derrida. The term not only covers the sense of stability and independence to which I referred in the introduction, but is also at times shorthand for what Derrida calls the "privileging" of presence. This, crudely put, is the view that all knowledge, discourse, and (it follows) action must in various ways be geared to, and support, "presence" in the previous, narrower sense. The privileging of presence, I will argue, is Derrida's characteristic version of ousia. His failure to distinguish it from presence itself, being inconsistent, does not impeach the challenging nature of his philosophical practice. But it makes it difficult to account reflectively for that practice, and obscures its relation to the "political" sphere as more traditionally conceived. I will call this situation the "Derridean Knot," and will suggest that the knot can be unraveled by *unambiguously* taking ousia—the "privileging" of presence in its many guises—rather than presence itself as the object of Derridean challenge.

Derrida's criticism of Heidegger, as quoted above, shows the challenging, liberating aspect of his own thought. For it shows that among the many problems addressed by Derrida's concern with domesticity is that of domination. It is bad enough, one would think, that Heidegger's thought could be domestic, or even domesticated. But if his thought is actually "dominated" by the proximity of Being, and if, moreover, this domination is exercised through devices as unphilosophical as metaphors, then we must hope that Heidegger (and we) could be freed from it. And in general, Derrida's thought *seems* to promise a sort of emancipation. Consider the following:

> ... It can be shown that these presuppositions and all the oppositions thus accredited form a system: we circulate from one to the other within the same structure. . . . A reflection must be undertaken today in which "positive" discovery and the "deconstruction" of the history of metaphysics, in all its concepts, supervise one another respectively, minutely, laboriously. Without that, any *epistemological liberation* risks being illusory or limited, merely proposing practical conveniences or notional simplifications whose bases remain untouched by criticism.[5]

We "circulate" from one presupposition/opposition to another within the same closed structure, as from room to room of a house whose outside doors may, for all we know, be locked. In order to achieve a liberation which is more than illusory or limited, a "deconstruction" of metaphysical concepts is necessary. Deconstruction thus promises a genuine (if "epistemological") liberation, and this promise is, I will argue, constitutive for Derridean discourse. On at least one level of that discourse, a promise of liberation *must* be held out—just as, on another level, it *must* be retracted.

The promise is ambiguous not only as to its status but with respect to its content, for Derrida is unclear as to what we are to be liberated *from*. On the level of his actual practice, as I will argue, the promised liberation seeks to free us from the kind of domination I have associated with ousia; as will be seen, this means liberation from the philosophical domination of presence. But when Derrida is reflecting upon his own enterprise, the promised liberation is often not from the domination of presence, but from presence itself: not from the "imperialism" of the logos, but from logos *tout court*.[6]

It is therefore unsurprising that, as the term *epistemological* itself suggests, the domination to be challenged resides in thought and language, and especially in what is called "philosophy" or "metaphysics":

> Very schematically: an opposition of metaphysical concepts (for example, speech/writing, presence/absence) is never the face-to-face of two terms, but a hierarchy and an order of subordination. . . . Deconstruction does not consist in passing from one concept to another but in the overturning and displacement of a conceptual order, as well as of the nonconceptual order with respect to which that conceptual order is articulated.[7]

For Derrida, Heidegger's valorization of authenticity over inauthenticity, and more generally his preference for proximity over distance, are instances of this still wider genus of binary domination. "Overturning" and "displacing" such domination becomes liberation when we recognize that in the modern world, domination (as opposed, for example, to authority) tends to be viewed as an evil. We moderns cannot become aware of domination *as* domination without wishing to be free of it. Merely by overturning and displacing, and indeed simply by exposing, cases of domination inherent in metaphysics, Derrida awakens in modern readers the wish to be free of them. Simply by highlighting the nature of metaphysical domination— for example, by using and justifying phrases such as "logocentric repression" and "subordination"—Derrida's discourse inevitably awakens the wish to be free of that repression and subordination, and tacitly holds out a promise that such liberation is possible. For what could be more wrong than intentionally to awaken in someone a wish that can never be granted? What could be more in tune with modernity than the Kantian formula that Ought implies Can?

The liberation so promised is, to be sure, restricted in scope: as the overturning and displacing of a conceptual order, it is not directly aimed at such "nonconceptual orders" as writers, readers, or societies. It aims at "freeing" the subordinate terms themselves, not the humans who use them (many criticisms of Derrida by, for example, old-line social theorists rest upon a prejudiced absolutizing of this distinction).[8] These repressed terms have, at least since the ancient *Eklogê enantiôn,* been defined in the West merely as "different" from their dominating partner: as evil, for example, is traditionally defined as the absence of good, error as the deficiency of cognition, darkness as the privation of light—or the female as the sickness of the male.[9] A Derridean example of one such subordinated term is "writing" (*écriture*), and writing is in a pitiable state indeed: it is a

> theme which is debased, marginalized, repressed, displaced, but [which nonetheless] exercises a permanent and obsessive pressure from the place where it is contained.[10]

Writing thus seems to be in an intellectual position akin to the repression of the ancient wife, enclosed within her home and not to be spoken of—and yet permanently and obsessively indispensable to the well-being and public behavior of her husband.

We are here approaching one of Derrida's most original insights: that the repressions and oppressions of society at large are not unlike what happens in and to its most basic texts.[11] Though Derrida's primary concern, of course —and for reasons yet to be broached—is with binary domination as it operates in texts, such domination is a much more pervasive phenomenon than that. For through its importance to metaphysics, binary domination turns out to be central as well to other discourses and practices which metaphysics grounds and articulates.[12] Derrida, indeed, does not hesitate to attribute enormous breadth to its sway. Pedagogical institutions such as the university, in perpetuating the domination of metaphysics, themselves fall victim to it.[13] The discourse of ethnology, with all its malign Eurocentric consequences for the Third World, also belongs to the metaphysical domain.[14] Science itself, in spite of some challenges, is also part and parcel of binary domination.[15] Such binary oppositions as inside/outside (with the former, as in Heidegger, dominating) inhere not only in learned discourse but in all our language. For all are shot through by the quest for a "transcendental signified"—a quest which

> is not imposed from outside by some such thing as "philosophy," but by everything which connects our language, our culture, our "system of thinking" to history and to the system of metaphysics.[16]

The sway of metaphysics—the conceptual order predicated upon binary domination—thus comes to implicate the entirety of the Occident, "with all [its] methods of analysis, explication, reading, and interpretation."[17]

2. "DECONSTRUCTIVE" "PROCEDURE"

We still do not know exactly what constitutes that sway. We have seen that the "from which" of the deconstructive promise of liberation is extremely broad: deconstruction comes to "instigate the subversion of every kingdom."[18] Such global subversion, promising liberation from omnipresent and multifarious evils, cannot of course be a single uniform process. Derrida's texts contain numerous and varied enterprises of overturning and displacement, and, as with Hegel, his greatest achievements lie in the concrete gestures by which he carries out these enterprises. As mentioned above, I do not seek here to inventory those gestures or establish their rationales, necessary though that is. My aim here is merely to understand deconstruction's promise of liberation in a general way, and this requires at least a general, if unavoidably schematic and provisional, formulation of deconstructive procedure. Such a formulation can be gleaned from certain of Derrida's texts—in particular "Signature, événement, contexte" and the discussion of method in "L'exorbitant."[19] As presented there, the liberation of metaphysical terms from their binary domination by other terms comports, in general, three phases. They do not follow one another in any kind of neat temporal succession, but must be worked on simultaneously.

(1) The subordinate term in a binary (e.g., writing, absence, distance, inauthenticity) is no longer relegated to being merely "different" from its opposite, but is thematized on its own account: the binary is inverted and what I will call a "counter-binary" is produced. (*A sudden horror and rage against what it had loved, a bolt of contempt for what had been its duty . . .*)

(2) The effects of this inversion are then measured: we locate the domicile of the original differentiation (*écart*) of the two terms, which preceded the setting in place of their binary opposition (*this "at my house" is everything that the soul has loved up to now!*).

(3) This domicile is given a name. Out of the "differantial" relation of the newly valorized term to the formerly dominant one there emerges, in the third phase, a new term—*pharmakon* is only one of them—which is no longer complicitous with the ancient hierarchy of domination, but permits us to fathom the ground and lack of ground for the original binary with which we began. That binary is thus not merely inverted (as in step 1, which would only amount to substituting a new relation of metaphysical domination for the old one), but displaced or rendered "non-pertinent."[20] (*An insurgent, willful, volcanic demand for wandering, for foreign places; for becoming foreign . . .*)

It is important to (3) that the name which is given to the new "concept" be an old one already in use in the language (such as *hymen, play, writing, violence*). This "paleonymy" means that the production of new meaning does not simply run its course in the pure ether of Derrida's thought, but announces itself as a disturbance of or intervention in our inherited language.[21] (*Perhaps a sacrilegious grip and glance backward, back to what it had until then worshiped and loved, perhaps a blaze of shame for what it has been doing, and simultaneously a jubilation that it has done it, an intoxicated, internal, exuberant shudder . . .*)

For present purposes, these are the basic steps of what has come to be known as "deconstruction." Many things remain to be clarified in it, including most particularly the precise nature of the emancipatory displacement in (3). The aim of my general and provisional formulation here is not to achieve a definitive analysis of what Derrida is all about, but to permit a crucial set of questions:

The metaphysical binary, with its instatement of one side of an opposition as intelligible and valuable, sounds (if, at present, only vaguely) like a conceptual version of the Aristotelian dominance of form over matter which I sketched in the introduction and have explicated elsewhere. Are Derrida's gestures of "overturning" and "displacing" directed against the three traits of domination inherent in ousia? Is the assignment of otherness and difference to one member of the pair anything other than its relegation to the traditional unintelligibility of matter, to be disposed by form?[22] Is the cohabitation of the two terms in what I have called a common "domicile" their collocation, if not behind a wall, at least in a region apart (*a l'écart*)? And is not to render this opposition "nonpertinent" simply to deprive it of effect, of initiative?

3. DECONSTRUCTIVE CHALLENGES TO OUSIA IN GENERAL

In part, I will argue, the answer can only be Yes. Consider, for example, what Derrida has to say about the *pharmakon:*

> . . . it is not, in any sense of the word (metaphysical, physical, chemical, alchemical) an ousia. The *pharmakon* has no ideal identity, it is aneidetic. . . . This "medicine" is not something simple. But it is not, for all that, something composite, a sensible or empirical *syntheton.* . . . It is rather the anterior *milieu* in which differentiation in general is produced, as well as the opposition between the *eidos* and its other.[23]

Without form (*eidos*), the *pharmakon* is not a composite held together by form: it escapes the categories of form-in-matter. More than that, it is the *milieu* or domicile of differentiation of form and its other. It thus shows how that distinction—and the relations of domination which, for Aristotle, follow on it—is not ultimate. Operating in such ways on such binaries, Derrida in the course of his thinking, and without ever stating that he is doing it, calls into question all the basic ousiodic categories.[24] He questions, for example, the value of *archê* (form as dominant beginning) in general.[25] Similarly for the category of *telos* (form as dominant end).[26] *Eidos,* as we will see in more detail later, is called into question as the dominant present—when, for example, Derrida questions the role of the present as the "kernel" of time when time is conceived metaphysically:

> In spite of all the complexity of its structure, temporality has a center which is indisplaceable . . . a living kernel, and that is the punctuality of the present now.[27]

In this example and elsewhere, Derrida does not merely use ancient words (as Nietzsche did in recounting the Great Getting-Loose), but also explicitly questions them. In so doing, he specifically addresses the three ousiodic traits of boundary, disposition, and initiative. Boundary, the idea that any being must have an inside and an outside, is identified as one of the controlling moments of traditional logos, and Derrida deconstructs its appearances in the work of Hegel, Husserl, Heidegger, Kant, and Levinas.[28] The dispositive power of the form of a thing to order everything within its boundaries is also brought into question, under the name of the "center":

> The function of the center [as a point of presence, a fixed origin] was not only to orient, balance, and organize the structure . . . but above all to make sure that the organizing principle of the structure would limit what we might call the *play* (*jeu*) of the structure. By orienting and organizing the coherence of the system, the center of a structure permits the play of its elements inside the total form. . . .[29]

Once such ordering power was called into question, it was necessary

> to begin thinking that there was no center, that the center could not be thought in the form of a present-being, that the center had no natural site, that it was not a fixed locus but a function, a sort of nonlocus in which an infinite number of sign-substitutions came into play.[30]

Initiative also comes under Derrida's attack. Its cognitive dimension is questioned, for example, when he applauds Heidegger's refusal to understand beings in terms of just one of their characteristics—the characteristic which for Aristotle would have been their form as what is knowable in them (*Gramm.*, p. 38/22). Aristotle's own paradigmatic example of initiative—fatherhood—is the repeated object of Derrida's criticism. Writing (*écriture*) is for Derrida precisely what threatens the royal and the paternal (*Gramm.*, p. 139/91), and he challenges the latter in a variety of ways: in his valorization of the hymen as nonpenetration; in his critique of Levinas's approbation of fatherhood and the location of a "parricidal" moment in his thought; in his critique of Hegel's prefaces as the "fathers" to his books; in his characterization of Hegelian *Aufhebung* as "what comes back to the father"; in his related characterization of dissemination as what does *not* come back to the father; in his association of it with castration.[31] Finally—unlike the modern writers I mentioned in the introduction—Derrida does not exempt the subject from his critique of ousiodic structure. For the subject-object distinction, as he notes, relies on the distinction of inside and outside: on fixed and inviolable boundaries between subject and object.[32] As these examples show, deconstruction recurrently challenges the three axes of ousiodic domination, though without identifying them as such.

4. DECONSTRUCTIVE CHALLENGES TO OUSIODIC STRUCTURE IN THE TEXT

Derrida's challenge to ousia is not at its height, however, when he discusses general phenomena such as fatherhood, cognition, and "discourse," or when he impeaches general notions such as that of the center or the subject. It is pursued most relentlessly and circumspectly when he attacks, very specifically, ousiodic approaches to texts: our tendency, nothing if not familiar, to treat texts as exhibiting the structures of an ousia.

Such an approach sees a philosophical text as, in the Aristotelian sense, *informed* by the thesis for which it argues, and by the laws of logic which structure the arguments it contains. The "parts" of the text are so many lemmas in the overall argument, and its "matter" consists of the words in which it is written or spoken—words which have no function of their own, but merely convey (more or less successfully) the arguments and thesis which call them forth. This approach, moreover, attributes moving causes to the text. These include not only its author but also the external circumstances which occasion it and the realities of which it treats: the text is seen as faithfully replicating the form of an external reality.[33] Finally, a text so understood also has its final cause or *telos,* the unifying goal to which a "book" (Derrida's paradigm of the "onto-theological" ousiodic text) is directed.[34]

In short, the "ousiodic" view of philosophical texts is just our normal view of them. On this view, a text is the intentional product of its author ("moving cause"). If philosophical, it has a single shaping thesis ("form") and arguments for that thesis ("formal parts"). These arguments are couched in words ("material parts") made up of marks or sounds ("matter"). To the extent that the thesis actually generates, rather than merely orders, the arguments made on its behalf, it is "original." And, in keeping with traditional accounts of initiative, the form of the text—its thesis—should pass unchanged into the mind of the reader. Without, of course, the matter: we do not count it evidence of philosophical acumen if a reader is able to reproduce a text word for word, but only if she can accurately restate the arguments in her own terms.

The standard *philosophical* norms for reading and evaluating philosophical texts involve the elevation of the three main traits of ousia into nearly absolute standards of appreciation. Thus, if the thesis is not stated "comprehensibly," i.e., is not understandable by the reader exactly as the author understood it, we count it a defect of the text (not, of course, of our standard). If the arguments do not go together to establish the thesis, it is also a fault. If the author imports words or ideas from other authors without informing us, she is a plagiarist (footnotes thus constitute a frontier zone of intellectual exchange between the text and its predecessors). And so on.

Derrida's own version of textuality is conspicuous for its violations of this sort of ousiodic view. A Derridean text, first of all, has no secure boundaries: in one of his most famous phrases, *"il n'y a pas de hors-texte,"* there is no outside-of-the-text:[35]

> The text *affirms* the outside. . . . If there is nothing outside the text, that
> implies, with the transformation of the concept of text in general, that [the

text] itself is no longer the snug airtight inside of an interiority or of an identity to self . . . but rather a different putting into place of the effects of opening and closing.[36]

Associated with the view that texts are not strictly bounded but continually open up to, and close off from, other texts is the view that writing is never a *creatio ex nihil* but always the transforming of previous texts: the dispositive power of the author often extends only as far as ordering antecedently created parts. The anterior texts may persist in the present one, in varying ways and to varying degrees: as explicitly cited, or as consciously or unconsciously alluded to, echoed, avoided, and so on—down to the level on which every text, like the one of Nietzsche discussed in the introduction, reuses old words. Because of the continual persistence of older texts in newer ones, reading for Derrida is akin to X-raying a painting and finding other paintings underneath its surface (*Diss.*, pp. 352, 371, 397/316, 333, 357). Derrida's name for this persistence is "grafting" (*la greffe*). Grafting antecedent texts into her own is not something the writer does on particular occasions, then; any term is a graft, in which older texts radiate into those into which they are grafted, transforming them (*Diss.*, pp. 337, 395, 397/304, 355, 357). Finally, the view of a text as a series of grafts—in addition to depriving it of any localizable beginning or *archê*—"ruins its hegemonic center, subverts its authority as unity" (*Diss.*, p. 383/344; also see p. 364/328). Disposition is undone.

Opening the boundary of the text to antecedent texts thus leads to subverting the center: Derrida's questioning of dispositive power destabilizes the power of the central thesis to order the parts of the text as well as to generate them. Any discourse can be read to show that, far from being governed by a single central principle, it can be clarified from the point of view of any proposition in it:

> Like every discourse, like Hegel's, Bataille's discourse has the form of a structure of interpretations. Each proposition, which is already interpretive in nature, can be interpreted by another proposition. Therefore, if we proceed prudently and all the while remain in Bataille's text, we can detach an interpretation from its reinterpretation and submit it to another interpretation bound to other propositions of the system.[37]

Instead of an ousiodic unity provided by its single basic thesis or truth-claim, a text is here construed as susceptible to a variety of acts of unification, each of which begins from one of the propositions it contains. The dispositive power of the form is thus displaced in favor of an indeterminate multiplicity of relative readings, each proceeding from a different and provisional "center." To do this, for Derrida, is to install a general "slippage" in discourse, ultimately cracking the whole apart.[38] And so his term *dissemination* is advanced, together with his suspicion of the literary theme as a device for understanding a given work in a unified way, as anti-ousiodic:

> If there is no thematic unity or total sense which could be reappropriated over and above various textual instances, in some imaginary or intentional order or in a lived experience, the text is no longer the expression or the representation (fortunate or not) of some *truth* which would come to diffract or reassemble itself in a polysemic literature. It is for this hermeneutical concept of *polysemy* that it would be necessary to substitute that of *dissemination*. (*Diss.*, p. 294/262; also see pp. 282, 389/251, 350)

Similarly, once again, for the text's initiative, which would be its capacity to affect its readers by transferring its meanings and theses unchanged into their minds.[39] For Derrida, good reading is never the accurate reproduction of a text's finished and well-formed meaning, but is always creative—at once faithful and violent.[40] The writer—the moving cause, on the traditional view—dominates the resources of her language only partially, and what she cannot dominate is in part those elements of her expression that she herself is unaware of. Reading, precisely in being faithful to the text, must be true to this incompleteness of authorial dominance. It should always

> aim at a certain relation, unperceived by the writer, between what she commands and what she does not command among those schemas of her language of which she makes use. This relation is . . . a signifying structure which critical reading should *produce*.[41]

The play of success and failure in a text is thus significant in itself, which means that critical reading never simply reproduces in the mind of the reader what the writer wanted to convey. It transgresses the author's intentions, to produce new meanings: to create a new text, undreamed of by the "original" author. One must, as Derrida puts it, "read and write with a single gesture."[42]

Finally, texts as traditionally understood have their "matter," and Derrida is very explicit about what that is.

> It is not a simple analogy: writing, the letter, the sensible inscription have always been considered by the occidental tradition as the external *body* and *matter* of spirit, of breath, of the word, of the logos. (*Gramm.*, p. 52/35; emphasis added)

I suggested at the outset that Derrida viewed writing in terms that could apply to the oppressed ancient wife. Here we see it explicitly playing the role of matter in the text as traditionally understood. It is clear, then, why writing is a "menace" to metaphysics (*Gramm.*, p. 149/101). It plays, in fact, several roles that matter plays in the metaphysical tradition. First, it is enclosed and dominated by the central organizing themes of the book, thus becoming

> the good writing . . . comprehended . . . within a totality, and enveloped in a volume or book. The idea of the book is the idea of the totality . . . of the signifier. This totality of the signifier cannot be that which it is, a totality, unless a totality constituted by the signified preexists it, supervises its in-

scriptions and its signs, and is independent of them in its ideality. (*Gramm.,* p. 30/18)

The "signified" of the book—its theses, arguments, lessons, themes, and meanings—thus pre-exists and "supervises" its material realization; it plays the role of form, shaping the linguistic matter in which the book is inscribed. The destiny of writing, in this dispositive dominance of the signified, is—like that of an ancient woman—self-effacement:

> the philosophical text, although in fact it is always written, carries with it, precisely as its specifically philosophical characteristic, to efface itself before the content which it carries and, in general, teaches.[43]

Included in this effacement is what we might call matter's own fecundity, writing's capacity to disseminate new meanings independently of the central signified of the text:

> The effacement or the sublimation of seminal difference is the movement by which the remainder of the outside-the-book allows itself to be interiorized and *domesticated* in the onto-theology of the great book. (*Diss.,* p. 53/45; also cf. p. 285/253)

"Outside-the-book" (*hors-livre*), then, are all those material elements which, like the ancient slave, do not contribute to its meaning: not only the inexhaustible and fearsome fecundity of its words, but its typography and even the empty spaces on its pages.[44]

Finally, the materiality of the book is rendered docile by being "designated," somewhat as God, for Thomas Aquinas, rendered matter fit to receive its appropriate form. Designation passes here by way of the phonetic: since meaning is primarily carried by speech, the only parts of the material text which "count" are those which affect the sound of the words. The materiality of writing is thus "designated" as alphabetical, which "leads to interpreting every irruption into the book of the non-phonetic as a transitory crisis and an accident of passage" (*Gramm.,* p. 59/40)—as, Aristotle might say, a monstrosity.

From this derive Derrida's many gestures calling attention to the non-phonetic aspects of his own texts—from writing *différance* with an "a" to the typographical excesses of "Tympan" (*Marges,* i–xxv/x–xxix) and *La vérité en peinture,* as well as the even more blatant experiments from *Glas* onward. All of them prove to highlight the "nondesignated" aspects of writing: those aspects of it that are not coordinated with the spoken word. Derrida's efforts to highlight these aspects, and to think writing and dissemination independently of their "domestication" in the book, amount to an attempt to focus and valorize Aristotelian matter, matter which flees and resists form, on its own account. Small wonder that Derrida refers to writing so conceived with the Platonic formula *epékeina tês ousîas,* "beyond ousia."[45] Small wonder as well that those overall features of Derrida's thought which have drawn the most outrage from critics too numerous to mention—the denial of the "outside-the-text," the refusal even to consider a text's truth claims or argumentation, the highlighting instead of rhetorical anomalies and semantic infelicities, the devaluing of the author and her intentions, the battle against a single meaning, the odd look of his writings—should all be directed against ousiodic features of the text.[46]

5. CONCLUSION

But the individual text, however relentlessly Derrida may pursue its deconstruction, is merely an agent—or what I would call an "engine"—of the oppressive structures of metaphysics in general. One of the crucial merits of Derrida's thought is that he so rarely loses sight of this, no matter how eagerly he may pursue the minutiae of a single text. I have already noted passages in which Derrida claims, without arguing the point, that metaphysics is the core discourse of the West; metaphysics is, he writes in a footnote to *Positions*, "the most powerful, extended, durable, and systematic *discursive* formation of our culture" (*Pos.*, p. 68 n. 13/102 n. 21). The nature of metaphysics is not exhausted by its power, extension, and durability, then; it also exhibits, for Derrida, a particular systematic structure of its own. It is in fact what he calls a "closed" system, in two respects. First, it is conceptually closed: a small number of core concepts, in "systematic solidarity" with one another, direct the rest.[47] Among these are the concept of truth as objectivity (either in the traditional *adequatio* or in Heideggerean disclosure); the oppositions of intellectual to sensible, of signified to signifier, of proper to foreign, of activity to passivity, of light to shadow; and the presuppositions of simplicity of origin, continuity of all derivation and of the homogeneity of all orders.[48]

Second, metaphysics is historically closed: these determinations, oppositions, presuppositions, and so on have persisted relatively unchanged, and unchallenged, from Plato through Heidegger:

> The unity of this metaphysical tradition should be respected in its general permanence through all the marks of appurtenance, the genealogical sequences, the stricter routes of causality that organize [a given] text.[49]

The "core concepts" of metaphysics thus not only direct the rest of what happens in metaphysics, but provide its unity over time. I conclude that *metaphysics itself is for Derrida ousiodically structured.* It is not, for example, merely a set of tendencies or habits, but it has a dispositive form: the set of core concepts which unifies it, and directs the rest. Its boundaries, not easily known, are presumably those of the other discourses which operate in terms of those core concepts. Its initiative, also a matter of some difficulty and diffidence, seems for Derrida to reside in an effort to extend them to cover everything.

The inmost core of metaphysics for Derrida—the core of the core, that which establishes and directs the other systematic solidarities—is what he calls the "privileging of presence."[50] The other basic increments of metaphysics—being, consciousness, act and potentiality, sense, ideality, objectivity, truth, intuition, experience, telos, etc.—reduce to this.[51] Among what Derrida identifies as what I call the "core concepts" of metaphysics, those that are privileged—the intellectual, signified, proper, active, light, simplicity, continuity, and homogeneity—all denote various aspects of "presence." Philosophy itself being thoroughly metaphysical, no objection to the privileging of presence is possible within philosophy: "This privilege defines the very element of philosophical thought, it is . . . conscious thought itself, it directs every possible concept of truth and of sense" (*VP*, p. 70/62).

Derrida's work thus challenges the ousiodic structure of philosophical texts and of metaphysics itself. Since the core concepts of metaphysics are in turn the formative principles of other Western discourses, his thought achieves a vast pertinence. But this aspect of his work, never explicated by Derrida himself, is often lost entirely by readers—especially in America, where his importance for literary criticism has obscured the urgency of his challenge to metaphysics,[52] and where a leading analytical philosopher can dismiss his work as "a systematic method that rests upon a philosophy of language that is very weak."[53] Derrida's work, in fact, rests upon ways of reading—challenging—the history of philosophy that are very strong.

2

THE PRIVILEGE OF PRESENCE
AND THE DERRIDEAN KNOT

1. OVERALL STRUCTURE OF THE DERRIDEAN KNOT

The misunderstandings of Derrida to which I alluded at the end of the previous chapter have some plausibility because his challenges to structures of ousiodic domination are not theorized or even identified as such. To see why this is so is to enter into a Derridean problematic even more convoluted and uncertain than the Cartesian circle; I call it the "Derridean Knot." The strands from which this knot is tied are familiar to critics of Derrida. They include his occasional love of unintelligibility and the seeming irrelevance of much of his work to genuine liberation—its banality. What is new here is, first, the tracing of these problems to Derrida's position within an opposition he never states—the opposition of presence to ousia—and, second, the claim that relocating him within this opposition can actually salvage the emancipatory promise of his thought.

To uncover and clarify the Derridean Knot requires attention to Derrida's view of metaphysics as founded upon the "privileging of presence." "Presence" itself will turn out to function in no fewer than three different ways in his thought, each of which leads to a different view of what he is challenging and how. The Derridean Knot is the undecided intercoil of these three views.

My analysis in the previous chapter claimed that deconstruction is a liberating exercise directed against the founding gesture of all metaphysical binaries, the disposing and directing source of all possible truth and sense: the privileging of presence. It then makes sense to ask: What, for Derrida, is presence?

In spite of its convolutions and elusiveness, Derrida's view of the nature of presence is stated quite clearly in several places in his writings. To be "present" means most basically, as he puts it in "Force and Signification," to be "summed up (*résumée*) in some absolute simultaneity or instantaneity."[1] This concept of presence has for him undergone only one major modification in the history of the West: its transformation from an "objective" sense in which something is present if it exists on its own in a state of completion (which the tradition, following Aristotle, calls "actuality") into a "modern" sense of complete givenness to a subject (which Descartes called "clearness and distinctness").[2]

The above characterization of presence is importantly ambiguous. To be "summed up" means, in one sense, to be complete. Because a "present" being is complete, it does not require anything else to be or to be given. To be present is then to exist independently of other things, or to be given as a "transcendental signified." But in another sense, to be "summed up" is more than merely to be, or to be given, completely. That a being's completeness at some "absolute . . . instantaneity" sums it up may mean not only that it is complete and independent at that instant but also that what it is right then is all it ever "really" is. This sense of "summing up" is more extended than the other, for what gets summed up is the thing over the entire duration of its existence. Such summing up attributes to a thing not only completeness and independence as a given moment, but the permanence of a substance—the kind attributed, for example, to the center conceived traditionally as "a fundamental immobility and a reassuring certitude, which itself is beyond the reach of play"[3] This extended version of presence arises, Derrida says, from a certain interpretation of time: one which takes the punctuality of the present moment as the "indisplaceable center" of time. It is only in virtue of such privileging of the present that we can presume that what the being is right now is what it has been and will be.[4]

These two characterizations of presence are clearly quite different from one another. For it is entirely possible to take something as being complete at a particular moment without going on to say that that momentary completeness "sums up" what it was earlier, and will be later—that its whole existence is determined from its completeness or givenness at this (or some) present moment. I will call the latter move the "privileging of presence," distinguishing it from the former characteristic, i.e., from what I will call "presence" itself.[5] This distinction is not always made by Derrida, and when he runs the two senses together, as he does in "Force and Signification," he generates what I call the Derridean Knot.

The first two strands of this knot become clear when we ask if Derrida is to be read as challenging presence in the narrower or in the more extended sense. Is he suggesting that nothing is ever complete or independent—that the concept "presence" has no referents? Or is he questioning not presence itself, but the second sense—its privileging? In that case he would be challenging not a concept at all, but a practice: what Heidegger calls the "onto-theological" practice of taking a concept which may (or may not) apply to some things and instating it as the paradigm for all, in this case as the founding validator of all knowledge and speech.[6] Derrida would be challenging, in other words, not presence itself, but the *dominance* of presence.

The first strand—that which views presence itself, rather than its privileging, as the object of challenge—contains two further possibilities. If something is not to *any* degree complete, it cannot present itself to us: we cannot experience or encounter it. If it is not independent enough of other things to be even *intellectually* detached from them, it cannot be referred to or spoken truly of. Some degree of completeness is thus necessary for truth and reference to be possible at all; and the possibilities of truth and reference are, clearly, conditions of our ordinary speech.[7] If we are to abandon them wholly, it appears that we not only cannot talk truly, we cannot talk at all. This generates a second snarl in the Derridean Knot. Given that presence, rather than its privileging, is taken as the object of Derrida's challenge, is it in fact the kind of presence that is required for truth and reference? If so, then Derrida can challenge presence only at the price of embracing unintelligibility. If not—if, for example, the kind of presence he challenges is merely a sort of absolutistic ideal needlessly foisted upon language by metaphysics—then it is unclear just what import Derrida's challenges to it will have.

The Derridean Knot is thus composed of two main strands, one of which bifurcates. Strand I, to give it a name, takes the object of challenge to be presence itself, which then must be construed either as a condition for speech (Ia) or as a mere ideal in terms of which metaphysicians have regarded speech (Ib). Strand II says that Derrida's thought challenges not presence at all, but its privileging. The knot is a knot because Derrida never decides which strand to pursue: all three run together throughout his discourse, which therefore appears at times genuinely emancipatory (II), at times willfully unintelligible (Ia), and at times banal (Ib).

Thus, in one passage of "La différance," Derrida simultaneously puts into question "the authority of presence [and] of its simple symmetrical opposite, absence or lack"; he seems, in other words, to challenge authority, or privilege, rather than presence.[8] On the other hand, the famous argument against the "transcendental signified," given elsewhere in "La différance" and again in *Positions*, suggests that the object of what Barbara Johnson has called "deconstructive critique"[9] is presence itself, not its privilege. A transcendental signified would be something that is, in Derrida's sense, present in that it "refers only to itself": it is entirely detachable from other things, and hence can be located on what I called the first level of Derrida's characterization of presence. His argument, which I will not recount, is that nothing is ever given that way:

> The play of differences supposes, in short, syntheses or referrals which forbid that at any moment, or in any sense, a simple element could be *present* in itself and not refer to anything but itself.[10]

The problem here is with the descriptive capacities of the notion of presence. Derrida's claim is that presence is a concept which has no referents. It is problematic in itself, independently of any structures of domination: even right now at this instant nothing "really" is present as anything.

Derrida does not cut or untangle this knot. His characterization of presence above, for example, runs the two main strands rather neatly together; the very phrase "privileging of presence" cuts neatly down the middle. Moreover, Derrida (like Heidegger) never distinguishes presence—*parousia* —from ousia. His writings either simply employ them as synonyms[11] or, more reflectively, point out that any ousia must be given and therefore must be present, so that presence is a condition of ousia. An example of the latter is the words just preceding a passage I quoted earlier from "Plato's Pharmacy":

> . . . having no stable essence, nor "proper" character, [the *pharmakon*] is not, in any sense of this word (metaphysical, physical, chemical, alchemical) a substance.[12]

This more reflective way of conflating ousia and presence can be seen most clearly in a metaphysical binary I have not yet discussed: that of form and matter. This, for Derrida, is an "inaugural opposition of metaphysics" (*VP,* pp. 5, 70/6, 63), and in it form dominates. But "form" for Derrida is just another name for presence: it is "that in the thing in general which presents itself, lets itself be seen, gives itself to thought."[13] But this captures only Aristotle's wider sense of *eidos*—that which denoted any determinate property.[14] His narrower, and more pregnant, sense of *eidos* as essence (or as what the Medievals would call "substantial form") is missing. Missing along with it are the very specific kinds of domination that essence exercises over matter. For if the only problem with ousia is that it is given, then its structure of internal domination is implicitly unproblematic.[15]

Similarly with the account of the center to which I referred above: it is because the center is "a point of presence, a fixed origin" that it can reduce the play of the structure it centers. Domination by the center is not denied here; but it is viewed as the inevitable result of the center's presence, so that presence remains the direct object of challenge. In both cases, we see a reduction of ousiodic structure to mere completeness and independence—to presence. And this reduction, as I suggested in the introduction, seems to be a perpetuation of "modern" philosophy's obsession with the substrate—with presence.

2. STRAND IA: GLOBAL LIBERATION

Challenges to presence and to the dominance of presence are not, of course, necessarily separate: if we challenge presence itself effectively, any privileging of it falls away. This is presumably why Derrida's thought can at places take itself to be challenging presence, while actually exhibiting multiple and various challenges to ousiodic structure. But because the knot is a knot, Derrida also really challenges presence itself, and these challenges take two forms. When presence is viewed as grounding the concepts of truth and meaning to which our speech appeals, speech itself must be contested together with it. The other path, as I have noted, is to say that all or some of our actual discursive practices trade upon a less absolutistic sense of presence. In the former case, I will argue, deconstruction becomes unintelligible and the liberation it promises impossible; in the latter case, it becomes banal, and its liberation unnecessary.

Derrida sometimes runs these two distinct ways of viewing presence so neatly together as to suggest that he is not entirely unaware of the distinction. An example occurs in "La différance": ". . . the signified concept is never present in itself, in a sufficient presence that would refer only to itself."[16]

What is "sufficient" presence, and how does it differ from presence *tout court*? Is a more relaxed version of presence possible in which a signified refers *mostly* to itself? Or, perhaps, a little bit to itself? Or is "sufficient" presence all there is, so that when Derrida claims that all truth and sense derive from it, he means that truth and sense are impossible without the complete self-referentiality of objects of discourse? In which case, his denial of such presence will lead inexorably to a valorization of unintelligibility.

Derrida certainly seems to appeal to unintelligibility in places, especially when he is attacking such notions as articulation, truth, identity, and being. Differance itself, having like the *pharmakon* no stable essence, is strictly speaking "unnameable," and deconstruction "feels its way [*tâtonne*] across the inherited concepts towards the unnameable." Derrida also seems to agree with Levinas that "violence appears with *articulation*": to put anything into words is to do violence to it.[17] Among the concepts which must be deconstructed is, in particular, that of truth, for the privilege of presence, we saw, "directs every possible concept of truth and of sense." Together with the concept of truth goes that of experience, a concept which is "quite embarrassing" because of its connections to modern theories of subjectivity (*Gramm.*, p. 89/60).

While "no philosophy responsible for its language can renounce *ipseity* in general," such self-identity is precisely what differance disrupts; while dissemination, for its part, ". . . disseminates itself without ever having been itself and without returning to itself."[18] Identity of some sort has, of course, traditionally been associated with being—with that which is indicated by the copula. For Derrida, the "is" of the copula is "an indication of presence" which "procures this calm, this consciousness of ideal mastery, this power of consciousness in the act of showing"—which renders it just a "phantasm of mastery" of the West.[19] In connection with Plato, and therefore "more or less immediately [with] the whole history of occidental philosophy," Derrida thus denounces the "presumed possibility" of "a *logos*, deciding and decidable, of or on the *on* (being-present)." In short, Derrida's liberation of discourse from "all the occidental methods of analysis, explication, reading or interpretation" seems to direct us toward

> a writing without presence, without absence, without history, without cause, without *archê*, without *telos*, absolutely deranging every dialectic, every theology, every teleology, every ontology.[20]

Some of these discourses are quite well deranged; but one wonders how to make sense of what is left. What are we to make of a discourse which refuses to appeal to the copula or to any notion of nameability, truth, articulation, experience, being, analysis, explication, reading, or interpretation? The global nature of that *from* which deconstruction seeks liberation is matched by the emptiness of that *for* which it would free us.

These passages from Derrida, though they explicitly appeal to unintelligibility, are not evidence that he propounds a mere nihilistic sophistry; nor are they ironical tropes or mere slips of his pen. Rather, they result from a genuine and instructive *prôtê hamartia:* that of taking "presence" for the object of challenge while simultaneously regarding it as globally constitutive of discourse. Conceived on that basis, "liberation" can indeed only be a groping for the unintelligible.

To say that liberation from metaphysics includes the sacrifice of intelligibility itself, moreover, amounts to saying that there simply is no way out of metaphysics: deconstruction's promise of liberation, necessarily made, must now with equal necessity be retracted. Derrida, again, is quite explicit about our inability to escape from metaphysics, for metaphysics is embedded in all our language:

> There is no sense in passing up the concepts of metaphysics in order to shake metaphysics. We have no language—no syntax and no lexicon—which is foreign to this history: we cannot enunciate any destructuring proposition that has not already had to slip itself into the form, the logic, and the implicit postulates of the very thing which it wishes to challenge.[21]

Hence, it is impossible to get out of metaphysics: it is a house which sits in no surroundings, and every door leads back inside.

> One must then attempt to free oneself from this language. Not to *attempt* to get free, for that is impossible without forgetting our history. But to dream of it. Not to *get free* of it, which would have no sense and would deprive us of the light of sense. But to resist as long as possible.[22]

Our incapacity to free ourselves from metaphysics leads back, again, to an appeal to unintelligibility. For it means that Derrida's own writings are essentially double: they must use metaphysical concepts to undo metaphysical concepts, and thus ineluctably carry forward the tradition they attack. In this "double reading," "every gesture is equivocal."[23]

The goals of deconstruction so understood fall rather short of traditional concepts of emancipation, even of "epistemological liberation." In fact, Derrida says, the aim of his thought is not to undo metaphysics, but to enable us to see it better: to know its limits, indeed to render its concepts "enigmatic," and to make the whole edifice "tremble" (while leaving it, alas, in place).[24]

3. STRAND IB: BANAL LIBERATION

If presence is both the object of critique and constitutive for discourse, then there can be no effective critical discourse. But Derrida, I suggested, also takes the other path. He also views the completeness, or complete givenness, of a being all at once as a sort of ideal, not as something that must actually be achieved in order for speech to become possible. On this approach, our actual ways of speaking operate, or can operate, on a relaxed version of presence and of other metaphysical concepts:

> The absolute *parousia* of the literal meaning, as presence-to-self of the logos in the voice, in absolute hearing-oneself-speak, should be *situated* as a function responding to an indestructible but relative necessity, at the interior of a system which comprehends it. Which amounts to *situating* metaphysics of the onto-theology of the logos.[25]

The problem here is not with parousia but with "absolute" parousia. It is to be solved not by shaking the indispensable oppressions of presence, but by "situating" them. This situating amounts to seeing the basic concepts of metaphysics, together with the oppositions that define them, not as primary but as derived: as effects, not rules, of play. In such a case, "the form (presence, evidence) would not be the final recourse, the last instance to which any possible sign would refer," but would be, like an author's intention, "inscribed within a system which it no longer dominates."[26] The important step in this is to see metaphysics not as a matter of certain concepts (and still less as a matter of all concepts), but as a sort of work that concepts do: "There is no concept which is metaphysical in itself. There is a work—metaphysical or not—on conceptual systems."[27] This allows us to modify the "work" of a concept without trying to abandon that concept altogether.

Thus, for example, truth is to be viewed not as "authoritative" for all discourse, but as a piece in a game, or as a "function." The concept of origin, or of the fundamental signified, is likewise a function, "indispensable but situated," in a wider system of signification (instituted by the interdiction of, presumably, differance).[28] Theorization by means of such concepts is not impossible—only limited.[29]

Of what, then, are these concepts to be "functions"? One is tempted at first to say, "of our projects and purposes": that philosophical and other concepts do their job within the horizons of what we humans need to have done, and that they are to be "situated" as advancing—or hampering—human undertakings. But if we read Derrida in that way, he becomes quite banal. For what is more obvious, especially to those who are acquainted with empiricism and pragmatism, than the view that concepts are important because of the work that they do; that absolute knowledge and final truth are impossible; and that there is no ultimate and unimpeachable authority?[30]

Though Derrida has never turned his own systematic attention to the classical empiricists, it is clear he is not among them—not because he is a rationalist or a skeptic, but because in his view empiricism (and its offshoot, pragmatism) never undertook an adequate examination or critique of metaphysics. This, for Derrida, is not because empiricists were unaware of the importance of metaphysics, or of its baneful influences, but because they failed to acknowledge the systematic solidarity of its fundamental concepts. As the *traditional* other of philosophy, empiricism challenges the coherence of the logos; but it does this in an incoherent way. Because of its own incoherence, empiricism will not allow any radical challenge to its own nature to be even formulated, let alone argued for. It becomes not merely dominant but imperialistic: each displacement, each nonmetaphysical (or "transmetaphysical") concept becomes merely a personal error.

The great strength of empiricism for Derrida thus lies in its fatal error: no systematic mistake can be acknowledged by an approach which does not view itself as a system.[31] Only by taking account of metaphysics not as a set of isolated or even repeated errors, but as what it is—the "most powerful, extended, durable, and systematic" discourse of our culture—can we "avoid empiricistic improvisation, false discoveries, etc., and give a systematic character to deconstruction" (*Pos.*, p. 68 n. 13/102 n. 21). Hence, the critique of empiricism

> is a matter first of all of showing clearly the systematic and historical solidarity of the concepts and gestures of thought which [we] often thought could be innocently separated. (*Gramm.*, p. 25/13f)

It is, in my terms, a matter of challenging the ousiodic structures implicated in empiricism itself.

Derrida can, I think, be rescued from the humanistic banality in which we seem to have left him. In accordance with the deeper lessons of his critical suggestions concerning empiricism, we can say that metaphysical concepts such as truth should be seen as functions not of human purposes and projects, but of the overall systematic solidarity, or ousiodic structure, of metaphysics itself. But this "rescue" would lead to yet another question. When we see individual metaphysical concepts as functions of the whole, are we not, like Hegel, according absolute status to that whole? Are we not instating metaphysics itself as an absolute? Are we not echoing the hoary claim that "the true is the whole"? And, in particular, do we not restore to its founding gesture—the privileging of presence—absolute status as the ground of all sense, unchallengeable either within philosophy or without it?

The "rescue" fails because this, of course, is precisely what Derrida is attacking. But in so doing, he is not challenging presence itself, in either of its senses. Rather, he is challenging the power of metaphysics to "situate" us: its capacity, in virtue of its single founding gesture, to send us to our proper place and consign us to our proper function. He is challenging, in short, the ousiodic structure of metaphysics. And so, once again, he comes out with an attack on ousia. But as with his others, it is an attack that never speaks its name. (*A victory? Over what? Over whom? Riddlesome, suggestive, questionable victory, but for all that—the first victory: This sort of unfortunate and painful thing belongs to the story of the Great Demarcation.*)

4. UNTANGLING THE KNOT: THE NAME OF CHALLENGE

Derridean challenge, or deconstruction, cannot speak its name, I suggest, in two senses. The first is that it cannot say the name of its object (which is "ousia"), but considers itself to be attacking presence. I have explored this move, and its multiple effects, in the foregoing. The second name deconstruction cannot speak is the name in which it challenges ousia. In its global mode, deconstruction's emancipatory promise is in the name of a groping toward an unnameable writing without presence, absence, history, etc. In its banal mode, it moves toward a "situated" view of metaphysical oppositions.

But Derrida, I will argue, is actually challenging ousiodic structure in the name of something quite specific. This can be seen by considering another thing that pushes Derrida to the view that presence, rather than ousia, is the problem. This is that while, as we saw, he tirelessly locates and challenges the oppression inherent in what he calls "metaphysical binaries," *his thought does not challenge binary structure as such.* There are for Derrida, in fact, a number of "good" binaries. Among these are difference/differance, the latter as "origin" of the former; differance/presence, the latter as "effect" of the former; differance vs. the sensible/intellectual distinction, which it "founds"; differance vs. *all* the other oppositions of language, of which it is the "common root"; effect of play vs. rule of play; presentation/nonpresentation, with differance as the nonpresentable which makes presentation possible;

premise/conclusion; effacement/effacement of effacement; form/unform (trace); trace/God; trace/being-originary.[32]

These binaries might be justified by recalling that, as I noted above, deconstruction brings with it a first gesture of reversal, in which the formerly subordinated term of a binary is valorized as against the formerly superordinate term. In addition to the traditional metaphysical binaries, which are oppressive, deconstruction itself thus forms a set of what I have called "counter-binaries." Produced at just one stage of deconstructive reading, counter-binaries are presumably "good" for Derrida in somewhat the same way that the dictatorship of the proletariat was "good" for Marx: as the first step out of a bad situation.

But these considerations will not apply to all the above examples. For a counter-binary is reached in the first phase of deconstruction, by taking a traditional metaphysical binary and thinking its subordinate term in its own right. Because it is a mere inversion of the original binary, it and the terms it contains remain, as I noted earlier, metaphysical. The binaries I have just listed, however, contain such specifically Derridean terms as "differance" and "trace." They are not strictly metaphysical, then, and cannot be accounted for in this way.

On my earlier schematic account of deconstruction, specifically Derridean terms entered only in the third stage: as names for that which differentiates the terms of the original binary and permits us to fathom the ground and lack of ground of both the original binary and the counter-binary. That such specifically Derridean terms as "trace" and "differance" are asserted to be part of binaries in the examples above indicates that those binaries are neither original binaries nor counter-binaries, then, but a third kind. In this third kind of binary, which I will call a "meta-binary" and of which the above list provides some examples, the first two stages of the deconstructive process, yielding a third term which at once locates and displaces the opposition of the first two, result in a situation in which that third term stands over against *both* of the others. This is explicitly the case when "differance," for example, is said to found the sensible/intellectual opposition, and more generally when it is asserted to be at the origin of all metaphysical oppositions. Or when the *pharmakon* is said to be "the anterior *milieu* in which differentiation in general is produced, as well as the opposition between the *eidos* and its other."[33]

In addition to the metaphysical binaries with which it starts, and the counter-binaries through which it proceeds, deconstruction thus seems to end in a third set, meta-binaries. In such binaries, the two original terms are both opposed to a third term which at once situates and displaces their mutual opposition. Thus, in the metaphysical tradition, the sensible world is commonly devalued in favor of the intelligible world, and that is one binary. When we attempt (as Hume did) to think sensible experience apart from such devaluation, and perhaps even devalue the intellectual in its name, we produce what I call a counter-binary. When differance is shown (as Derrida undertakes) to be the condition of both binaries, we get a meta-binary. Deconstruction thus does not challenge binary structure as such, but is *a passage from binaries through binaries to binaries.*

But what distinguishes a "bad" metaphysical binary from a "good" Derridean one? In order fully to think through his own procedures, Derrida would have to show why it is that his final meta-binaries are exempt from the domination and other oppressions characteristic of metaphysics. This would amount to explaining the nature of the emancipatory displacement in the third step of my schematic sketch of deconstruction above, and in so doing Derrida would have to specify that in the name of which he challenges the ousiodic structure of metaphysical binaries. Any such specification would have to appeal to the nonmetaphysical nature of the third term—to the fact that a term such as "differance" or "trace," not being thought on the basis of presence, does not designate anything that can be summed up or given all at once. It would place Derrida, I will now argue, into immediate proximity with both Hegel and Heidegger.

The proximity to Hegel is evident from the fact that an appeal to the non-givenness, or undecideability, of the meaning of the third term is the only way to distinguish deconstruction from Hegelian *Aufhebung.*[34] In *Aufhebung,* the third term grounds and situates the opposition of two other terms—indeed, in the case of the "Logic of Essence," it does so precisely by grounding and overcoming the dominance that one term has over the other (as when the dominance of substance over accident is overcome in favor of mutual reciprocity).[35] But the third term itself is metaphysical, in the sense that its meaning is, like that of the other two, something fully present. And this means that the third, *aufhebende* term does not disrupt or displace the original opposition, but goes on to enter, with its own opposite, into a further opposition, which is resolved in the same way. The systematicity of Hegelian discourse is thus established. That discourse situates oppositions, but never displaces them, and this is an effect of the "presence" attributed by Hegel to his unifying and situating third terms.

For Derrida, by contrast, two metaphysical terms are brought into oppositional proximity by a third term which designates nothing completely given. What constitutes the binary is thus grasped as a non-given, a lack. A metaphysical binary is thus deconstructed, and a meta-binary is produced, by and around a gap: an absence, indeed, but a dynamic and creative one, rather than a "simple" and "symmetric" one. This places Derrida into proximity to Heidegger, whose philosophy (as I noted in the introduction) contains a relentless examination of such dynamic absences (*diakena*) and of how they are accessible to us.

The metaphysical binary and the counter-binary can be seen as stages in a sequential play which concludes with the meta-binary: all are phases in the emergence of a single "being." That being is structured in its emergence, then, by a dynamic gap: what, with respect to Heidegger, I have called a "diakenon." A Derridean diakenon gathers a binary, places its components into indeterminable relation, by:

1. Taking it up as a traditional metaphysical binary;

2. Reversing it;

3. Situating and displacing the reversal, showing it to take place around a third term which cannot be defined in terms of presence.

Derridean diakena turn out to operate rather as their Heideggerean fore-runners did.[36] In his essay "Andenken," for example, Heidegger begins from the traditional ousiodic view of the poem of that name as a bounded whole structured by a single theme, that of remembrance; produced by an author, Friedrich Hölderlin, out of certain circumstances in his life; and aimed at being clearly understood by the reader. Heidegger then "reverses" this understanding by pointing to features of individual words in the poem, not subordinating them to its thematic message but understanding each of them in terms of an irreducible plurality of basic meanings to the word "an-denken." In this he produces a whole series of what I call "counter-bina-ries." What makes them all possible, of course, is the word "andenken" itself, which is thus the *écart* of the different ways of understanding the poem. But "andeken" is, itself, indefinable: its different meanings cannot be brought into the transparency of a larger, *"aufhebende"* meaning. Its relation to the counter-binaries Heidegger has produced is thus that of a meta-binary: it brings traditional and reversed ways of reading the poem into interplay.

If Derrida successfully escapes the earlier Heidegger, who valorized au-thenticity because of his view of world as comprising nearness, it is anything but certain that he has escaped from the later Heidegger, who valorizes nothing at the complete expense of anything else (even the statements of physics, Heidegger says, are "correct," *richtig*),[37] but advances diakenic alter-natives to older categories.

The foregoing considerations are, of course, quite foreign to Derrida. He never discusses the kind of path his thinking takes as it moves from bina-ry through binary to binary, or discusses in detail how a diakenon such as differance unifies the different binaries whose traversal brings it to play. It cannot be otherwise, for the unifying or "gathering" side of Heideggerean discourse—the sense in which, for Heidegger, any pathway or text is the progressive (but disjointed) revelation of a single thing or word—is criti-cized by Derrida, in *Specters of Marx*, as merely another form of privileging: "Heidegger . . . [always] gives priority to gathering and to the same (*Ver-sammlung, Fuge, legein,* and so on) over . . . a difference whose uniqueness . . . will never be assured in the One."[38] The only place in Derrida where anything gets unified or brought together is in the "summing up" of a thing by its givenness at just one moment. And that is not, as it is for Heidegger, an "appropriating event" in which we participate, but a mere artifact of the privileging of presence.[39]

It should be evident from the above examples that Derrida has an even larger and more brilliant set of anti-ousiodic gestures than does Heidegger. But, like Heidegger and even more consequentially, he fails to perceive this; and the failure is because of where he follows and departs from Heidegger. Derrida follows Heidegger when he takes presence, rather than ousia, for the object of his critique. He departs from him in that, for Derrida, with presence gone there is no other way for a being to attain unity over time. The "single development" and "individual thing" which Heideggerean diakena unify—and through the togetherness of which they become accessible *as* diakena—are unthinkable for Derrida except metaphysically, however often his writings in fact contain them. Hence differance, like other Derridean terms, does not designate unification through a nothing, but radical dispersal or dissemination. Hence, too, his writings do not contain any discussion of the unity of the three kinds of binary through which deconstruction moves. It cannot be otherwise.

This leads to another difference with Heidegger. In order for a process or thing to be diakenically unified, its phases or components must for Heidegger not only be encountered or understood together; each must, at the outset, be understood in its own right. When Heidegger says that "none of the [regions of the Fourfold] makes itself obdurate in its separate particularity,"[40] he does not deny separate particularity—independence—to them altogether; he denies only its "perdurance," i.e., its *ständige Anwesenheit*. His instatement of diakenic interplay thus always begins with faithful description; in "Andenken," this is extended to an actual reprinting of the entirety of Hölderlin's poem at the beginning of the essay. There is then a level, for Heidegger as for Hume, where description works: the level on which the various momentary phases of an interplay can be described separately, where things can be reliably taken "as" what they are.

In terms of my account of the two levels in Derrida's characterization of presence, Heidegger allows for the givenness of something at a particular moment, and hence for reference and truth. His real challenge to presence occurs only at the second level—where something present (*anwesend*) is taken to be the only kind of unifying factor a thing can exhibit over time. When Derrida takes presence rather than its privilege for his object of challenge, he moves to a level where even these momentary phases are instances of presence, and are subject to deconstruction.[41] Rejecting "transcendental signifieds" but not binaries as such, Derrida is pushed to the view that presence itself, rather than its privileging, is the object of his critique. This bars him from a full understanding of his own procedures and keeps them at the level of mere challenge.

5. CONCLUSION

I have argued that Derrida challenges ousiodic structure in many different and effective ways. I have also argued that when he reflects on this, he is tied into a complex knot generated from two moments of indecision. The first is a failure to specify whether the object of his challenge is presence itself or its "privileging." The former option, insofar as Derrida actually chooses it, leads to a second moment of indecision: whether presence so construed is a condition for our speech or an ideal foisted upon it by metaphysicians. Thence emerge two Derridas, aligned as thinkers have been since Hegel: on a Left-Right axis. The Derrida of the Left is a radical critic of metaphysics who is trapped within the metaphysical heritage of his own language. The Derrida of the Right is one whose "critical" repertoire does not go beyond the banalities of empiricism or pragmatism.

The common move of the Derrida of the Left and that of the Right is to take presence itself as the object of his challenge. For the Derrida of the Left, presence is a condition of all our discourse, and in criticizing it he only lands in valorizations of unintelligibility. For the Derrida of the Right, presence is not the indispensable condition of speech but a sort of ideal construct; our ordinary speech itself is then untouched by his critique, and he feels his way "across the inherited concepts," not "towards the unnameable," but towards the Wittgenstein who "leaves everything as it is."[42]

Neither of these Derridas is able to keep the promise of liberation made by his thought. That promise can, I suggest, be redeemed only by first returning to the point from which the two Derridas emerged: the first moment of indecision, Derrida's failure to specify whether the object of his challenge is presence itself or its ousiodic privileging. And then by taking, definitively, the route offered by strand II in the knot: seeing the privileging of presence, not presence itself, as the problem.

But then the privileging of presence reveals itself to be but one instance of a broader sort of privileging: the structures of domination inherent in what I call ousia. For privileging presence amounts to saying that what a being is, and what it will be, can be given in some undivided moment. This accords to that moment the capacity to order a bounded domain: the prior and posterior of the thing are determined by its current state. The representation of such presence then becomes the goal of all cognitive discourse, which after all seeks only to show us how things *are*. Presence comes to dominate—as Derrida shows—our entire conceptual apparatus. Philosophical texts are viewed as ordered by what turn out to be forms of presence—in paramount place, the truth of the thesis of a given text, and the validity of the laws of logic by which that thesis is argued for.

Seeing deconstruction as aiming at ousiodic structure, the strand II which

Derrida also often follows leads to the genuinely emancipatory gestures of his thought that I have adduced here, and to many others as well. But that productivity is at the price of making ousia, not presence, the true object of challenge. Were he unambiguously to do that, Derrida would be led to an object of challenge that is not global. "Presence" itself, as well as truth and reference, could be retained by a critical discourse they were not allowed to dominate—one that acknowledged that the Before and After of a thing need not be determined, even in thought, by its Now. This specific object of challenge—ousiodic structure—is also not a mere chimerical ideal of "absolute parousia," foisted upon us by metaphysicians for reasons unknown. Its philosophical and discursive manifestations are clearly complicitous with manifold structures of domination resident in the human world. As itself resident within philosophical texts, it constitutes what I have suggested is the final redoubt of such structures of domination.

There would then be, in addition to the Derridas of the Left and Right, a Derrida of the Middle, whose challenges to ousia would become in theory what they already are in practice. They would lead philosophy beyond very ancient confines: we would no longer accord to texts, simply because they are philosophical, the ousiodic structure of searches for truth. Philosophy could be seen to begin where Plato and Aristotle both had it begin: in wonder and eros, where ousiodic structure breaks down so that searches may begin. At those moments, philosophy cannot help but transgress our very notions of intelligibility; and Derrida's thought would show us how to experience, or remain with, such specific absences of meaning. His meta-binaries would be ways of answering to the points of meaninglessness within philosophical texts without closing them off or terminating them. He would, in short, show us "philosophy" as a developed form of what I call "abnormal poetic interaction": interaction in which an utterance has no meaning at all, yet claims intelligibility. As an instance of nonterminating poetic interaction, indeed "the most powerful, extended, durable, and systematic" case of it, philosophy would enter into the service of freedom, and onto the first stage of the Great Demarcation.

OUSIODIC STRUCTURE VS. THE SPEECH COMMUNITY IN RICHARD RORTY

*In the background of this bustling and roaming—for the
freed spirit is restless and underway . . . as if wandering in a
desert—stands the question mark of an ever more dangerous
curiosity: "Can we not overturn all values? . . . Is everything
perhaps false in its final ground? And if we are deceived, are
we not—precisely because of that—also deceivers? Must we
not also be deceivers?" Such questions guide and entice the
freed spirit, leading it ever farther forth, ever farther off.
Solitude encircles and encoils it, ever more threatening, more
suffocating, more heart stifling, choking—solitude, fearsome
goddess and mater saeva cupidinum, fierce mother of the
passions.—But who today knows what solitude is?*

Heidegger's sin, for Richard Rorty, was to commit himself to a certain sort
of solitude. As Rorty puts it in "Pragmatism without Method,"

> . . . what needs criticism is [Heidegger's] inhumanism—his attempt to find
> Dewey's "connection of man . . . with the enveloping world . . ." by cutting
> himself off from connection with other men. . . . To Heidegger, technologi-
> cal civilization was something so un-Thoughtful, so un-Greek, that only re-
> fusal to speak any of the words associated with it could help. But this could
> help only a very few. For Heidegger there is no community that plays the
> role that the Christians played for Tillich or the Americans for Dewey. So
> there is no attempt to help such a community find its way by helping it to
> reweave its beliefs, and thus its language.[1]

This supposed commitment to solitude, in turn, follows from what Rorty
calls Heidegger's "reification" of language. Rorty finds this exemplified in
Heideggerean passages such as this:

> Man acts as though he were the shaper and master of language, while in
> fact language remains the mistress of man. . . . For strictly, it is language

that speaks. Man first speaks when, and only when, he responds to language by listening to its appeal.[2]

Because Heidegger thus hypostasizes language on its own unique ontological level, Rorty argues, his thought can take itself to be a response to language alone. Heidegger's solitude is his response to a reified language that itself is solitary.

Rorty's reading of Heidegger is suspect, to say the least. The man for whom Rorty can find "no community that plays the role that . . . the Americans [played] for Dewey" almost destroyed his own career in 1933 in an effort to place the university at the disposal of the German people.[3] And much of Heidegger's later work consists, precisely, in an attempt to *escape* solitude: in a relentless pursuit of dialogue (*Gespräch*) with thinkers and poets.[4] Such pursuit is necessary for Heidegger because, as I have argued elsewhere, language for him exhibits what I call diakenic kinds of unity: it is, strictly, nothing over and above actual words and texts. The "speaking of language" is thus not for Heidegger the self-expression of a hypostasized *archê,* but a gathering of words around the kind of defining Nothing that is at work, for example, in Hölderlin's poem "Andenken."[5] If language is the mistress of man, it is not through her ontological plenitude but via the dynamic, gathering fissure at her core—a fissure which can manifest itself only in linguistic encounter with the other, i.e., in dialogue. Rorty's criticism of Heidegger, missing this, reads Heidegger back into a history which Heidegger himself sought to escape: the history of presence.

To see what is really at stake in this, we must go beyond Rorty's treatment of Heidegger altogether. For what Rorty wants to challenge is the entire approach he calls "foundationalism," which seeks unchangeable grounds for philosophical and other discourse. Rorty's Heidegger, seeking to base his thought on the speaking of a "reified" language, is an important case of such foundationalism. And Rorty's criticism of Heidegger, like his criticism of foundationalism in general, seeks to *free* us from it. His version of liberation will not be merely, or even in the first instance, "epistemological," like Derrida's. Rather, Rorty takes the primary locus of the ousiodic structures he criticizes to be not discourses as such, but the communities which use and are structured by them: "speech communities."

Rorty's critique of foundationalism is most relentless not when he treats Heidegger, but in his complex discussion of what is clearly the most radical and rigorous foundationalist project in contemporary philosophy: what he calls "analytical philosophy." In this chapter, I will argue that what Rorty criticizes in the community of analytical philosophers turns out to be its ousiodic structure. I will then show that in spite of the problems he brings out in that structure, ousia in Rorty's view structures not only analytical philosophy, but speech communities in general and as such. This means that for Rorty to challenge it consistently would place him outside all speech communities—a project as impossible for him as escaping from metaphysics would be for Derrida. The result, as I will argue in the next chapter, is a project of irony neither as global as the project of the Derrida of the Left, nor as banal as that of the Derrida of the Right—but shot through with inconsistencies. These can be removed by seeing (a) that what really bothers Rorty about foundationalism in general is the ousiodic structure it imparts to the speech communities structured by it, and (b) that speech communities are not necessarily ousiodically structured—a step which moves Rorty into proximity with Hegel.

1. OUSIODIC STRUCTURE AND ANALYTICAL PHILOSOPHY

Though still dominant in American universities, analytical philosophy for Rorty has lost sight of its own nature. Its view of itself, accurate enough some decades ago, now amounts to little more than fantasy. Rorty's challenge to it moves, accordingly, on two levels. One of these, running for example through Rorty's *Philosophy and the Mirror of Nature*, confronts the fantasy, which I will call "Analytical Philosophy," with the realities of contemporary culture. Analytical Philosophy, so viewed, is an idealized community of inquiry defined by a penchant for drawing suspiciously fixed and clear distinctions—between what is rational and what is not, what is meaningful and what meaningless, what is true and what false, what is good and what bad philosophy. Philosophers committed to such a vision of their discipline draw these distinctions, Rorty contends, in the service of foundationalism. Their devotion to it manifests itself in many ways. They admire science, for example, because, as they see it, science shares and indeed shapes the search for foundations. Philosophy is for them an autonomous discipline, differing from other discourses in being of "second intention": it reflects upon other disciplines because it has, unlike those more specialized fields, a set of overall basic principles by which all of them can be judged.[6]

Analytical Philosophy's second-order status, which for Rorty establishes its "purity," marks clear boundaries for philosophy itself. Its commitment to basic principles—in the first instance, presumably, the directives for thought codified in the predicate calculus—generates the problems and shapes the debates that are taken up within those boundaries (such philosophy contains, for example, little discussion or use of such antifoundationalist methods as dialectic). Finally, Analytical Philosophy's mission to reflect critically on other disciplines reflects the claim that it can, in virtue of its own rational form or basic principles, affect the world beyond its boundaries. As I will argue shortly, this trait amounts to a very strong type of what I call "disposition." For the moment, it is clear that Analytical Philosophy is a community of inquiry which sees itself as ousiodically structured: it has boundaries, disposition, and initiative. Rorty's confrontation with it thus includes a challenge to ousiodic structure as the blueprint for philosophical community. As with Derrida, however, this challenge to ousiodic structure is never identified as such.

While the idealizations of Analytical Philosophy had some relevance to the American situation in the first two decades after World War II, they had lost it by the early 1980s.[7] By then the American philosophical community was not structured around any single set of enduring problems, as Analytical Philosophy had been; it was based in university philosophy departments which varied widely in the kinds of problems and issues they took to be important. Nor did philosophy have any distinctive tools for solving those problems.[8] It defined itself by adherence not to a quasi-scientific set of methods, but merely to an "argumentative" style which eschewed allusion and indirection. Its unity, or rational form, was merely "stylistic and sociological."[9] What I am calling "analytical philosophy" is, in short, the Quinean successor to Analytical Philosophy.

Taking as its materials whatever issues that philosophers find interesting, and dealing with them in an argumentative style common to all inquiry, contemporary analytical philosophy seems to constitute a non-ousiodic community: it has no center or form dictating to the various philosophy departments that constitute it, and issues migrate freely—or at least randomly—into it through those departments. It seems, then, that Rorty's confrontation with Analytical Philosophy criticizes the boundaries and dispositive form which it claimed for itself. It does so on behalf of a more realistic view, which does not describe philosophy in terms derived from the old idealizations. Described in these new terms—i.e., apart from the continued adherence of many of its practitioners to the outdated ideals of Analytical Philosophy—analytical philosophy is, in Rorty's view, doing quite well; indeed, it constitutes a "precious cultural resource."[10]

In view of remarks like that, Giovanna Borradori has maintained that analytical philosophy "remains untouched by [Rorty's] attack."[11] In fact, if we look closely at how Rorty describes analytical philosophy, all is not quite well with it. For Analytical Philosophy's strong claims to disposition and initiative have, in Rorty's description of its successor, been only selectively weakened —and in ways, moreover, which render them vague and inconsistent.

Like its predecessor, analytical philosophy claims an ability to "classify, comprehend, and criticize the rest of culture."[12] This amounts to claiming not merely a form of the ousiodic trait of initiative, but a strong form. For it means not only that analytical philosophy aims to order (classify) other discourses, but that its comprehension of them is complete and critical. What is justified in them is merely what passes the test of philosophy's own conceptual grid. Other discourses, having only the legitimacy analytical philosophy accords to them, should relate to each other only in ways that it prescribes. Analytical philosophy thus claims the power not merely to affect the intellectual world beyond its boundaries, but actually to organize that world. Such power would be virtually dispositive in character.

But this claim to initiative is a problematic one. As Rorty notes, analytical philosophers had by 1981 learned to keep their criticisms of other disciplines largely to themselves. Instead of launching open attempts to show how other discourses are inadequate, as some Analytical Philosophers did, analytical philosophers merely held aloof from them—to such an extent, Rorty writes, that analytical philosophy "has pretty well closed itself off from contact with non-analytic philosophy, and lives in its own world."[13] Analytical philosophy as described by Rorty thus has an inconsistent relation to other discourses: on the one hand, it holds aloof from them, resting securely within its own borders. On the other, it claims, *sotto voce*, to comprehend and judge them.

What happens within its boundaries is also doubly determined. On the one hand, which issues come to be discussed in a philosophical way is, we saw, decided merely by the sociological constraint that an analytical philosopher should belong to a "good" philosophy department (Rorty calls this "the institutional tail wagging the scientific dog").[14] But such discussion, as I noted above, must still be argumentative in style. And this, in Rorty's view, is what determines which thinkers and issues are allowed to be "philosophical," or even rational at all. Indeed, it is in the name of that argumentative "style" that analytical philosophy claims to criticize other discourses, and even (quietly) seeks the exclusion of those, such as Continental philosophy and literary theory, which it finds insufficiently argumentative—just as Logical Positivism had (loudly) excoriated metaphysics as insufficiently scientific.[15]

In Rorty's account of analytical philosophy, then, the ousiodic structures of Analytical Philosophy are maintained, but in weakened and inconsistent ways. The unity provided to Analytical Philosophy by a shared set of problems and procedures for dealing with them (itself an effect of Analytical Philosophy's empiricist foundationalism) is weakened into a mere—but still coercive—argumentative "style." The claim to classify and judge other discourses, while not abandoned, subsides into prudent aloofness. In the importance of the "institutional tail" and in the circumspection of its public stance, analytical philosophy exhibits ousiodic structure under attack.

The weakness and inconsistency of analytical philosophy are evident from Rorty's descriptions of it, but he does not make them explicit. Explicitly, his criticism of the ousiodic structure of analytical philosophy is, again, that it is unrealistic. Its target is the trait that analytical philosophy most clearly shares with its forebear: its pretension to order and judge other discourses, or what I call its claim to initiative. As in the case of Analytical Philosophy, Rorty considers this claim to be fantastical. For Western culture as a whole, on Rorty's view, has abandoned the search for ultimate ordering principles, and by now needs their philosophical-scientific type about as much as it needs their older, religious version: not at all.[16] The standards analytical philosophers seek to impose upon the intellectual marketplace are thus obsolete. Their inability to accept this has led to their aloofness: they have retreated into a sort of priesthood apart, a community of foundationalists with its own boundaries, rational form, and initiative. That community, moreover, is a distinctively "modern" one in that it can see nothing beyond its boundaries but unfathomable chaos.[17]

In short, Rorty thinks that, like Heidegger's, the foundationalism of analytical philosophers issues in intellectual isolation. His criticism of Heidegger, in fact, can be viewed as claiming that Heidegger's thought also exhibits, in a very different way, ousiodic structure: language as the dominatrix of man exercises such disposition over humans that thinkers (e.g., Heidegger himself) relate to language alone, rather than to other people. Behind the boundaries established by Heidegger's disconnectedness, then, language reigns supreme.

Rorty's criticism of Heidegger is carried out in the name of community: he does not argue directly that Heidegger's view of language is false, but undermines it by describing it as "simply a stage in the [solitary] hypostatization of Martin Heidegger himself."[18] When he turns to A(a)nalytical P(p)hilosophy, by contrast, his critique is explicitly carried out in the name of truth. Analytical Philosophy is criticized for being a mere fantasy of ousiodic structure, without factual embodiment today. Its successor, analytical philosophy, is described as weakening that structure inconsistently. The resulting situation is described not as the march of reason, but as increasing isolation and irrelevance.

What Rorty's criticism of Heidegger and his confrontation with A(a)nalytical P(p)hilosophy both share is that they depend on his ability to describe their targets accurately, but in new terms and from new perspectives. Whether or not Heidegger's views on language are true, Rorty's own description of them must be if his criticism is to go through. A(a)nalytical P(p)hilosophy's pretensions are unjustified only if Rorty's description of the actual state of affairs is true. Both the criticism and the confrontation thus operate via what Rorty calls "redescription," which I will discuss in the next chapter.

If we look at the decisive common feature of Analytical Philosophy and analytical philosophy, however, a paradoxical feature of Rorty's critique emerges. Empirical foundationalism was a classic case of what Arthur Fine calls "truth mongering": coming up with some general account of truth and asserting it to be the goal of all responsible inquiry.[19] As carried out in A(a)nalytical P(p)hilosophy, this move presupposes two beliefs about truth: that it is the sole goal of responsible inquiry, and that it is a property of assertions.[20]

It was by taking assertionistic, scientific truth for the paramount goal of inquiry, then, that Analytical Philosophy established itself as empirical foundationalism. One of the founding moments of Analytical Philosophy, though Rorty does not discuss it as such, came when Gottlob Frege excluded from "science" (including his own inquiry) all senses of "true" other than that which applies to sentences, so that the goal of inquiry is a certain type of sentence—a true one.[21] That gesture, moreover, has survived the weakening of Analytical Philosophy into analytical philosophy. For Frege's views, expressed peremptorily if at all, are attributable to virtually everyone identified with A(a)nalytical P(p)hilosophy. To Frege, who was no ordinary truthmonger, the gesture had a merely pragmatic justification. When elevated to the status of an insight into the nature of truth itself,[22] it led to a number of doctrines characteristic of Analytical Philosophy in its heyday: that the basic unit of language is the basic bearer of truth, the sentence or proposition; that the basic epistemic component of the mind is the psychologized sentence, the belief; that the basic phenomenon of morality is moral choice, in which an individual undertakes to make true one of a variety of possible descriptions of the world; that the basic unit of society is such individual choice, etc.

As Roger Scruton has written, "in philosophy . . . truth is all-important, and determines the structure of the discipline."[23] The two beliefs about truth mentioned above, whether stated or unstated, remained largely definitive for analytical philosophy at the time of Rorty's writing. In all the diverse and ingenious inquiries that proceed in the name of analytical philosophy, and in all the elegant solutions and dissolutions that those investigations yield, we see the refusal, both radical and rigorous, to articulate or countenance any goals for inquiry other than that of assertional truth. The strategies and procedures for securing such truth are what analytical philosophy calls "reason," which is thus reduced to the predicate calculus and derivatives. The issues concerning such truth—those of reference, to which meaning is reduced; of realism and instrumentalism, to which science is reduced; the possibility of consciousness, to which the burgeoning field of Artificial Intelligence is reduced; and the norms of moral choice, to which human goodness is reduced—are the issues which analytical philosophy raises. The concept of truth, then, is analytical philosophy's bounding and disposing form—just as it was in the case of Analytical Philosophy.

Such truth, I noted in the introduction, is the excellence of presence: an entity is present if true propositions can be formulated concerning it. Thus, the problems with both Analytical Philosophy and analytical philosophy derive from their devotion to presence. It is a devotion Rorty both questions and shares. For as I have noted, his own challenges to analytical philosophy are themselves in the name of truth. How, then, can he escape the basic charge which lies behind those he actually levels—that of truthmongering? (*In the background of this bustling and roaming . . . stands the question mark of an ever more dangerous curiosity: . . .*)

2. OUSIODIC STRUCTURE AND SPEECH COMMUNITY

Rorty's confrontation with A(a)nalytical P(p)hilosophy thus turns out, like Derrida's overthrow and displacement of metaphysics, to embody unstated challenges to its ousiodic structure. But the paradox I just mentioned suggests that Rorty's challenge has limits. For he himself, it seems, adopts the same kind of structure for his own discourse that he criticizes in the case of A(a)nalytical P(p)hilosophy. In this section, I will argue that the reason for this is that all discourse for Rorty remains bound to truth in the same ways that analytical philosophy, for him, is bound to truth. The result is that the openness and formlessness which Rorty attributes to analytical philosophy are not carried over into his general view of speech communities as such, which remain ousiodically structured.

Contingency, Irony, and Solidarity, though highly critical of Analytical Philosophy, remains in a way true to what I have identified as its founding exclusion. We hear early on that where there are no sentences there is no truth; indeed, it is because only sentences can be true that truth for Rorty is something we make rather than find. As he puts it:

> To say that truth is not out there is simply to say that where there are no sentences there is no truth, that sentences are elements of human languages, and that human languages are human creations. . . . Only sentences can be true, and . . . human beings make truths by making languages in which to phrase sentences.[24]

The references to "human beings" here show that Rorty is not talking merely about A(a)nalytical P(p)hilosophy, or his own discourse: he is making some general observations on the nature of speech communities as such. And one such observation is that truth, for Rorty as for A(a)nalytical P(p)hilosophers, is always and only a property of assertions.[25]

Rorty's adherence to the other side of analytical philosophy's founding exclusion—the view that all responsible inquiry aims at truth—is subtle and original, and seems to work like this: Sentences require words for their formulation. Unlike such philosophers of language as Donald Davidson, Rorty holds that not all words gain their meaning exclusively from their use in sentences, i.e., from the conditions under which they assert truths. As Wittgenstein argued in *Philosophical Investigations,* at least some words are better understood as social practices which can cue and articulate other social practices. They should be understood not solely in terms of their descriptive capacities, but in terms of what I call their parametric functions. The parametric functioning of a word can be investigated by relating it to and evaluating such practices: by arguing for sentences such as "word y enables us to articulate such-and-such phenomena in a socially useful way," or (more generally) "word z triggers such-and-such socially useful practices."

Thus, we might argue that calling retarded children "exceptional," though it does not capture what it is that makes them unusual, is more humane than calling them "retarded" (to say nothing of other epithets). In such argument we would be establishing the truth of a sentence, such as "it is humane to refer to retarded children as 'exceptional.'"

But what about "humaneness" itself? Is it, with its positive associations, a pragmatically virtuous word? For Rorty, who operates with an argumentative view of reason, such questions get less arguable as the words questioned get more basic. Though he alludes to the procedure (*CIS*, pp. 57, 73), he will not, for example, establish that "humaneness" is a good word as an Hegelian might: by *showing* that at the core of its manifold meanings lies a disciplined set of ambiguities which are not adventitious but are dialectically generated and refined.[26] Nor will he do as Heidegger would: *show* that the different meanings of a word are diakenically gathered over history by an emptiness, that they "swing in a hidden rule" which his own thought does not describe, but puts into play simply by showing them.[27]

Rather, "humaneness" must for Rorty be validated as a useful word by argumentative appeal to some external criterion. Such appeal would have to go beyond citing and organizing what has already been declared good because humane and appeal to some still higher value, such as "facilitating disparate practices." The issue could then be captured in standard propositional form: the sentence "to be good is to be capable of facilitating disparate practices" would be a topic for traditional philosophical debate.[28] But such debate has to end somewhere, and so Rorty arrives at the view that every language has some terms, and very important ones, that cannot be argued for at all (*CIS*, p. 9). Rorty calls this the "final vocabulary" of the language, or more precisely of a particular speech community.

Connected with the view that all reason is argumentative, i.e., aims at establishing the truth of sentences or propositions, is a stronger view: the view that truth is the only virtue that can be argued for, and hence is the only standard for rational evaluation. This stronger view is in general quite implausible—we continually argue whether one course of action is "better" than another in various senses, or whether a painting is "beautiful," and Rorty himself argues, as I noted, that Heideggerean philosophy is defective because it is solitary, not because it is untrue. But he appears nonetheless to hold this stronger view with respect to final vocabularies. The only way to evaluate languages, it appears, is with respect to the fidelity they allow to reality.[29] But that is impossible for Rorty, for the world "does not provide us with any criterion of choice" between alternative vocabularies. There is then for Rorty "nothing which validates a person's or a culture's final vocabulary" (*CIS*, p. 20).

Any passage from one such vocabulary to another is, therefore, not rational: though causes of the movement can be given, reasons for it cannot.[30] Rorty does state that some vocabularies are "better tools [than others] for dealing with the world for one or another purpose" (*CIS*, pp. 21, 197). But this appeal to usefulness does not mean that it can stand in the place of the discredited truth as a rational tool for evaluating final vocabularies. For the purposes for which a vocabulary comes into existence and is used are in Rorty's view themselves immanent to that vocabulary, in which they are formulated and agreed to be possible and important. No general account of what makes vocabularies useful—and might make some more useful than others—is possible.[31]

Limiting himself to traditional, indeed analytical, views of reason as restricted to arguing for the truth of assertions, Rorty has arrived at the general view that the basic terms in which those assertions are couched cannot themselves be either argued for or criticized. He converts this, I will now argue, into a general view of speech communities as bounded and disposed, i.e., ousiodically structured.

The boundaries of the Rortyan speech community can be seen from what Rorty advocates for philosophy. With his view that final vocabularies are unwarranted, we may say, Rorty has disposed of Analytical Philosophy's pretensions to necessary truth. But he conflates traditional philosophy's necessity-claim (its claim to know things that cannot be other than they are) with its universality-claim (its claim to know things which are true for everyone).[32] The lack of necessity then means lack of universality, and so Rorty advocates that philosophy become a sort of local discourse, in which one palavers only with those "who share enough of one's beliefs to make fruitful conversation possible."[33] Each philosophical community (like analytical philosophy) would admit only those who agree with a sufficient number of its basic beliefs, and thus would be securely bounded.

In this, philosophical communities are like other speech communities for Rorty; and the walls separating such speech communities from one another are unbreachable indeed. We can see this by noting that while the basic beliefs of a particular speech community may only seldom be explicitly *formulated* as beliefs, they are always *conveyed* by its basic words. This is why a language game for Rorty is not merely a set of verbal practices but "a set of agreements about what is possible and important" (*CIS*, p. 48). Simply by playing a language game in which a particular set of words is basic, a speech community conveys its collective belief in their importance; but it usually does this without saying so. Thus, for example, analytical philosophers almost never state their basic belief that assertional truth is the only articulable goal of rational inquiry, and many would be surprised (if not offended) to hear it put that way. But that belief is evident in the way they use "truth" and allied terms, and in the general reduction of philosophy to argument which Rorty notes and deplores.

Because basic beliefs commonly operate as unstated restrictions on the use of certain important words, someone who does not share the basic beliefs of a particular speech community is less likely to find herself arguing with its members than unable to talk with them at all. The only way to understand members of another speech community, in fact, is either to talk in their language—adopt their basic commitments—or make them talk in yours, i.e., adopt yours. The final vocabulary of a speech community thus gives it determinate, indeed unbreachable, boundaries: disparate speech communities are walled off from one another, not merely through disagreement, but through mutual incomprehension. In true modern style, moreover, each such community tends to see itself as the only one: all other speech communities, being unintelligible to my own, will be dismissed by me as "irrational" (see *CIS*, p 48). (*The freed spirit is restless and underway . . . as if wandering in a desert . . .*)

The final vocabulary of a speech community not only bounds it but governs what debates arise within it and how they are conducted: it determines how its members will see themselves and "describe everything that is important" (*CIS*, p. 74). The evaluative commitments conveyed by a speech community's final vocabulary thus constitute a dispositive form—not only for the debates that go on in that community, but for that community's members themselves. For in Rorty's view, "human beings are simply incarnated vocabularies" (*CIS*, p. 88): the vocabulary of a given speech community generates the nondiscursive practices and institutions of that community. So it is unsurprising that a new vocabulary causes later generations "to look for appropriate new forms of nonlinguistic behavior, for example, the adoption of new scientific equipment or new social institutions" (*CIS*, pp. 9, 88; also cf. pp. 20, 41, 53). The final vocabulary, then, cannot be changed without transforming the community it structures into something new. It constitutes, to use a traditional term, the "essence" of that community.

In sum: a speech community's final vocabulary, conveying the basic beliefs which constitute the community as a speech community, is both a bounding and disposing form for that community. It decides who can speak within that community, and orders it by governing what institutions and practices they adopt. The only structure of traditional ousia which the Rortyan speech community lacks—indeed, as Rorty's criticisms of A(a)nalytical P(p)hilosophy show, ought to lack—is, as will be seen in more detail later, initiative: the power to affect the world outside, especially other discourses.

Rorty's claim that the basic words of a speech community cannot be argued for or against has left him open to all sorts of criticism as a relativist, and in particular seems to leave him in what Thomas McCarthy has called his "ethnocentric predicament."[34] For, as people like McCarthy and Hilary Putnam[35] were quick to point out, Rorty's speech communities, cut off from everything beyond themselves, would have no reason ever to try to improve critically upon their own ways and beliefs. If I am right, the real target of these criticisms is Rorty's apparent reinstatement of ousiodic structure for speech communities in general.

He appears, in fact, to be advocating just the kind of aloof solitude for which he has criticized Heidegger and analytical philosophy. For all his challenges to analytical philosophy's ousiodic structure, for example, he sees it as functioning, within its own community, undisturbed and smoothly: it is in his view, as I have noted, a valuable cultural resource, and (after abandoning its claim to order and evaluate all other discourses) it should continue as it is.[36] This is presumably welcome news for those committed to traditional ousiodic structure as a way of conceptualizing philosophical community. It would also, however, be welcome news for racists, sexists, cultists, fundamentalists, and just about everyone who prefers to keep her basic beliefs unchallenged. For it leaves each speech community in undisturbed solitude, asking only that it renounce its initiative to prescribe to other such communities. (*Solitude encircles and encoils it, ever more threatening, more suffocating, more heart stifling, choking . . .*)

IRONY AND REDESCRIPTION AS
CHALLENGES TO OUSIA

As I suggested in the previous chapter, Rorty's challenge to ousia seems to have limits, and rather strict ones at that. Any speech community is for him ousiodically structured by its own final vocabulary. Since all human communities are speech communities (*CIS*, pp. 36f), we appear to be left with a view of human beings as at the disposal of self-enclosed, unchallengeable vocabularies which wall them off from everyone who does not share their basic commitments. If not a truly "ethnocentric predicament," because a speech community is not an *ethnos,* this is clearly an ousiodic one. It leaves Rorty able to challenge only the exercise of initiative by such communities: the claim of one speech community to understand and judge others in the terms of its own final vocabulary.

But Rorty's position is more complex. His challenges to ousiodic structure are not in fact limited to arguing for its merely fantastical nature and showing inconsistencies and weaknesses in its actual operation—procedures which, we saw, were also open to Derrida. He also contests it in a way that Derrida explicitly refuses: by formulating an alternative to it. This alternative is developed in Rorty's reconceived visions of the philosophical community and of speech communities in general, and in his account of the kind of person who founds such communities: the "ironist." Rorty's discussion of final or basic vocabularies, and his advocacy of irony as the way to dethrone them, will amount to yet another challenge to ousiodic structure, this time not on the level of philosophy but on that of speech communities in general.

1. THE IRONIST

Rorty's 1986 "On Ethnocentrism: A Reply to Clifford Geertz" showed that a complacent solitude of speech communities was not what he advocated.[1] *Contingency, Irony, and Solidarity,* on which my account of Rortyan irony will focus, shows that rejecting it is central to his enterprise. For the clubby smugness associated by so many people with essays such as "Solidarity or Objectivity?" is just what the book most vigorously attacks. We can begin to see this by noting one important sense in which Rorty is not a relativist. He is perfectly willing to accept that in *every* carefully conducted debate someone is right and someone is wrong (*CIS,* pp. 6, 47f). But he emphasizes those cases where argument never gets going because the two parties have no common vocabulary in which to engage one another. Because the basic terms of the arguers—their final vocabularies—cannot be argued for or against, responsible inquiry into the value of those terms is impossible. So far, Rorty agrees fully with analytical philosophy. He differs from it because he wants not to render all inquiries "responsible" by his own lights, but the opposite: to proliferate cases where responsible inquiry is impossible.

These cases, if closed to responsible investigation, are open to what Rorty calls "irony." For all speech communities, lacking foundations, are open to the withering words of the "ironist"—of one who worries about her own basic beliefs or vocabularies and shows that they cannot be final. (*"Can we not overturn all values? . . . Is everything perhaps false in its final ground? And if we are deceived, are we not—precisely because of that—also deceivers? Must we not also be deceivers?"*)

It is irony, then, which for Rorty brings about the "death" of final vocabularies and of the ousiodic intellectual communities which they found. Rorty's story of such death will have two stages. As will be revisited in more detail later, for Rorty the withering attention of the ironist is not drawn by specific problems encountered by the final vocabulary of the community, for (as the case of analytical philosophy shows) from the point of view of that community there may be no such problems. What bothers the ironist is simply the view that the basic vocabulary is "final," not in Rorty's own sense that it is too basic to be argued for, but in the stronger sense that it cannot be improved upon and is eternally valid: that it is viewed as no mere idiosyncratic historical project, but the last word, the one to which inquiry and history have converged, the one which renders further inquiry and history superfluous.[2]

This is why a speech community can function perfectly well by its own lights, and still fall victim to irony. It is not as if the ordering principles of a final vocabulary were somehow challenged by the very materials they were supposed to order—as consciousness is repeatedly challenged in Hegel's *Phenomenology*, or as Hegelian philosophy itself is to be challenged, to its own advantage, by transformations in the discourses whose basic concepts it orders. Rather, the speech community is perceived by its members to be functioning successfully on its own terms. The fact that those terms are not the only possible ones cannot be recognized by those who take them as their foundation. And it is that very general foundationalist gesture, common to all non-ironical speech communities, against which Rortyan irony is directed.

In the second stage of Rorty's presentation, the ironist, in addition to questioning vocabularies, also tries to invent new ones. The creation of new vocabularies is the positive outcome of Rorty's critique of foundationalism, and is the alternative he proposes to traditional, foundationalistic (and especially analytical) philosophy.

On the one hand, Rorty construes the ironist to be motivated by Harold Bloom's "anxiety of influence": she wants to show that she is not a "copy or a replica" of other people, but personally unique (*CIS*, pp. 23f). Since human beings are for Rorty incarnated vocabularies, the only way to be unique is to have a unique vocabulary—and the only way to get that is to create it oneself, rather than spend one's life "shoving around already coined pieces" (*CIS*, pp. 23f). In doing this, the ironist ceases to be determined by the vocabulary she has inherited, but actually creates one. Together with it, since she herself is an incarnate vocabulary, she creates nothing less than her own mind, thus achieving what Rorty calls "autonomy" (*CIS*, pp. 27, 97; also cf. pp. 20, 80). The ironist remains, to be sure, at the disposal of her language; she does not become something more than an incarnate vocabulary. But it is now a vocabulary which she herself has generated and organized.

So conceived, the self of the ironist appears to manifest the three traits of boundary, disposition, and initiative. The boundaries of her self are indicated by the all-important distinction between words that she herself generates and those that come to her from outside; her single dispositive and creative form is manifest in the uniqueness of the personal "impress" she seeks to give to everything she thinks (*CIS*, pp. 23f, 43). She may even attain a sort of initiative, for "with luck . . . her [new] language will strike the next generation as inevitable. *Their* behavings will bear [her] impress" (*CIS*, p. 29). The autonomy attributed to the ironist here thus seems quite like the traditional Kantian variety—except that what the ironist "gives herself" is not a universal law sanctioned by reason, but a contingent vocabulary sanctioned only, and temporarily, by her own uniqueness. It is "just another set of little human things," but one "around which one makes one's life center." Rorty does not hesitate, echoing Kant, to call such centering an "unconditional commandment" (*CIS*, pp. 37, 93; also cf. p. 33).

Rorty thus seems to be challenging not ousiodic structure itself but the idea that the central, dispositive form of such structure can be rational and necessary. Elsewhere in *Contingency, Irony, and Solidarity*, however, Rorty rejects the concept of such a centered self, so that the invention of a new vocabulary proves to be not a single project of re-creating a distinct self, but a piecemeal effort:

> If there is no center to the self, then, there are only different ways of weaving new candidates for belief and desire into antecedently existing webs of belief and desire. (*CIS*, p. 83f; also cf. pp. 10, 88)

When we try and put these two accounts together, we seem to have a story in which the ironist begins with concern for her own unique identity, but in fact discovers that she is nothing more than a set of reweavings. Something like this is suggested at the end of Rorty's discussion of the self:

> But if we avoid Nietzsche's inverted Platonism—his suggestion that a life of self-creation can be as complete and as autonomous as Plato thought a life of contemplation might be—then we shall be content to think of any human life as the always incomplete, yet sometimes heroic, reweaving of such a web. (*CIS*, p. 43)

The ousiodic self constituted by the anxiety of influence thus appears to be an idealization—like Analytical Philosophy. But there is a difference. The idealizations of Analytical Philosophy, we saw, can for Rorty profitably be abandoned by analytical philosophers. But the project of a uniquely distinctive self is constitutive for the ironist: if her aim is to establish the uniqueness of her personal impress, to "create a style so distinctive as to make one's books incommensurable with those of one's precursors" (*CIS*, p. 126), then mere piecemeal reweaving will not suffice, and the ironist must be maintained in her original illusion. Rorty in fact leaves the two accounts unreconciled: in spite of the above quote, he also assures us that "some people have actually succeeded in re-creating themselves" (*CIS*, p. xiv).

The invention of a new vocabulary centers for Rorty on a conceptual practice he calls "redescription." Assuming that we know what it is to describe something, what Rorty means by redescription follows cleanly: it is to describe something in new terms—in what Rorty calls "metaphors." A metaphor, for Rorty, is in the first instance a meaningless sound and as such is not, in the usual sense, linguistic at all. Uttering one in the course of a conversation is a gesture, more like *doing* something than *saying* something— like suddenly making a face or kissing your interlocutor (*CIS*, p. 18). We may presume that such actions arouse responses from those at whom they are directed; when the uttering of a metaphor and the response to it are repeated and become patterns, we have what Wittgenstein might call a new language-game, and what Rorty would call a new set of agreements about what is possible and important. The kind of ironical discourse with which Rorty seeks to supplement the traditional, truth-oriented variety is thus redescription. By using words in radically new ways to describe things as they have never been described before, Rorty starts a game in which he hopes that others will join (see *CIS*, p. 12).

Redescription is central not merely to Rorty's reflections on irony, but to his own practice of challenge as well. Rorty's criticism of Heidegger, I noted, relied upon redescribing Heidegger's hypostatization of language as in fact the hypostatization of Martin Heidegger. His critique of Analytical Philosophy, I also noted, was achieved by describing the actual practices of philosophers in late-twentieth-century America in ways they had not been described before; his critique of analytical philosophy reposed on the redescription of it as inconsistently perpetuating weakened versions of the ousiodic structures of its parent. His discussion of speech communities claims to be a description, again in new terms, of the ways they actually function; and his account of irony itself relies on the redescription of such ironic philosophers as Hegel, Heidegger, and Nietzsche.

2. PROBLEMS WITH IRONY

Both Rorty's views on redescription and his practice of it are, I think, deeply and importantly problematic. On the theoretical level, Rorty's use of "redescription" rather than "reorganization" or "reconnection," or any of many other "re-" words, to describe what he is about is no innocent terminological matter. Its obvious reference to description ineluctably sends Rorty back to the idea of the mind's "Glassy Essence," which he combated so effectively in *Philosophy and the Mirror of Nature*.[3] This can be seen by looking at two respects in which Rorty's account of redescription, based as we saw on his account of metaphor, is in tension with it.

First, the account of metaphor as gesture aims to exclude from it any cognitive value. But if metaphors are wholly noncognitive, how can we use them to "describe," to say nothing of "*re*describe"? A meaningless sound does not describe anything. But throughout *CIS*, Rorty talks as if the job of the ironist is not, say, to "reorganize" our practices by "reorganizing" our language, but to "rearrange" things by "describing" them differently (*CIS*, p. 99). And if revolutionary, metaphorical language is *re*descriptive, then normal language (which for Rorty is constituted by the fading of metaphors into true or false sentences: *CIS*, p. 8) must be descriptive. In both its revolutionary and ordinary modes, then, language's main job is to describe, to make statements about, reality—a traditional component of the Glassy Essence view of the mind. Rorty's relation to truth and presence thus becomes complex and ambiguous. While retaining truth as the general goal of responsible inquiry, Rorty wants to reject it for his own ironical version. But the rejection is partial, because irony is *re*description and hence is merely a new way of saying true things. Irony, in other words, is the irresponsible passage from one set of possible true assertions to another.

A second incompatibility between the accounts of metaphor and redescription is the disappearance, in the latter notion, of the interactive context so vital to Rorty's original account of metaphor. While metaphors are sounds to be dropped into conversations, redescription appears to be an essentially solitary activity. The scientist, for example, can redescribe nature, even when she is the only person in it. One can also redescribe oneself, which is, in principle at least, a wholly private activity. When one redescribes other people, one may do so from a distance so vast that a salient feature of such redescription is its potential cruelty (*CIS*, pp. 16f, 27, 91f). Absent any conversational context, redescription becomes the activity of an isolated ego, one whose relation to her audience is (as we will see Rorty take his own to be) wholly contingent. We are again conveyed to the Glassy Essence, now to the solipsism associated with it.[4] (*Such questions guide and entice the freed spirit, leading it ever farther forth, ever farther off. Solitude encircles and encoils it . . .*)

Once detached from human contexts, redescription also becomes, like the notion of "truth" itself, impossibly general. It can, for example, be performed on all possible objects (the examples in the preceding paragraph alone come under such general and traditional headings as Nature, Self, Other, I, It, and They). What Kant did in rendering his *état civil* of the mind's faculties, what Einstein did by defining mass in terms of energy, and what the Nazis did in calling Jews *Ungeziefer* would all, it appears, be equally cases of "redescription."

Contingency, Irony, and Solidarity thus does not adequately explain why redescription is re*descriptive;* if I am right, it should not be. The "re-" also, I think, makes problems for Rorty, because his likening of metaphors to activities such as making faces fails to do justice to what he recognizes is the paramount way in which a metaphor differs from a funny face or a kiss: that it is composed of previously existing words.[5] Thus, he writes:

> Metaphors are unfamiliar uses of old words, but such uses are only possible against the background of *other* old words being used in old familiar ways. A language which was "all metaphor" would be a language which had no use, hence, not a language but just babble. (*CIS*, p. 41; emphasis added)

What is missing here is the recognition that the "background" of a metaphor includes not merely *other* words being used in the old ways, but the old uses of the words of the metaphor itself. Part of the "meaning," for example, of "the butterfly of a smile spreads across her face" is the traditional meanings of "spread" and "butterfly" (including their traditional incompatibility, not just with smiles and faces, but with each other).[6] No metaphor is entirely new: its creation is a matter of *bricolage*, of finding new uses for old tools and materials. But this is exactly what Rorty wants redescription *not* to be. He wants it to come up with radically new language-games and words in order to supply the side of inquiry too basic for argument: the irresponsible side (*CIS*, pp. 24, 27). Hence the generality in his conception of redescription: for Rorty, words do not grow from the dialectical transformation of earlier words, but from the wholesale rejection of earlier vocabularies. Such rejection is to free the ironist, including Rorty himself, from the past: in spite of his recurrent discussions of historical figures, philosophy for him is to be *exclusively* validated by its relation to the future.[7]

But finding tensions in Rorty's theoretical account of redescription may not be particularly helpful. To ask him for a conceptually adequate account of redescription would be to demand a philosophically responsible account of irresponsibility. And this would be to awaken philosophy's ancient problematic of the Other in a uniquely twisted way. For we would not be demanding that Rorty, the responsible philosopher, give a philosophical account of what he excludes from philosophy. We would be demanding that Rorty, the irresponsible redescriber, abandon his own approach,[8] become his own Other, and give that Other's account of himself.

The difficulties with redescription, however, are not merely theoretical. Rorty's practice of it leads, I think, to two main groups of problems, both of which derive from the problematic role of truth in his own thought. One of these concerns his understanding of previous philosophers and of his own relation to them. Rorty's accounts of thinkers and texts are interesting, vigorous, and sometimes deeply illuminating. But they are often inaccurate. *Contingency, Irony, and Solidarity*, in particular, is a well-tended garden of misprision. The real Hegel said that history has faded to "gray on gray," and that the discord of the times forces philosophers to turn away from it to form a "priesthood apart."[9] Rorty's Hegel is relentlessly public and characteristically ends his narratives of history with the remark that "and so Germany became Top Nation" (*CIS*, p. 104). The real Heidegger hinted that language is a (diakenic) "house" in which we "dwell."[10] Rorty's Heidegger says that it is a "divinity" of which we are "emanations" (*CIS*, p. 11). Derrida's *Post Card* says that "the post card is neither public nor private."[11] Rorty's *Post Card* is a series, not of postcards, but of love letters, and "nothing is more private than a love letter" (*CIS*, p. 126). Rorty's Habermas fully agrees with Rorty, the bourgeois liberal, on political matters (*CIS*, pp. 66f). The real Habermas, as Thomas McCarthy has remarked, wrote *The Theory of Communicative Action* to show how capitalism has undermined democracy.[12] And so on. Though Rorty discusses a wide range of texts, in ways that are consciously intended to break *disciplinary* boundaries (*CIS*, pp. 96–103), he never violates the boundaries of his own personal impress and vocabulary. His readings, in short, often justify his references to ironist history in general as "fantasy" (*CIS*, pp. 125, 141).

These misreadings sever important and valid connections between Rorty and his predecessors. Such connections are important to Rorty because

> ... the ironist's nominalism and historicism will not permit him to think of his work as establishing a relation to real essence; he can only establish a relation to the past. (*CIS*, p. 101)

But the first chapter of *Contingency, Irony, and Solidarity,* for example, contains a string of striking theses about language: that it is not a medium, that it has a variety of functions, that all relations of language to the world are causal, that language originates in metaphor, and others. All are to be found in Hegel, who even asserted, à la Rorty's account of metaphor, that words when first used by the philosopher mean absolutely nothing.[13] And the great doctrine that Rorty wants to draw and make into a criterion and exclusionary test for any philosophy—the view that it should be wholly private—was not only suggested by Hegel at the end of the *Lectures on the Philosophy of Religion.* It was practiced and transcended by the later Heidegger.[14]

As to Rorty's connection with what will follow him—that, he says, is a matter of luck (*CIS*, p. 37). The future is thus, like the past, a realm of sheer contingency. It is not, as death is for Heidegger, an emptiness which actively structures our lives here and now by compelling us to make definitive choices;[15] Rorty does not advance the theses that he does because the future awaits. He advances them because he thinks they are true; his attitude toward the future is merely the hope that he will get lucky and others will follow him. (*Solitude encircles and encoils it, ever more threatening, more suffocating, more heart stifling, choking . . .*)

Partly responsible for these misreadings, it seems, is that Rorty takes redescription as his object—it is, in all its vagueness, what he expects to find texts doing. He seeks, in other words, to operate on a textual level where argument is wholly absent. But the new vocabularies which even ironists like Derrida, Heidegger, and Nietzsche seek to introduce are largely defined contextually, in and through the arguments made with them. If we abjure the arguments, we lose most of the words. More generally, it is as if the absence of any account of the "re-" in redescription absolves Rorty from sustained encounter with the texts he discusses. Thus freed, he can operate without regard to the constraints of assertional truth, with its demand that we "get things right" about what we discuss (see *CIS*, pp. 6f, 16).

Rorty also runs into problems in connecting his own discourse with contemporary realities. An example is evident from *Contingency, Irony, and Solidarity*'s political argument. Politics in general is not a field with which Rorty deals easily. Consider his idea, given elsewhere, of a "concrete note" on which to conclude a discussion of political matters:

> Suppose that somewhere, someday, the newly elected government of a large industrialized country decreed that everybody should get the same income, regardless of occupation or disability.[16]

Such "concretion" is high-flown indeed.[17] I adduce it merely to show how Rorty's own discourse is radically disconnected. With truth abjured, the relation between that discourse and reality itself is tenuous, and hence Rorty's statements about texts and politics are misleading. With redescription directed only against the wholly general issue of the final nature of vocabularies, rather than specific problems with them, Rorty's thought cannot grasp its own relations to its predecessors. Finally, with redescription radically general and the abjured truth the only standard by which to evaluate vocabularies, their merits and failings cannot be compared at all (cf. *CIS*, pp. 14f, 19, 20, 48, 75). The various vocabularies we have are cast adrift from one another, and among them floats Rorty's own discourse—free of any nonfantasized relation to the past and of anything more than a contingent relation to the future. As with traditional discourses, Rorty's own is now protected by inviolable boundaries, within which his own vocabulary reigns—for a while —unchallenged. (. . . *Solitude, fearsome goddess and* mater saeva cupidinum, *fierce mother of the passions.*)

3. DETERMINATE NEGATION AND PROXIMITY TO HEGEL

Rorty's own thought, then, ends in a solitude not unlike that which he himself criticizes in the cases of Heidegger and analytical philosophy. That solitude, I have argued, is an artifact of the ousiodic structure that Rorty applies to speech communities and discourses, including his own. For in spite of his important challenges to ousiodic structure, Rorty clearly makes an unreflective parametric use of ousia to structure his own discourse: his challenges to ousiodic structure therefore remain sporadic and inconsistent. We can see more clearly how this comes about by placing Rorty's thought into closer proximity to Hegel, whom he regards as the founder of an ironist tradition in philosophy.[18]

When presence (truth) is first ironized and then reinstated by redescriptions couched in a new vocabulary, the old edifice for Rorty is not merely displaced or made to tremble, as with Derrida; it is abandoned altogether. Rorty implies this when he fails to see the middle ground between inventing something entirely new and reducing new inventions to past states of affairs:

> . . . our geniuses invent problems and programs *de novo*, rather than being presented with them by the subject-matter itself, or by the "current state of research.". . . It is a mark of humanistic culture *not* to try to reduce the new to the old. . . .[19]

The contrast with Derrida is double: Rorty not only abandons the old edifice

altogether, but can do so because he has another domicile to go to. Derrida
—the Derrida of the Left, anyway—refused to countenance any such refuge
from metaphysics because presence itself, its central villain, was a condition
of all speech. For Rorty, different final vocabularies are as different as can
be—which does not mean, as I have been arguing, that presence does not
continue to trouble his thought.

It is because the ironist has another domicile to go to—the "entirely new"
final vocabulary that she herself invents—that Rorty comes into proximity to
Hegel, whose philosophy (as Rorty notes) is deeply concerned with such
basic vocabulary shifts (cf. *CIS*, pp. 7, 55, 78f). Like Hegel, Rorty tells a
general story of such shifts: of the downfall of a final vocabulary and the
community of inquiry it structures, and the rise of a new one. Like Hegel's,
Rorty's story has in general two stages: where Hegel had negation and the
reinstatement of positivity through the negation of negation, Rorty has
the withering force of irony and the creativity of redescription. But unlike
Hegel's, and even more resolutely than Habermas's (as will be seen), Rorty's
story is undialectical.

Hegelian dialectics, of course, is structured by what Hegel calls "determinate negation."[20] In such negation, each new stage negates something specific about the previous stage in order to cope with a problem which has
arisen within that stage; the older stage thus provides guidance, if sometimes only of a "negative" sort, to its successor. For Rorty, by contrast, the
defining features of "dialectics" are its concern with vocabularies rather
than with propositions, and its "partial substitution of redescription for inference." Negation and inversion do not belong to dialectics at all, and a
"more up-to-date" name for it, in Rorty's view, would be "literary criticism"
(*CIS*, pp. 78f). Dialectics thus does not, for Rorty, include seeing how an
older vocabulary might have guided the emergence of a newer one. Indeed,
since the new one will be entirely new, such guidance is impossible (*CIS*,
p. 197). Hence, when dialectics becomes a matter of establishing or recon-
structing specific interconnections in a sequence of vocabularies, it immediately becomes for Rorty either misleading (as with Nietzsche) or intrinsically suspect (as with Hegel himself: *CIS*, pp. 100, 134).

Because Rortyan redescription is not motivated by anything specific in
the old vocabulary, the new vocabulary shares nothing specific with the old:
it is not a "determinate negation" of it. Nor can the two define themselves
through their mutual difference, as was the case for Heideggerean and Derridean diakenicity. Instead, they lapse into mutual indifference—and Rorty
falls victim to one of the least attractive of modern myths, the idea that the
intellect of a human being can somehow create the way God's does: *de novo*,
after all, only means *intellectualiter ex nihil.*

Taking itself for a completely radical *inventio de novo*, redescription produces, and because of its generality must produce, a free float of various
disparate discourses, each with its own final vocabulary and hence with its

own ousiodic structure. The fate of each new vocabulary is therefore to be merely one more human project, "to be filed among the others" like that of Freud (*CIS*, p. 39). It would be congenial to Rorty if this coexistence of vocabularies were of the liberal type: each vocabulary would flourish independently of the others and without bothering them. Actually, Rorty suggests something stronger: enough overlap in vocabularies to permit people who share a political space to care about one another (*CIS*, pp. 92f). But he needs something stronger still. For sharing-and-caring coexistence, like the liberal variety, would permit the unchecked proliferation of vocabularies,[21] and this conflicts with Rorty's pragmatism. Pragmatically speaking, vocabularies are different ways to conceptualize a problem or situation. A person who had infinitely many of them would be unable to settle on any finite number as "best" for the situation at hand, and hence would be unable to act. The more vocabularies we have at our disposal, the closer we come to this situation. We need our vocabularies to be finely textured, but not to have too many words for harmony, i.e., for accessibility in time of need (*CIS*, pp. 12, 32, 55). In other words, we need them to exhibit both harmony and diversity.

The unity of harmony and diversity is a standard of evaluation deeply rooted in the philosophical tradition. It is one version of what Aristotle conceived as order over size and called *to kalon* (often translated as "beauty"). Most importantly in the present perspective, it is what Hegel viewed as the reconciliation of contradiction and called *Wahrheit* (often translated as "truth").[22] To give a "dialectical" account of the development of one discourse out of another would not for Hegel be to describe how that development actually occurred, because his dialectics do not pursue truth. Rather, it would be to show that the development can be reconstructed as one in which a sequence of specific problems arises and is resolved, at each stage, by a minimal change in the preceding state of affairs.[23] Such a reconstruction, while (often) untrue to the historical facts, omits no problem or solution, and brings them all into a harmonious whole. It is thus an exercise in harmony over diversity, not in truth. And as Hegel carries it out, it is a way of relating one discourse (his own, for example) to those which precede and follow it. The question is not so much of *seeing* the relations as of *establishing* them, and so Hegelian dialectic is a way of overcoming solitude. (—*But who today knows what* solitude *is?*)

It is remarkable that Rorty in fact appeals to this idea of harmony over diversity throughout the extended argument of *Contingency, Irony, and Solidarity*. The final utopian dream of the book, for example, is of the gradual expansion of the liberal community to include increasingly diverse types of people, a (single) "ever larger and more variegated *ethnos*" (*CIS*, p. 198; also p. 192). The radical separation of public and private vocabularies, for which Rorty argues throughout the book, is asserted at its end to "make it possible for one person to be both" public liberal and private ironist: to harmonize two radically diverse components of her humanity (*CIS*, p. 198). It is in order that all poetic productions can abandon their claims to unique insight into the nature of things and coexist with others in a "beautiful mosaic" that they are to be put through the same "dialectical mill" by the ironist (*CIS*, pp. 76, 81).

There is no problem with such evaluative use of harmony over diversity except that it provides ample means not merely to show but to *argue* that some final vocabularies are better than others. If, for example, two current vocabularies are at odds, then it is good to produce a third one which accomplishes what they both do without the conflicts (*CIS*, p. 12); but any vocabulary which, in this version of Hegelian *Aufhebung*, can replace others will not only be better than they, but arguably better. Rorty himself gives an excellent example of such argument in chapter 3 of *CIS*, where he argues that the project of giving liberal culture a foundation conflicts with the basic vocabularies which nourish that culture (those of contemporary art and science) as well as with liberal practices already underway.

Arguments such as this do not claim that some vocabulary is bad because it contains a great many words for what does not exist, and lacks names for many things that do; they are not about the "truth" of vocabularies. They may, in fact, make no determinate appeal to the extralinguistic world at all:[24] they are committed only to the view that, whatever reality may be like, we will cope better with it if our vocabularies are fine-grained and harmonious, detailed yet accessible. When Rorty argues this way, he subverts his own declarations about the limits of argument and breaks his promise to confine himself to simply getting on with his redescriptions, rather than argue for them.[25]

Rorty never discusses, or even acknowledges, the argumentative side of his approach. Like the problems I discussed previously, this omission is traceable, I think, to his failure to dissociate himself entirely from the problematics of truth. In his accounts of textual and political realities, Rorty had abjured truth too globally; here, on the other side of the coin, he binds it too tightly to evaluation. This is evident from the nature of the various challenges to ousia that we have seen in Rorty: they all relied not merely upon being more useful than the descriptions they replaced, but on being truer.

4. CONCLUSION

Rorty is thus at once very close to, and very far from, Derrida as I have presented him in the first two chapters of this book. Where the Derrida of the Left abjures presence to the point of occasionally lauding unintelligibility, Rorty sees nothing wrong with retaining it as the single criterion of thought; escape from presence is not for him even an impossible dream. The goal of his discourse is not to displace or question truth, but to come up with a radically new set of truths[26]—radically new because couched in a radically new vocabulary, one of luck and contingency rather than of reason and necessity. He is thus able to escape Derridean valorizations of unintelligibility, and to articulate new places for thought to go.

Together with their common concern with truth and presence goes a failure on the part of both Derrida and Rorty to recognize that what they are challenging is often ousiodic structure. The result of this failure to perceive what they themselves are doing is a set of fateful inconsistencies in both thinkers. Derrida, for example, makes and then retracts his promise of liberation, while his discourse becomes by twists both unintelligible and banal, as well as (at still other times) genuinely emancipatory. Rorty also both makes and retracts promises of escape from ousiodic structure. He critiques ousiodic views of the self and philosophy, but applies equally ousiodic views to the self of the ironist and to the structure of speech communities, and ends by being himself enclosed in ousiodic solitude.[27]

For Rorty to accept a more overtly Hegelian view of the emergence of new final vocabularies would mean for him to challenge ousia in a more thorough and consistent way. And that would mean depriving the speech community itself of the ousiodic structure Rorty continues to attribute to it. The boundaries of the speech community were determined, we saw, via the uniqueness of its final vocabulary, which made it impossible for outsiders to engage in "worthwhile" discussion with insiders. Once it is admitted that any such vocabulary is to some extent the transformation of an antecedent vocabulary, it becomes itself "determined" by that vocabulary: some of the commitments and concerns of the parent vocabulary carry over into it. A dialogue between both would be possible, and there would be at least one other speech community with which any new one could talk: its own parent community.

When a new vocabulary emerges via determinate negation, the inventor of the new vocabulary—Rorty's "ironist"—assumes, moreover, an argumentative burden: she must point to the specific problems with the old vocabulary that her new one is supposed to solve or dissolve (as Rorty himself points out the problems with the contemporary vocabulary of liberal culture in chapter 3 of *Contingency, Irony, and Solidarity*). She is not free, then, simply to float free among earlier vocabularies, but must relate determinately to some of them. She must show, in fact, that she understands them better than they understand themselves (as Rorty implicitly claims to understand A(a)nalytical P(p)hilosophy better than its own practitioners). Hence, the new vocabulary does not rest securely within its own boundaries, as Rorty would have it, but actively, and even critically, engages other vocabularies. Such engagement, moreover, may have the result of transforming both, as each sees and states problems with the other better than the other can.

Finally, the fact that the ironist's new words would not be given meanings wholly *de novo* but would carry their own specific histories, and the trajectories of those histories, with them into her new vocabulary means that her dispositive power is impeached. Her words, in virtue of their histories, will shape her thought even as it reshapes them—a more realistic picture, I suggest, than Rorty's version of an intellectual *creatio ex nihil.*

I advance the foregoing considerations as a redescription of Rorty himself: as a truer account of his own practices than he himself can give. The reason he cannot give it himself is his unspoken reinstatement of ousiodic structure in the speech community as such. That, I argued, is in turn an artifact of his restriction of reason to merely argumentative ends and instruments. Rorty is quite right that reason which is geared merely to arguing for the truth of sentences cannot critique the basic terms in which those sentences are couched. But he is wrong not to explore other forms of reason— dialectical reconstruction, for example. Thus bound to truth, Rorty's style of thinking continues what I have called the modern obsession with presence, at the expense of ousia.

Modified in the concrete and dialectical direction I am suggesting here, Rorty would see ousia—rather than merely static finality—as the true object of his challenge. His invention of new vocabularies would begin, in fact, where Derrida leaves off: with a conceptual order that has been destabilized and made to "tremble." The destabilizing agent would be a specific lack of fit between a vocabulary and the realities of the situation: the kind of mismatch that leads to phantasms such as those of Analytical Philosophy. Such a mismatch cannot, of course, be clearly understood or conceptually defined at first, precisely because the words for it are lacking. It would be a felt discord between our words and what we have to use them for, a sense of meaninglessness or of a gap in the language: a specific case of what Rorty would call the ironist's discontent.[28] Like the Derrida of the Middle, the dialectical Rorty would take such cases of meaninglessness to be what I call abnormal poetic elicitors. But where Derrida leaves us in the "nonterminating" experience of such abnormality, Rorty shows us how to think about restoring normalcy—if only for a while. His thought would thus count as a philosophical version of what I call "abnormal terminating poetic interaction": interaction in which a meaning is invented for an utterance which, as uttered, has no meaning at all. Rorty's thought would come out of its solitude and explicitly into the service of freedom: into the Great Demarcation.

CENTRALITY AS A CHALLENGE
TO OUSIA IN JÜRGEN HABERMAS

*. . . A feeling of birdlike freedom, birdlike panorama, birdlike
frolicsomeness, a third condition in which curiosity and tender
contempt have bound themselves together. A "free spirit"—this
cool phrase does good in that condition, it virtually warms. . . .
One lives, no longer in the shackles of love and hate, without Yes
or No, voluntarily near, voluntarily far, most happily slipping
away, turning aside, fluttering forth, off again, again flying
upward; one is pampered, as is everyone who has seen a monstrous great variety beneath her—and one becomes a counterpart to those who concern themselves with things that do not
concern them. Indeed: by this time sheer things concern her—
and how many things!—which no longer trouble her!*

For Habermas, Heidegger's philosophical sins, like his personal ones, are
many and serious. In *The Philosophical Discourse of Modernity,* he traces them
back to Heidegger's original failure to free himself from the transcendental
"philosophy of consciousness" which surrounded him in Germany.[1] Heidegger certainly, on Habermas's reading, *undertook* to overcome such approaches to philosophy, but he was so imbued with them that his undertaking amounted to an attempt to overleap his own shadow, reaching his new
standpoint definitively and at once:

> Heidegger frees himself so little from the problematic of transcendental
> consciousness that he can leap out of the basic conceptual cage [*Gehäuse*]
> of the philosophy of consciousness in no other way than by the path of
> abstract negation. (*PDM*, p. 165/138)

Habermas's accusation of "abstract negation" seems to land Heidegger in
proximity to the Rorty of my previous chapter, for whom a new vocabulary
emerges via just such an abstract, wholesale leap out of previous ones. It also

places him near the Derrida of the Left, whose global liberation from all intelligibility was similarly abstract. But any reading of Heidegger which makes him sound like Rorty should be, in virtue of the distance I noted between the two at the beginning of chapter 3, *prima facie* dubious. Like that of Derrida, Heidegger's abstractness is in fact only one side of his thought. When we turn to important Heideggerean texts Habermas never discusses, such as "Andenken" and "The Thing," we see that what Habermas views as Heidegger's "abstract negation" of old categories by his own new ones is really a diakenic interplay between the two sets of categories.[2] Its emptiness is not abstract but is concretized by the phenomena it gathers.

An accusation of abstract negation is made, one would think, in the name of determinate negation, and so of some version of the Hegelian dialectics from which that notion comes. This suspicion, I will argue, is justified. In contrast to Rorty, who, as I argued, is resolutely undialectical, Habermas makes use of both the concept and the procedures of determinate negation in his own thought. This enables him to do what Rorty cannot: to connect his own discourse with others in specific and argued ways. But Habermas will dispense entirely with one crucial element of Rorty's (and Hegel's) thought: its thoroughly provisional nature. For Habermas, there is a final ground, a vocabulary which takes itself to be, in Rorty's words,

> no mere idiosyncratic historical project, but the last word, the one to which inquiry and history have converged, the one which renders further inquiry and history superfluous. (*CIS*, p. 96)

The strength of Habermas's appeal to finality—which, as will be seen in the next chapter, invokes ousiodic structure for Habermas's own thought—means that Habermas's dialecticality, like his reading of Heidegger, is incomplete: it stops at the boundaries of his own theory of communicative action. In this respect, Habermas is what I define as a "modern" philosopher, and his attitude to presence is the reverse of that of the other philosophers of the Great Demarcation. They cannot focus on ousia because they question presence; Habermas, because he defends it. The common topic, that of presence, is more important than the different positions taken on that topic.

1. WORLD, PHILOSOPHY, AND OUSIA

What allows Heidegger's negation of previous categories to remain merely abstract is, in Habermas's view, his concept of world (*PDM*, p. 175/147). As Habermas sees it, world functions in *Being and Time* as a sort of replacement for the traditional transcendental subject, in that it provides the basic ground and horizon for our experience of phenomena. But unlike the traditional subject, world for Heidegger is in no sense to be identified with us—not with humans as we empirically exist, or with some transcendental stratum of ourselves. Rather, it is grounded in Being, which therefore "directs" and "dispenses" us from outside. This leads Heidegger, in Habermas's view, to abandon his own existential concept of freedom:

> Dasein no longer counts as the author of world-projections, in the light of which beings at once show and withdraw themselves; rather the *productivity* of the world-disclosing creation of meaning passes to Being itself. (*PDM*, p. 181/152)

This domination of Being over meaning, if I may call it that, is only reinforced (Habermas claims) in Heidegger's later work, in which everything is immediately directed by Being. In particular, sociopolitical responsibility, like the creation of meaning,

> passes over from the conscientious project of the individual concerned about his existence to an anonymous dispensation of Being that demands subjection, is contingent, and prejudices the course of concrete history. (*PDM*, p. 183/155)

Human beings are thus trapped in contingent worlds; they cannot get out of them any more than Heidegger himself could get out of the philosophical milieu in which he was educated.

What Habermas is criticizing in Heidegger is the project of *Seinsgeschichte*. The "dispensation of Being" to which he refers is Heidegger's view that Being, in Heidegger's words, "*dominates* [*durchherrscht*] all the phenomena that distinguish the age":[3] that it has what I call dispositive power over a given epoch of its history, including the individuals who live and act in that epoch. Habermas does not, to be sure, contest the view that human beings can be trapped by history; his own historical sensitivity, not to mention his youth in Hitler's Germany, prevents such naïveté. Rather, his criticism is that for Heidegger there is not—and need not be—any way out of such a trap. Merely by seeking such escape, Habermas issues the first of several challenges to ousiodic structure I will discuss in this chapter—here, as the boundary and disposition of Heideggerean world.

At first, it does not appear that philosophy for Habermas can help us out of such historical traps. The opening pages of his major work, *The Theory of Communicative Action,* argue that philosophy after Hegel surrendered both its totality-claim—its pretension to yield substantive theories of nature and/or of transcendental subjectivity—and its claim to foundationality: it can no longer hope to present even the conceptual basis for such substantive theories. Elsewhere, he suggests that only two roles are left open for it: those of "place holder" and "interpreter."[4]

As place-holder, philosophy is fragmented into just one element of scientific paradigm formation. It is typical, writes Habermas, for scientific research traditions to start off with claims that are universal, and hence nonempirical.[5] Such "philosophical thoughts," indeed, are necessary to the constitution of new scientific paradigms, for a proposed research program can have no claim upon other researchers if it is grounded solely in the hunches, intuitions, or genius of a single individual. But being universal, such claims are nonempirical, and tend to be dismissed by scientists. It is up to the philosopher to take them seriously: to examine how and to what extent they might be justified.

Philosophy's other role is as interpreter, in which it undertakes to translate into ordinary language the specialized discourses that the modern age has produced, thereby mediating them with one another and with the "life world" in general.[6] This, too, dissolves philosophy: its translations of specialized discourses are carried out with reference not to some realm of meaning that it possesses for itself (as with Analytical Philosophy on Rorty's description), but to the everyday practices of the life world. Since we all inhabit the life world, no specialists are required to interpret and articulate it. All of what Habermas calls "discourse" does so, as we shall see; philosophy at most does it more reflectively.[7] Hence, no *philosophical* specialists are required to mediate specialized discourses with the life world: those who conduct such discourse can do it themselves.

Philosophy for Habermas has thus lost its ousiodic character even more decisively than for Rorty. As with Rorty, it has no specific procedures or methods for carrying out its disparate tasks of investigation and interpretation. But in contrast to Rorty's "disconnected" view of philosophical discourse, which left each version of it undisturbed behind the unbreachable boundaries of its incommensurability with other discourses, for Habermas philosophy's very content is provided by other discourses. Philosophy thus has no secure boundaries, and is also not able to generate or order other discourses. It investigates their claims to universal truth and harmonizes them with the language of the life world; but, as we will see, this is in order not to dictate to them, but to be legitimated by them.

Habermas's vision of philosophy's dual role as place-holder and interpreter is then a challenge to ousiodic structure for philosophy. But philosophy seems for Habermas to be trapped within what he calls the "life world," no less than it was trapped within "world" for Heidegger. This, as he characterizes it, is a "reservoir of taken-for-granteds, of unshaken convictions that participants in communication draw upon in cooperative processes of interpretation" (*TKH*, vol. 2, p. 189/124). As such, it constitutes—like Heideggerean "world"—a basic domain of meaningfulness within which we can act and interact, but from which we cannot exit:

> In the situation of an action, the life world forms a horizon behind which we cannot go. . . . Accordingly, it is strictly meaningless for members of a sociocultural life world to inquire whether the culture in whose light they deal with external nature, society, and internal nature is empirically dependent on anything *else*. (*TKH*, vol. 2, p. 225/149)

Habermas then applies this to his own theory of communicative action, which

> insofar as it relates to structures of the life world, [must] explicate a
> background knowledge over which no one can dispose at will. . . . Whether
> a life world . . . eludes the phenomenologist's inquiring gaze or is opened
> up to it does not depend on just *choosing* to adopt a theoretical attitude.
> The totality of the background knowledge constitutive for the construc-
> tion of the life world is no more at his disposition than at that of any social
> scientist. . . . The context of its emergence does not remain external to the
> theory. . . . (*TKH*, vol. 2, pp. 589–591/400f)

The life world is thus for Habermas the "necessary" foundation of the theory of communicative action in the Greek sense of *anankê:* not as what is log-ically deducible from self-evident premises or true in all possible worlds, but as what we simply must put up with. Unless the theory of communicative action is somehow very different from philosophy itself, then, neither seems able to free us from the traps of history.

We have not, however, exhausted Habermas's view of philosophy's eman-cipatory potential. We can get clearer on this by noting that the two overall tasks Habermas has allocated to philosophy (or into which he has dissolved it) are very different from one another—as different as logical definition and critical argumentation are from hermeneutical articulation and inter-pretation. Are they mutually indifferent? Are they both imposed on philoso-phy merely through contingencies of history? Or is there something com-mon to both tasks, and to the myriad ways in which each must be concretely carried out, which requires that they should fall to a single discipline?

The last, I will argue, is the case. Both the examination of claims to uni-versal truth and the articulation of the life world need to be carried out by a discipline which is in a certain sense "central" to the diverse materials it treats. It is this peculiar sense of centrality—a non-ousiodic sense, as will be seen—which, from a Habermasian perspective, can unify philosophy with itself as an emancipatory enterprise.

Habermas certainly discusses the sense in which philosophy, i.e., his own theory of communicative action, claims what I will call centrality. But I will argue in chapter 6 that he also, and usually, understands philosophy as re-quired to claim something quite different: universality, i.e., truth for every-one. This approach is consonant, of course, with his view that *any* research paradigm must make universality-claims. But it is, I will also argue, wrong: universality, and truth itself, can be dispensed with by the theory of commu-nicative action, while centrality cannot. The theory of communicative ac-tion is thus distinguished from other research programs by the fact that it *replaces* (universal) truth with a peculiar form of centrality. It does this by way of various challenges to ousiodic structure. But Habermas, because of his explicit concern with truth and universality rather than with centrality—or, as I will argue, because of his obsession with presence rather than ousia—fails to see any of this.

2. CENTRALITY AND MODERNITY

We have now seen two challenges to ousia by Habermas: his critique of the Heideggerean conception of world, and his rejection of the view that philosophy can be an autonomous discipline with boundaries, methods, and procedures all its own. Like the other thinkers of the Great Demarcation, Habermas never identifies these challenges as such; that is part of what makes them "challenges" in the first place. The thematic of ousia is in fact rather deeply buried in Habermas's thought. I will seek to uncover it here via an excavation of his concern with a competing parameter, that of centrality. This immediately raises the question of what a "center" is, and to avoid mere stipulation, I will suppose that "centers" are what they have always been. The "always" here, as always in philosophy since the Greeks, means "since the Greeks": since the codification of ousia, in whose story the concept of center plays roles both complicitous and subversive.

The *kentron* was a goad or spike.[8] With the entry of mathematics into Greece one type of *kentron* was the leg of a compass, which could be jabbed down anywhere to begin the construction of a *kuklos,* a circle. Eventually, the circle as a whole was viewed as derived from its center: the *kentron* was no longer established by the actual jab of a compass, but was a midpoint (a *meson*) which itself established the rest of the circle and whose own origin was arbitrary, unquestioned.[9] Generating the periphery, and ordering it as equidistant, the center was viewed as what I call the circle's dispositive form. In this way, centrality became parametrically complicitous with ousia: something could be placed within an ousiodic framework by finding or giving it an identifiable center.

When a circle rotates, its midpoint does not, and so is unchanging; this rendered the mathematical concept of the *kentron* exportable into other types of discourse. Aristotle biologized it when he traced the movements of animals to the leverage of their limbs against (relatively) unmoved movers at their centers.[10] Plotinus and Augustine ontologized it: centrality in their *cosmoi* was assigned to God or the One, the unchanging source of all things.[11] In modernity, philosophy itself came to be viewed as an unmoved center for the discourses that constitute the human world. It was subjectivized by Descartes, whose *Meditations* trade on a view of the ego as an Archimedean point of leverage capable of establishing itself anywhere by the self-reflection of the *cogito,* and then of philosophically generating from itself the ordered totality of knowledge.[12] Kant gave it practical significance: reason, articulated in philosophy, oriented the *thinker* as the midday sun, in the center of the sky, oriented the sailor. It oriented the *actor* when his action originated—as it ought to at all times and places—from reason itself, autonomously legislating the categorical imperative.[13] The concept of philosophy as a central, unmoved, legislative discourse finally carried into Husserl's view of the ego as a "well-defined central point of emanation" for meaning itself, accessible through phenomenological investigation.[14]

But the intellectual career of the philosophical center ended on the threshold of the linguistic turn. For there is no single obvious generative source for language, which is normally experienced as an interplay in which speakers reciprocally yield the stage, opening themselves to engage one another. When philosophy became linguistic—or when, as Derrida puts it, language "invaded the universal problematic"—it became necessary to conceive of the center differently: not as a stable "present-being" but as "a sort of non-locus in which an infinite number of sign-substitutions comes into play."[15] "Infinite sign-substitutions" are of course precisely what philosophy, as rationally warranted discourse, is designed to prevent. With this reconception of centers generally, philosophy itself lost all claim to centrality among human discourses.

At least in the *mathematical* sense of "center." For there are also Western conceptions of centrality which challenge ousia. In Bronze Age Greece, for example, we find another sort of *kentron:* the sharp point or goad at the center of a *kuklos*—the circle formed by the typical single-handled shield. Such a central spike was hardly the unmoved source of the shield's movement, for it was wholly dependent on the arm which held the shield. It was also (paradoxically, if we take the term in its mathematical or ousiodic sense) dependent on the circumference: it was because the *kentron* was a *meson*, at the midpoint of the shield, that the shield's weight was equally balanced there and would not divert the impetus of any forward thrust. The center was a spike, rather than a mere boss, because at that point the defensive weapon could become offensive. The concentrated energy of the arm, augmented but not deflected by the balanced weight of the whole shield, could be used in close quarters to push at the enemy, goading him to stumble or retreat.[16]

The concept of a center which, far from generating the periphery, derives its status from balancing the forces of that periphery is explicated in Hegel's Logic, where the *Zentrum* of a field is constituted through the interactions of objects in that field. Its activity consists only in mediating these with one another—as if the sun were nothing more than the intersection of the gravitational pulls of all the planets.[17] The *Zentrum* is merely the sum of the forces operating among a set of (Hegelian) Substances: it is the point at which the most vectors of reciprocal interaction meet. Hegel seems to surpass the Bronze Age artisans, however: as *merely* such a mediator, the *Zentrum* can impart no additional thrust to what it mediates. An illustration of this occurs in the "Preface" to Hegel's *Philosophy of Right:* philosophy as a central discourse can only articulate the structures of the state. It cannot undertake to change, or even to criticize, what it comprehends.[18]

I will argue in the next section that Habermas's thought exhibits a "shield-like" type of centrality, and in this challenges ousiodic structure in philosophy. It seeks to take discourses which, left to themselves, are politically neutral or even defensive formations of a culture under threat[19] and, by bringing them together, to give them an offensive, critical thrust. The theory of communicative action is to be "central," not in the sense that it generates other discourses but, to the contrary, in that they all come together in it. (. . . *A feeling of birdlike freedom, birdlike panorama, birdlike frolicsomeness, a third condition in which curiosity and tender contempt have bound themselves together.*)

But is such heteronomy compatible with the critical thrust Habermas wishes to give philosophy? Is there a point at which his intellectual "shield" can become offensive? To answer this, we must clarify the complex centrality he assigns to philosophy, with particular reference to his own theory of communicative action. And before doing that, we must understand a problem to which his account of philosophical centrality is keyed.

In order to examine the diverse universality-claims raised by new paradigms in the empirical sciences, philosophy must for Habermas include an account of rationality in general. It thus aims at giving a formal (hence nontotalistic) account of reason (*TKH*, vol. 1, pp. 15–24/1–7). The question immediately arises of whether reason *is* unified: of whether a single, central account of the formal conditions of something called "rationality" is possible. The current answer, for Habermas, is clearly No. The panoply of discourses in the contemporary intellectual world, especially in modern social theory, may after Max Weber be styled a new "polytheism," in which figures such as Marx, Durkheim, Mead, Freud, Piaget, and Weber himself serve as deities. The paradigms these thinkers have introduced, Habermas writes, remain today *gleichberechtigt,* on equal intellectual footing.[20] Their fundamental heterogeneity impeaches the unity of reason. To rescue it requires reunifying them on a higher level, in a more general social theory which legitimates itself as objective precisely by achieving such unification:

> The more freely it can take up, explain, criticize, and carry on the intentions of earlier theory traditions, the more impervious [any social theory] is to the danger that particular interests are being brought to bear unnoticed on its own theoretical perspectives. (*TKH*, vol. 1, pp. 201f/140)

This general social theory is for Habermas his own theory of communicative action. The passage cited reveals a tension in it. On the one hand, "taking up," "criticizing," and "carrying on" are (as I will show later in more detail) clear allusions to the three moments of Hegelian *Aufhebung:* preserving, destroying, and raising to a higher level. So conceived, general social theory is parasitic upon the diverse other paradigms which it integrates, operating as a sort of Hegelian *Zentrum* and thereby establishing what I will call its own "centrality." That is why the polytheistic discourses of the contemporary age are not legitimated by being sublated into general social theory, but the reverse: such theory achieves, through this process, assurance of its own generality and impartiality. It does not order the discourses it "sublates," but secures its own legitimacy from them.

Habermas is also saying here, however, that general social theory is to retain, unlike an Hegelian *Zentrum,* a "theoretical perspective" independent of the paradigms it integrates. What makes this perspective proper to general social theory is precisely its universality. Other inhabitants of the pantheon of modern social theory are, Habermas tells us, "internally connected" to the life world in which they arise; their very plurality shows that the interests and aspirations which they serve to articulate are not universal, but merely those of components of that life world—of various groups and interests within the overall social order (*TKH,* vol. 1, p. 201/140). General social theory is to be free of such particularity. (*A "free spirit"—this cool phrase does good in that condition, it virtually warms . . .*)

The *Aufhebung* that Habermas has invoked must then validate general social theory, not as a mere *Zentrum* but as having its own proper theoretical standpoint. That standpoint must itself be legitimated independently of the discourses it takes up—in a further theory which both is universal and yields norms by which to criticize "particular" interests and theories. This universal *normative* theory is the formal theory of rationality to which we have seen Habermas relegate philosophy. The theory of communicative action itself, as general *social* theory, is to hold the middle ground between this theory of formal rationality and the intellectual polytheism of the modern age. Its aim is to show that the formal structures of a unified reason are at work in all the varieties of modern social theory.

That the need is for a general *social* theory points to philosophy's relation to modern society itself. Since the disparate social discourses of modernity are internally connected to the social contexts in which they arise and gain influence, those contexts themselves in turn exhibit Weberian polytheism. They do so, for Habermas (following Weber), as a result of the historical process of modernization, which has split the unified premodern human world into three distinct domains. Each of these domains has its own patterns of argumentation and separate social sphere: the "objectivating" rationality present in the sciences, geared to the production of technological means for the pursuit of various ends, has in the modern world been set off against the "moral-practical" rationality socially embedded in the legal system and ethical norms of a society, and against the "aesthetic-practical" rationality embedded primarily in the institutions of the art world (*TKH,* vol. 1, pp. 329f/240f).

For Weber, the differentiation of these subsystems is a defining characteristic of modernity. In it, they break from their foundations in the old world order and, in Habermas's words, "become independent, following their own dynamics" (*TKH,* vol. 1, p. 320/233). Thus separated from the others, each of them is bounded, constituting what Habermas calls a "grandiose exclusivity," and each is governed exclusively by its own "inner logic," according to which its basic ideal is connected with an interest, which institutions and patterns of action are generated and ordered to secure (*TKH,* vol. 1, p. 328/240). In addition to these versions of boundary and disposition, the modern subsystems also exhibit a kind of initiative, here (as with Rorty) problematic: the various applications of the peculiar inner logic of one sphere to the others (*TKH,* vol. 1, p. 329/240), as when all rationality is viewed as scientific, or in the aestheticization of politics. The differentiation of the life world, which is Habermas's term for the overall process producing this separation, is thus its multiple "ousiodification": the changing of what were formerly loose, interdependent textures of lived interaction into separate realms, each governed by its own inner logic.

The differentiation of these three systems constitutes the "signature of modernity," and renders the unity of reason historically counterfactual. It is, therefore, a process Habermas must criticize. The critical thrust of the theory of communicative action, then, cannot be restricted to criticism of paradigms in the social sciences; it must aim at modern society itself (*TKH,* vol. 2, pp. 549f/397f). It must provide a way to show that the three subsystems of modernity are occlusions of all that remains of philosophy's subject matter: of the deeper, more inclusive structures of a unified, formal rationality (Cf. *TKH,* vol. 1, p. 458/342, and vol. 2, pp. 584f/397f). This criticism will contain yet another set of Habermasian challenges to ousiodic structure.

Diogenes Laertius recounts that Plato, after the death of Socrates, burnt the tragedies which he had written and danced before the flames, crying, "Come out, Hephaestus, Plato has need of thee."[21] The words echo those which, in the *Iliad,* summon Hephaestus to make the shield of Achilles, the shield which depicts all that is noble about the Achaean way of life. Plato's shield—his *Republic*—is, however, more than a conservative glorification of Athenian tradition. Centered on the Theory of Forms, it argues that Athens must be radically transformed if what is good in it is to be saved. So, I suggest, for Habermas and modernity. His general social theory is to articulate and justify the achievements of the modern era, and so to be a critical shield for it.[22] But the shield is not to be merely defensive: it must obtain, at its center, an offensive critical thrust. The question is whether a discourse which merely claims a central position *among* a variety of other discourses, rather than a universal position *above* them, can generate that sort of critical thrust.

3. THE CENTRALITY OF THE THEORY OF COMMUNICATIVE ACTION

The center in question must be a theory of *communicative* rationality for at least two reasons. After losing its pretension to foundational authority, philosophy can dictate nothing to the various paradigms of social theory. These must instead be put into a mutual learning process in which the claims of each are inspected and, when disputes arise, the better argument prevails—

a constellation in which no center can be more than a *Zentrum*. In the course of staging this constellation, Habermas discusses a variety of texts and issues that go far beyond the philosophical and literary themes discussed by Derrida and Rorty. This is because of the internal connection I have already noted between social theory and modernity itself. Thinkers such as Durkheim, Marx, and Weber claim to be uncovering the basic social structures operating in our lives. By discussing them, Habermas is able to relate his thought to concrete issues. In so doing, as we have seen, he places his thought under an explicitly double burden: he must both "get these thinkers right," i.e., say true things about them, and make their critical confrontation productive for his own enterprise. Abstraction (e.g., in the form of attributing everything to a privileging of presence, as Derrida does) and fantasy (as in Rorty's accounts of historical and social realities) have no place here.

This complex undertaking calls for a "theory of discourse" to show the formal conditions of such argumentation—for a theory of rationality which sees reason as communicative and argumentative, rather than as the "subject centered reason" of an isolated individual (*TKH*, vol. 1, pp. 339f/249). In addition, if the norms for rationality are to apply critically to modern society, reason and society should not be generically different kinds of thing. Subject-centered views, taking reason to be the activity of an isolated and ahistorical thinker, locate it in something which is radically other than society. They raise the question of whether we can call societies "rational" at all. This problem does not arise for a view of reason which sees it as intrinsically social, and so the normative structure of rationality is best understood in communicative terms.

The concept around which Habermas develops his general social theory is thus one of *communicative* action, which is interaction in which any utterance can be criticized from three points of view: with regard to its truth, to its "appropriateness" as conforming to a legitimate social norm, and to its "truthfulness" as an expression of the speaker's mental state (*TKH*, vol. 1, pp. 148f, 412/99, 307). If one of these validity-claims is actually challenged by a hearer of the utterance, the speaker must attempt to validate, by argument, the particular claim which has been challenged.

Such an attempt constitutes a second level of communication, which Habermas calls "discourse." The aim of discourse is to reach consensus with others on an utterance's truth, appropriateness, or truthfulness.[23] It begins with a challenge to just one of the three claims made by the utterance, which is then examined separately of the others. Because discourse separates one validity-claim from the rest in this way, it is characteristic of the modern world.[24] Because the justifications advanced in discourse in part examine and in part appeal to unquestioned background beliefs (*TKH*, vol. 1, pp. 71, 107f, 150f/42, 790f, 100f), discourse includes the articulation and scrutiny —the interpretation—of the life world. (*One lives, no longer in the shackles of*

love and hate, without Yes or No, voluntarily near, voluntarily far, most happily slip-
ping away, turning aside, fluttering forth, off again, again flying upward . . .)

All three validity-claims, however, are present on the level of communicative action, which is thus a sort of central switchyard for validity-claims—
thence for the ideals of Truth, Goodness, and Beauty,[25] and thence again
for the three seemingly independent subsystems of modernity which these
structure. It is through the concept of communicative action, then, that philosophy can confront modernity in a critical way: each of the validity-claims
raised together in communicative action corresponds to just one of the
components of rationality that modernity has separated from each other,
and so in communicative action the unity of reason is still present.

Communicative action so conceived can only be central to modernity itself on two conditions: if modernity really consists in these three subsystems, each discursively structured around a particular kind of validity-claim;
and if utterances in communicative action really make validity-claims of all
three types. The former condition is a matter for sociologists (particularly
Weber) to decide with their various particular social theories, and for Habermas to underwrite by bringing these *gleichberechtigt* theories together
around his own theory. But the special status of the validity-claims with respect to communicative action—that every utterance in it makes all three,
and that only these three are thus universally made—is an issue for the general theory of communicative rationality that Habermasian philosophy is
to provide.

Habermas does not derive the validity-claims from some a priori domain
such as transcendental subjectivity: his account of communicative action is
advanced as a "reconstruction" of the ways we actually use language in the
modern life world (*TKH*, vol. 2, pp. 171–228/113–152). The reconstruction
proceeds not by direct appeals to the life world (which, again, is a matter for
particular social theories), but by the kind of *Aufhebung* we saw him refer to
earlier. That *Aufhebung*, which I will now discuss in greater detail, is thus a
critical unification of particular social theories around the theory of communicative action. (. . . *one is pampered, as is everyone who has seen a monstrous*
great variety beneath *him.*)

If theories as wholes were like the propositions of which they are built,
they would be true or false. But Habermas does not accept that analogy.
Highly general theories cannot simply be tested against reality as many
propositions can, and the *gleichberechtigt* social theories Habermas discusses
have already passed that test as much as any such theory can. He is left, then,
only with the rule of thumb that if two theories contradict one another, one
or both must be suspect. The appropriate procedure in such a case is, for
him, not to test each against reality, but to attempt to remove the contradiction via rational argumentation. The revisions required by this, however,
must be mutual: no discourse, and certainly not philosophy, is entitled to
primary status as an unmoved mover to which all others must conform.

Habermas's picture is thus of a plurality of discourses, each adjusting itself to accommodate the rational insights of the others.[26]

This picture can be fleshed out by noting one respect in which theories differ from propositions for Habermas: theories, like living organisms, develop over time. Habermas generally refers to such developing conceptual "organisms" as "directions of research" or as "learning processes"; each is a "coherent argumentation developed around constant thematic cores" and leads to a "cumulative production of knowledge."[27] The theory of communicative action is central, not simply because it statically *coheres* with other discourses, but because they dynamically *converge* on it. Sometimes they converge, so to speak, of themselves: all Habermas has to do is reveal the fact.[28] At other times, apparently, it is up to him to bring theories which are not converging into a common universe of discourse.[29] In either case, while not a criterion of truth,

> the ability to appropriate and work up the best traditions is indeed a sign of a social theory's powers to connect with others [*Anschlußfähigkeit*] and strength of comprehension. (*TKH,* vol. 2, p. 298/200; translation slightly altered)

To participate in a common rational discourse means, however, to be reciprocally open to criticism from other participants; for such discourse, as a case of communicative action, allows one's own validity-claims to be challenged, examined, and abandoned if found wanting. Communicative action, in virtue of the criticizable validity-claims it raises, thus contains an intrinsic critical potential which enables the participants in a common discourse reciprocally to "penetrate a given context, to burst it open from within, and to transcend it" (*TKH,* vol. 1, pp. 172–176/117–120). By providing a common universe of discourse for divergent paradigms in social theory, for example, the theory of communicative action unlocks their capacities for mutual and self-criticism; and this, we may take it, is for Habermas another indication of its merit.[30]

The above reference to *Anschlußfähigkeit* suggests a third way, in addition to convergence and the unlocking of critical potential, in which a social theory can be evaluated for Habermas: through its effects. The usefulness of a theory for further research "can only be verified in its ramifications for research in the social sciences and philosophy," and is not for its proponent to judge. But Habermas is aware that it matters to a theory whether other research directions can make use of it, and he devotes much of the closing section of *The Theory of Communicative Action* to a discussion of such possible ramifications.[31]

What makes Habermas's theory a "good" one is therefore, in part, that other theories converge on it, have their critical potential unlocked by it, and ramify from it into subsequent research. Balanced at the midpoint of a number of discourses and imparting critical thrust to them, Habermas's theory of communicative action exhibits the kind of shieldlike centrality I discussed earlier.

As such, it exhibits in concrete form the challenge to ousiodic structure in philosophy which is reflectively advanced in Habermas's account of philosophy as place-holder and interpreter. The "boundaries" of philosophy are not established from within, by philosophy itself, but by the rational learning processes which converge on it and give it content. It does not dispose or order them, but simply brings out their convergence via a critique from which it is itself not exempt. Initiative is exercised by the central theory not independently of others but in that other discourses, of their own accord, take up its insights. In sum: Habermasian centrality at this point is a dynamic reciprocity in which mutually independent discourses transform one another in specific ways. As such, it embodies a challenge to ousiodic structure in philosophy.

But this Habermasian challenge to ousiodic structure in the name of dynamic centrality will turn out to have important limits. Two problems with it are already becoming visible. One follows from the fact that establishing the centrality of the theory does not, in and of itself, require evaluating or even making any truth-claim. None needs to be *evaluated*, not merely because of the problems with testing general theories against reality that I noted earlier, but also because of the simple fact that to ask whether the statements in some other theory can be made compatible with those in one's own is not to ask whether any statement in either theory is true. None needs to be *made* because compatibility can be established by procedures that are almost syntactic. Any theory makes and entails both "positive" and "negative" assertions: statements that "S is P" and statements that "S is not P." Two theories are incompatible when, for some "S" and some "P," one theory contains a positive assertion and the other a negative. Compatibility can be achieved by simply changing one of the assertions to match the other: by adding or deleting a negation.[32]

Things are not really so simple (or so syntactic), of course, because one statement in a theory can rarely be changed in isolation. We must also go through the theory and change all those statements which either entail it or are entailed by it. And we might add at least one other constraint: that the overall number of changes be minimal. If a particular change in the other theory requires many further changes in that theory, for example, but the corresponding change in my own theory requires only a few, I may decide to change my own theory. The important point is that *none of these changes needs to be directed by the truth of any statement,* and the syntactic changes we make—adding or deleting negations—are not themselves statements, either. Establishing a theory as central thus does not require, as communicative action does, making assertions which claim to be true. It aims rather at the Hegelian goal, which I have discussed elsewhere,[33] of harmonizing diversity—here, the diversity of other theories.

This raises the question of whether Habermas's own activity in advancing the theory of communicative action is itself an instance of communicative action. Insofar as Habermas advances the theory as central, it seems not to be. For centrality is not one of the kinds of validity with which communicative action is concerned. Centrality can be established without making any of his three validity-claims, since we could agree with Habermas that his theory is central without even discussing whether it is true, appropriate, or truthful. But if the theory of communicative action is merely central, then the norms and structures of communicative action do not apply to it—and the universality which Habermas repeatedly claims is violated by the very theory which claims it. This is the first problem, then, with conceiving the theory of communicative action to be central rather than true: it would turn it into a theory of rational legitimation which is unable to account for its own legitimacy.

Second, there is doubt as to whether a theory produced and validated by such *Aufhebung* can be as critical as Habermas wants. For it can never achieve anything more than the integration of a finite number of other discourses. All of them are parts of its life world and so may be biased by deep structures of that life world. To achieve full critical independence by such procedures is thus impossible: it would require us to go beyond establishing the convergence of any set of theories actually in place in our life world to achieve an integration of all possible theories in the relevant domain. It would require achieving, not centrality, but universality.

As will be seen, Habermas clearly makes not merely a centrality-claim but a universality-claim for the theory of communicative action.[34] It is clear what he stands to gain by sustaining such a claim. First, the theory would be able to account for its own legitimacy. For a universality-claim, unlike a centrality-claim, is a variety of truth-claim: to claim that a structure is "universal" for a given domain is not to reshape theories, but to claim that sentences which describe that structure are true everywhere in that domain. If its universality-claim could be justified, the theory of communicative action could be advanced and decided in a case of communicative action: it would establish the conditions of its own legitimacy. Moreover, if the theory truly states the conditions of all rational discourse—or even, as "What Is Universal Pragmatics?" has it, the conditions of all speech[35]—then its centrality to all such speech will follow: no social theory, as a theory of human interaction, could avoid deep reliance upon, and hence confirming convergence with, it.

But Habermas's universality-claim raises obvious problems as well. The question of whether such universality is possible has virtually governed the history of Habermas's reception, and has led to a welter of literature by Habermas and his critics.[36] My approach in the next chapter will be to look briefly at the strategies Habermas himself proposes for validating his universality-claim. Those strategies will turn out to be geared to establishing the claim only as central or plausible—not as definitively true. I will then discuss four possible motivations for issuing the claim as merely plausible. These will all turn out to be problematic, and in the final section I will return to the centrality-claim. I will argue that Habermas's whole project deserves to be called "philosophical" in the un-Habermasian sense that it claims not universal truth, but centrality within the modern life world. That centrality will be double: the theory of communicative action will not merely be central to the theoretical discourses of social science, but will also mediate between them and the life world which it articulates. Through being centered on the life world, I will argue, it can acquire a critical perspective independent of the social theories it unifies without the need for a universality-claim. The price will be an acceptance of Hegelian dialecticality which goes beyond Habermas's and applies to the structures of communicative action itself.

6

UNIVERSALITY, CENTRALITY, AND THE
THEORY OF COMMUNICATIVE ACTION

The previous chapter argued that, like Derrida and Rorty, Habermas presents an important challenge to philosophy's claims to ground and order other discourses. Unlike Derrida, he presents an alternative to traditional conceptions of philosophy, and unlike Rorty that alternative does not sever connections with other discourses entirely. But Habermas's efforts to theorize this in a coherent way run into problems. In chapters 1 and 2, I argued that Derrida fails to distinguish clearly between *ousia* and *parousia,* or presence. Habermas exhibits an oddly parallel failure to distinguish between centrality and universality. The result is that his texts—and much of the literature they have inspired—do not clearly engage what will be the central problem of this chapter: whether he really needs to make a universality-claim at all.

1. WHY UNIVERSALITY?

That Habermas does make a claim of universality for the structures and norms of communicative action is beyond doubt. Strongly universal validity claims are for him, as we saw, typical of new paradigms in the social sciences. The theory of communicative action makes such claims when it asserts that *all* speech, to be rational, must claim truth, sincerity, and appropriateness. This assertion does not for Habermas express merely the current state of social science, or even that of the modern life world. The following is his clearest response to Max Weber's question as to whether or not rationalization (with its concomitant, modernization) is a phenomenon restricted to the West:

> [The three validity-claims of communicative action] form a system—however fraught with internal tensions—that did indeed first appear in the form of Occidental rationalism but that, beyond the peculiarity of this specific culture, lays a claim to a universal validity binding on all "civilized men." (*TKH*, vol. 1, p. 259/184)

This sort of universality goes well beyond the centrality that I discussed in the previous chapter. The claim is that communicative action, with its trio of validity-claims, is basic not only to social theories currently available within the modern life world, but to all "civilized" human beings. This strong universality-claim raises two questions: can Habermas justify it? And why would he make it?

The question of justification, as I noted in the previous chapter, has generated an enormous literature. But it can be answered with suspicious ease. At the end of the introduction to *The Theory of Communicative Action,* Habermas distinguishes three possible strategies for justifying the kind of universality-claim he has advanced without appealing to metaphysical or transcendental support:

(1) The account of validity claims can be formulated out of speaker-intuitions, and then be empirically tested against as varied a sample of speakers as can be found. This can, at least, render the account "plausible."

(2) We can try and show the empirical usefulness of the account in various fields.

(3) We can examine critically the history of social theory, to see what problems are present in it and how those theories could be improved when supplemented by the concept of communicative rationality.[1]

Habermas carries these strategies out in an impressive variety of ways: his discussions of speech act theory, for example (*TKH*, vol 1., pp. 367–452/ 273–337), can be assimilated to (1), and those of Weber and other social theorists to (3). The kind of analysis of legal thought pursued in his *Justification and Application* could be assimilated to (2).[2] There is a problem with *all* this, however: strategies (2) and (3) are ways of arguing not for the universality of the theory of communicative action, but for what I call its centrality. Once that is clearly distinguished from universality, their irrelevance to the latter is clear. And (1), as Habermas himself notes, can only render his theory "plausible." So, astonishingly, none of these strategies is even aimed at redeeming the strong universality-claim Habermas wants to make.

We could search further, to see if Habermas has at his disposal other argumentative resources which he does not mention (or, perhaps, recognize). But the overwhelming discrepancy, in the passage under discussion, between the problem Habermas states and the means he suggests for its solution is, I think, suspicious in itself. It is wiser to step back and ask just what sort of problem Habermas takes himself to have. What role does the universality-claim for communicative action have in his thought? What is that claim's status, and what is its motivation? What is gained by claiming universality instead of centrality?

At the end of *The Theory of Communicative Action*, Habermas returns to the issue of the contrast between what he calls the "strongly universalistic claim" of the theory of communicative action and the merely "hypothetical" and only "indirectly examinable" status of that claim (*TKH*, vol. 2, pp. 586f/ 399). It seems that he is attempting here not to prove his universality claim but only to advance it as a hypothesis plausible enough for discussion: he takes it not as a report of established fact, but precisely as a *claim*. This would explain the sketchy nature of his earlier discussion of how to justify that claim: he needs to validate it only as a topic for discussion, not as actually true. And it would mean that the crucial question concerning Habermasian universality changes from one concerning what can *justify* it into one concerning what can *motivate* it.

There are, I suggest, at least four possible motives. Two of them, I will argue, are dubious: assigning them to Habermas conflicts with what he says elsewhere. The other two, though they can be attributed to Habermas with more confidence, will turn out to be problematic in themselves. The result will be an enhanced suspicion that Habermas does not really need his universality-claim at all. (. . . *one becomes a counterpart to those who concern themselves with things that do not concern them.*)

First, in a passage I have already quoted from the book's introduction, the universality-claim is motivated by social science's claim to objectivity:

> . . . Theory formation is in danger of being limited from the start to a particular, culturally or historically bound perspective unless fundamental concepts are constructed in such a way that the concept of rationality they implicitly posit is encompassing and general, that is, satisfies universalistic claims. . . . We cannot expect objectivity in social/theoretical knowledge if the corresponding concepts of communicative action express a merely particular perspective on rationality, one interwoven with a particular cultural tradition. (*TKH*, vol. 1, p. 197/137)

Universality is thus claimed in the service of the "objectivity" expected for social/theoretical knowledge. But as a motivation for his own universality-claim, such an appeal to objectivity has a problem of which Habermas is clearly aware. For it assumes that the expectations involved are themselves legitimate. Perhaps the tendency of social scientists to make objective truth-claims is itself, like neopositivistic understandings of science in general, a fit object for critique. Habermas has in fact argued at book length both against making science so viewed into the paradigm of all knowledge, and against naively positivistic views of science itself; so we may assume that, in spite of appearances, he is not merely taking over the current self-interpretation of social science in making his universality-claim.[3]

The second possible motivation is similarly dubious, but somewhat more pressing in terms of the current investigation. Advancing universality claims in the service of objectivity means advancing them in the name of the most rigorous form of truth—and, it follows, of presence. When Habermas's overt linking of objectivity with universality (and so, tacitly, with presence) is combined with the fact that many of his criticisms of thinkers such as Derrida, Foucault, and Heidegger center on their (supposed) inability to make truth-claims,[4] he seems to be motivated by the "domination of presence" associated by Derrida with the metaphysical tradition.

In fact, however, he is not—not in any simplistic way, at least, and not on the present reading of that dominance. For one of Habermas's main targets, early and late, is precisely the view that truth is the single paramount goal or telos of speech and inquiry in general. In "A Return to Metaphysics?" he puts this point in almost the form of a lament:

> The occidental deference towards logos reduces reason to something that language performs in only one of its functions, in representing states of affairs. Ultimately, methodically pursuing questions of truth is the only thing that still counts as rational. Questions of justice and questions of taste, as well as questions regarding the truthful presentation of self, are all excluded from the sphere of the rational. Whatever surrounds and borders on the scientific culture that specializes in questions of truth, every context in which this culture is embedded and rooted, then appears to be irrational as such.[5]

In opposition to this, Habermas seeks to maintain what he calls "the equi-primordiality [*Gleichursprünglichkeit*] and equal value of the three fundamental linguistic functions."[6] For communicative action is oriented not just to truth (the excellence of presence) but to appropriateness and truthfulness as well.[7] Habermas does not, in the passages just referred to, shrink from calling the Occidental deference to logos by the name of "logocentrism." If he is under its spell, it is in no simple or direct way.

Habermas's desire, already mentioned, to give his theory of communicative action critical thrust provides a third, and more plausible, motivation for his universality-claim. Critical or self-critical potential is for Habermas primarily unlocked through dialogue with others. What brings such dialogue about is pre-eminently, for him, the making of a validity-claim which transcends the location of its utterance: as Kant pointed out, an assertion which only claims validity for me (or us) here and now is not open to criticism by others.[8] Habermas is then inviting not the adherence of others to his new research paradigm but their criticisms of it, and the "others" in question would be not merely denizens of the modern life world, but people the world over. Moreover, validity-claims whose purpose is merely to draw others into critical debate have to be provocative; they do not have to be proven. To be provocative, they need to be only plausible; and Habermas's explicitly available strategies can show that they are at least that.

The motivation for Habermas's universality-claim now appears to be pragmatic rather than theoretical. If such is the case, those claims are not, in Austin's language, constative speech acts at all. They are made in order to achieve a perlocutionary effect: to draw as many interlocutors as possible into the field of discussion. Their illocutionary status is similar to that of an invitation or summons.[9] But this motive, while I think it can reliably be assigned to Habermas, has problems of its own. For such an invitation need not be couched in the form of a universality-claim. If the point of making a universality-claim is to issue an invitation, why not simply issue one? If provocation is needed, why will the centrality-claim not suffice? If the radical separation of subsystems of rationality is truly a feature of most views of the modern world, the claim that a single form of reason is central to them all should be incitement enough. Why take the risk—no small one, in light of the Habermas literature—that one's universality-claim will be discussed only to be refuted? From this point of view, Habermas's advancing of his universality-claim as a topic for discussion appears to be misleading and even damaging.

A fourth and final possibility, one which I have also mentioned previously, is suggested by the passage I adduced above from the end of *The Theory of Communicative Action*. There, Habermas's motivation lies not in the nature of social science but in that of communicative action itself:

> the theory of communicative action aims at that moment of unconditionedness which is built into the conditions of consensus-formation by criticizable validity claims—*as* claims these transcend all spatial and temporal, all provincial limitations of the context of the moment. (*TKH*, vol. 2, pp. 586f/399f)

The "aiming at" referred to here means that the theory of communicative action is itself advanced as a case of communicative action. So it carries with it the kind of unconditional validity-claim that it attributes to communicative action in general. Habermas therefore makes his universality-claim because his own general theory has it that he must. Like the third motivation above, this one can plausibly be assigned to Habermas. But if my previous argumentation is correct, it is circular. For I argued that the theory of communicative action can also be seen as claiming only centrality. If so, then it is not itself an instance of communicative action. Why does Habermas think that it is? The answer, presumably, is that all rational discourse must in his view make universality-claims. Only if his own universality-claim has previously been accepted, then, does it follow that the theory of communicative action itself must be advanced in a case of communicative action.

Let us get clear on just what is at stake. Habermas argues, at enormous length and with accumulating persuasiveness, that various modern social theories—advanced by theorists as diverse as Durkheim, Marx, Mead, Parsons, and Weber, among many others—can be brought together around his own theory of communicative action. He also argues that those theories have internal problems which can be solved by evaluating them from the standpoint of communicative action, and that their critical and explanatory powers can be enhanced by such critical convergence. He shows, in other words, that the theory of communicative action is central to modern social theories. This makes indirectly plausible that it is also central to the modern life world itself, which those theories explain in important ways. Yet he goes on to make a universality-claim for his theory that he cannot begin to vindicate and which, on several accounts of its possible motivation, is unnecessary or even problematic. Why?

2. HABERMAS'S REINSTATEMENT OF OUSIA

Habermas's universality-claim appears to have neither justification nor motivation. It seems that we must turn—as many do—to personal whim: that Habermas, for example, wants to use universality-claims as a weapon to fight "enemies" such as Derrida, Foucault, and Heidegger. But between conscious motivation and personal whim there lies, in philosophy as elsewhere, a spectrum of intellectual gestures which can guide and structure thought without being transparent to the thinker—the spectrum of what I call parametric functioning. Habermas's adoption of a universality-claim seems, in fact, to exhibit what I have elsewhere called the "reinstatement" of ousia in Empiricist discourse: the unargued (because unrecognized) relocation of ousiodic structure from one level of reality to another.[10] To see whether this is so, I will examine here four levels on which ousiodic structure *may* be reinstated for Habermas: those of (a) the individual moral agent; (b) the community of people involved in a case of communicative action (which I will call the "communicative action community"); (c) the life world; and (d) the theory of communicative action itself. The first three levels will exhibit sporadic, ambivalent, and incomplete challenges to ousiodic structure. The fourth and final level will show an unambiguous, and I will claim unnecessary, reinstatement of ousiodic structure.

Levels (a) and (b) cannot be separated, for in Habermas's view it is the rational destiny of the individual moral agent to reidentify herself as a participant in a communicative action community. Such reidentification has both theoretical and practical aspects, and constitutes a general narrative structure which Habermas fleshes out in several different ways. Consider, first, moral theory. The moral agent, considered in isolation from any community, is in Habermas's view structured by what Max Weber called "purposive rationality"—reason which calculates how to achieve a given end. It is the one-sided development of such rationality which, in Weber's view, produces the differentiation of modernity's independent subsystems.[11] Habermas, as I have noted, agrees that these subsystems are kept wholly separate by modern thought; but he does not think that they are really as separate from one another as they seem. At fault in this, for Habermas, is not purposive rationality itself but the concept of it: what from the standpoint of such rationality appear as wholly distinct cultural subsystems are from the point of view of his own concept of communicative rationality merely one-sided developments of the three validity-claims which such rationality always contains (*TKH*, vol. 1, pp. 456f/340f).

Habermas overcomes purposive rationality by reconceiving it as what he calls "strategic" rationality and contrasting it with his communicative version. Communicative rationality is aimed not strategically at the success of the individual actor in achieving her purposes but at communicative understanding (*Verständigung*): agreement on all three validity-claims of an utterance.[12] This reconception of the moral agent, Habermas notes, goes beyond Weber and modernity to take issue with a long tradition in philosophy, for the concept of strategic action modifies not only Weber's purposive rationality but the Aristotelian concept of "teleological" action—an individual's choice and utilization of means to achieve some purpose.[13] As I have argued elsewhere, Aristotle's teleological concept of action is ousiodic in that it views moral action as the outcome of an ousiodic structure: that of the moral agent.[14] When strategic action is thus traced back to teleological action, it reveals its ousiodic roots; and in criticizing it, Habermas is also criticizing the ancient conception of moral agents as ousiodically structured. To be sure, the break with ousia is not identified as such. Teleological action as Habermas discusses it is hardly freighted with Aristotle's whole metaphysical ethics, according to which a rational agent has only one ultimate telos, the disposition of reason over his life; it refers, as Habermas defines it, to the effort to achieve any purpose whatever. But that certainly includes the Aristotelian overriding purpose, and so Habermas's break is with that as well.

This break with ousiodic structure in moral theory is a prototypical Habermasian *Aufhebung* of previous theory: Habermas modifies Weber's (and Aristotle's) concept so as to bring it into productive communication with his own view of moral agency as fundamentally dialogical. In *The Philosophical Discourse of Modernity,* a similar story is told more generally, again as one of philosophical progress and conceptual innovation:

> . . . the paradigm of self-consciousness, of the relation-to-self of a subject knowing and acting in isolation, [must be] replaced by a different one—by the paradigm of mutual understanding, that is, of the intersubjective relationship between individuals who are socialized through communication and reciprocally recognize one another. (*PDM*, p. 361/310)

Such replacement of social theories founded on the (ousiodic) paradigm of subject centered reason by Habermas's own dialogical theory is paralleled on a practical level in stories whose "protagonist" is not a theoretical paradigm but an acting individual, who sheds her isolated ego to enter into community with others. In "Moral Development and Ego-Identity,"[15] for example, the penultimate, Kohlbergian stage of the formation of individual identity is a Kantian stage at which the individual operates in accordance with universal moral principles that she gives to herself, and which thus have a legislative disposition over the actions they generate and order. The very capacity to conceive of an immanent, as opposed to an external, source of action presupposes boundaries to the moral self (as it did with Rorty's ironist). Thus bounded and governed, the Kantian/Kohlbergian moral agent is, like the Aristotelian *phronimos,* what I call ousiodically structured. This "monological" stage of moral maturity is superseded for Habermas, however, by a stage in which the individual repeatedly "constructs new identities" out of communicative interaction with others.[16] The supersession, which I will not discuss in greater detail, is, Habermas writes, a matter of "breaking down barriers, dependency."[17]

In "What Is Universal Pragmatics?" the story is linguistic: the supersession of the isolated, ousiodic moral ego occurs when the individual undertakes to redeem the validity-claims raised by any of her utterances, thereby forsaking strategic interaction and committing herself to communicative action.[18] Her utterance, in other words, does not remain at her disposition. It transgresses the boundaries set by her personal purposes, and enters a communicative context which is not governed by those purposes—drawing her along with it into a community structured by critical reciprocity.

The replacement of the isolated individual moral agent by the communicative action community thus occurs for Habermas in several places, and on both practical and theoretical levels: it is both a theoretical *Aufhebung* and a practical fate. The two levels thus share what amounts to a *general narrative structure* according to which an individual or an earlier social theory migrates from a self-enclosed purposive or conceptual domain into a mutually transformative, because critical, reciprocity with other individuals or theories. Consider how Habermas works on the theoretical level. Part of an overall social theory—Weber's views just on purposive rationality, for example—is detached from the rest of that theory and taken on its own. It then critically interacts not with the original theory but with Habermas's, into which it is incorporated—but which derives its legitimacy in part from it, so that it preserves a reciprocally critical relation to Habermas's theory. Similarly on the practical level: the individual's words or actions, perhaps intended strategically to realize her own purposes, migrate into a dialogical context in which they can be mutually criticized for the validity-claims they make.

In all its guises, the monological, strategic ego is, I have argued, an ousiodically structured one. Habermas's account of its necessary replacement by the communicative action community is thus a challenge to such structure. But what about that community itself? Does it embody ousiodic structure?

At first, it does not seem to. Consider the communicative action which occurs on the floor of the United States Senate, for example, and which is often more important than the speeches actually being given. It has a structure which in some respects is highly developed. It is, for one thing, formally restricted to senators, and so seems to have secure boundaries. But, in fact, any particular case of it will involve just those senators who actually participate; some may leave and others may arrive. When all of them depart, what I will call the "communicative action community" they constitute dissolves altogether. Even in such an "official" version, in other words, the communicative action community is not stably bounded like an Aristotelian household.

Second, no one member of such a community has a dominating position: in communicative action, any participant is able to challenge any utterance. When that actually happens and the interaction becomes discourse, speech roles are symmetrically distributed: every participant has an equal chance to speak and be heard.[19] The participants are not merely isolated denizens of a Rortyan cultural filing cabinet, for each can critically transform the others and be transformed by them in turn.

The first two levels on which Habermas may unknowingly relocate ousiodic structure, the individual moral agent and the communicative action community, thus seem rather to embody challenges to such structure. But ousia has not, it seems, died off entirely. For Habermas, tellingly, refers to understanding (*Verständigung*) as the "immanent telos of human speech" in general.[20] And this, if we are to read the word *telos* strictly (i.e., as the form of a thing coming to control its matter),[21] would suggest an instatement of the structures of communicative action themselves as the dispositive form, not merely for various communicative action communities but for all human language. If so, it seems, Habermas has *re*-instated ousiodic structure on the level of language itself. Habermas's challenges to ousia in the cases of the moral agent and communicative action community would then be merely preludes to its re-instatement on a larger level.

To see the extent to which this is the case requires some adjustments to Habermas's remark that understanding is the immanent telos of language. For Habermas, language as such does not constitute a single bounded domain; it is a medium of interaction and so of events, and there is an impressive variety of languages.[22] We can better gauge the degree to which Habermas is re-instating ousia by recalling that language for him exists, like all communicative phenomena, within the horizon of intelligibility furnished by a life world. This brings us to level (c): the level of the life world itself as a linguistically organized set of unquestioned background beliefs and common sense (*TKH*, vol. 2, p. 189/124). Does the life world exhibit ousiodic structure?

Here, Habermas's thought becomes decidedly ambivalent. At one point, for example, he characterizes the life world as "a context that, itself boundless, draws boundaries" (*TKH*, vol. 3, p. 201/132). But the sense in which it can "draw" boundaries without "having" them remains unclear. Elsewhere, in fact, Habermas explicitly refers to "limits" of the life world:

> When [interlocutors] go beyond the horizon of a specific situation, they cannot step into a void; they find themselves right away in another, now actualized, yet *preinterpreted* domain of what is culturally taken for granted. . . . Even new situations rise up from a life world. . . . [The life world] is immune from total revision . . . situations change, but *the limits of the life world itself cannot be transcended.* (*TKH*, vol, 2, pp. 191, 201/125, 132; emphasis added)

The Habermasian life world thus has (or somehow imposes) not merely boundaries but inviolable ones. It also turns out to have considerably more internal structure than Habermas suggests when he characterizes it, in a passage I have quoted earlier, as a "reservoir" of truisms or convictions (*TKH*, vol. 2, p. 189/124). For as Habermas implicitly argues in the first part of *The Theory of Communicative Action,* if the life world is linguistically structured, the telos of language itself must structure it: everything, certainly everything linguistic, that happens within its boundaries is (unless "strategic") either openly or covertly directed toward the achievement of communicative understanding. Hence, even such seemingly nonlinguistic phenomena such as dance are "limit cases" of action which is oriented to achieving understanding.[23]

This confirms that what Habermas contests in Heidegger's concept of world cannot have been its ousiodic structure as such, for Habermas's own concept of the life world also exhibits such structure.[24] Habermas's challenge to ousiodic structure here, like those of Derrida and Rorty, thus does not amount to a conscious critique of ousia itself. It is in fact the mirror of Rorty's: where Rorty contested not ousiodic structure as such but the rational necessity that he saw at the core of Analytical Philosophy, Habermas contests the irrationality and contingency that he finds at the core of Heidegger. From this follow Habermas's universalism, its contrast with Rorty's pluralism, and their common inability to criticize the very notion of "core" itself.

I have now traced Habermas's challenges to ousia through three of the four levels on which I suggested they might be located: from the individual moral agent through the communicative action community to the life world. It is notable that in the course of this, the challenges themselves have become weaker. It was clear that the individual moral agent for Habermas was comprehensible only in terms of a challenge to, indeed the abandonment of, its ousiodic structure: only, that is, insofar as such an agent yielded its isolated, "strategic" viewpoint and came to identify itself as a member of a communicative action community. That community itself was presented as porous and reciprocal, rather than as ousiodically structured. On the level of the life world, ousiodic structure was more securely, if inexplicitly, in place; the challenges to it were incomplete, unargued, and undeveloped— at times almost rhetorical in character. We now approach the final level: Habermas's own theory of the nature and status of communicative action.

If communicative understanding provides the ordering telos of interaction within the Habermasian life world, then the theory of communicative action is the reasoned setting forth of that ordering principle. As with philosophy generally, the theory does not leave what it treats unchanged. For though Habermas does not stress it, it is clear that the recognition, by those who accept his theory, that communicative understanding teleologically structures other forms of interaction will actually enhance its ability to do so. This, presumably, is why his general narrative of such recognition has both theoretical and practical aspects. On its theoretical side, the theory of communicative action converts the norms and structures of communicative action from unknown to known and renders them rationally legitimate. This then enhances their practical capacity to structure the life world itself, and, in short, enables them to be what they are. Like Kant's critical *état-civil* of the human mind,[25] the theory of communicative action is not merely a report of how the life world is structured; it is also and simultaneously the perfecting of that very structure. Whether it itself exhibits ousiodic structure, and how necessarily it does so, thus has implications for the levels I have previously discussed: for if it does, its own investment in ousiodic structure may communicate itself back down to those levels.

Habermas presents his theory of communicative action, in contrast to the more radical critiques of the postmodernists, in explicitly Hegelian language as a "determinate negation" of subject centered reason. His *Aufhebung* of earlier views is not, in his words, an "undialectical rejection of subjectivity," but a "critique testable step by step."[26] When presented as a determinate negation, Habermas's relocation of the telos of interaction from (the aims of) the individual participant to (the communicative understanding of) the speech community as a whole assumes a specific burden: it must introduce enough change to solve the problems with purposive rationality without going beyond what is necessary for those solutions. Does it do so?

There is, I suggest, an important gap between the content of communicative understanding, on the one hand, and its status as the telos of Habermas's tale of the "fate" of the ousiodic ego. It is clearly part of Habermas's narrative that the telos of speech should be not the achievement of individual purposes but some form of social integration. Also part of the tale is that such social integration cannot merely be agreement on the validity of truth-claims.[27] But the distinctive claim of the theory of communicative action—that the social integration at which *all* speech aims is constituted by rational agreement on, and only on, the three validity claims of truth, appropriateness, and truthfulness—is *not* part of this story. It is established by a variety of arguments which, in view of Habermas's own account of his argumentative strategies and what they are geared to, I did not find it necessary to discuss here—arguments which take their beginning not from the critique of subject centered reason but from an analysis of speech acts and from the Habermas-Weber account of the differentiation of the life world.[28]

It is here, then, that we find the limits of Habermas's challenge to ousia. The making and redeeming of the three validity-claims falls under the norms of a formal account of communicative rationality which itself, as normative, structures what can happen within the domain of rational speech. But it is not structured or transformed in turn by rational speech: the co-presence of three, and only three, validity-claims is not advanced as something that will be reciprocally modified by new debates within the life world. It is advanced as a permanent, necessary structuring principle of that world.

Viewed in this way, the theory of communicative action does not stand to other discourses in the reciprocally critical relation that Habermas, on the reflective level, advocates. Habermas is, on that level, quite aware that his theory of communicative action is open to challenge and critique; as we saw, it is no unmoved mover to which other discourses must conform. But it is not *designed*, as for example Hegel's philosophy was,[29] to be refuted. Though Habermas maintains, as I have noted, that no theory is entitled to the status of discursive "unmoved mover," his claim that communicative understanding is the universal telos of all linguistic interaction accords the theory which sets it forth just such status. Thus understood, the theory of communicative action is what Rorty calls "final," not in that it renders "further inquiry and history superfluous" but in that it makes of them only unfortunate necessities which may confirm or refute it, but cannot enrich it. The theory of communicative action itself thus embodies an unambiguous reinstatement of ousiodic structure in Habermas's own philosophy.

Habermas's theory of normed making-and-redeeming exercises what I call parametric functions over his own discourse: it leads him to see a variety of other things in terms of ousiodic structure. First, it sets theoretical boundaries to his thought through what I call "exterior" and "interior" exclusions of other discourses. Thus, though Habermas leaves space in his general account of rationalization complexes for a "social-aesthetic" rationality, that space is filled, as Thomas McCarthy points out, not with examples of such rationality, but with an "x."[30] McCarthy has shown that Habermas does not fully discharge the burden of proof he assumes with this emptiness, and that to do so would lead to inconsistencies with his treatment of Walter Benjamin.[31] Social-aesthetic rationality, then, is a case of what I call internal exclusion: though nominally a form of rational speech, it does not serve to fill out the nature of communicative action, and resides within his overall theory the way an ancient wife—who, for Aristotle, also has only a nominal form of reason[32]—resides within the household.

A case of external exclusion is Habermas's famous encounter with that multifarious combination of insight and delusion called "postmodernism." I will not attempt to trace in detail here the manifold embarrassments of this; Habermas's treatment of Heidegger can serve as an example. His reduction of Heidegger's later writings to *Seinsgeschichte*—thereby excluding *all* their interesting and plausible insights—reposes, I have argued elsewhere, on nothing more than failure to read the relevant texts.[33] What remains after this and other such exclusions is for Habermas a conceptual grid which constitutes, perhaps, the best available picture of the current intellectual economy of the Western world, at least of its Germanic and Anglo-Saxon components. But it is a picture which is painted from within—from a provisional center which itself is open to revision and refutation.

The ousiodic features of the theory of communicative action also guide Habermas's accounts of the other levels I have already discussed. Because what it sets forth is the telos of all communication occurring within life worlds, the theory must—in spite of what I pointed out as Habermas's own ambivalences—structure the life world around itself. Because concrete communicative action communities are parts of the life world, its norms acquire bounding and dispositive power over them, however transient and symmetrical they may be. Considered as I did previously—as the telos of one of Habermas's narratives of the replacement of subject centered reason—the communicative action community was that to which an individual moral agent yielded her isolated identity. Its boundaries were porous and no participant dominated. But when we arrive at it from the other direction—from the structures of communicative action itself—its own ousiodic structure becomes apparent. Only those who engage themselves to redeem rationally the validity-claims they make, for example, can join such a community; others must either remain "strategic" or undergo "reidentification" as communicative. The three validity-claims always raised in communicative action, and the ways those can be criticized and argued for, determine not only the kinds of speech that will be used to redeem them, but also the issues that will arise in such communities (issues concerning or presupposing their validity).

The dispositive power of the life world itself over those who inhabit it is further attested by the two ambivalent ways in which Habermas challenges it. One is his (unargued) claim that culture and language "do not restrict the scope for action."[34] If true, this would amount to saying that the life world does not have dispositive power to structure the behavior of those within it. But unless it is meant in the sense that my language does not impede me from achieving any purpose *which it allows me to formulate,* it is obviously false. We can, after all, speak only about what we have words for (*TKH,* vol. 2, pp. 90f, 224/56f, 149), and the words a given life world contains determine what can be formulated as ends, or as means, within it. An ancient Greek, for example, could not consciously act on the Kantian imperative to treat all other humans as ends and not as means, because classical Greek has no word which corresponds to ours for "human being."[35] She could not, indeed, consciously undertake even to act of her own free will —because classical Greek has no word for "will." Her language itself sets boundaries to what she can conceive, and so to her conscious actions.

This first effort to challenge the dispositive power of the life world thus draws Habermas into a claim which is clearly false and contradicts his remark, quoted above, about how the life world "draws boundaries." The other way in which the life world is challenged for Habermas is in discourse. There, as we saw, some element of the life world—some belief about the objective givens governing the situation, or a moral or social norm, for example—is thematized and criticized. In this, writes Habermas, "the life world loses its prejudgmental power over everyday communicative practice to the degree that actors owe their mutual understanding to their own interpretative performances" (*TKH,* vol. 2, p. 203/133). Participants in communicative action can, then, gain distance from their life world. But for Habermas this will not lead to a transgression of the boundaries of the life world altogether. Discourse is confined to examining utterances as regards their truth, appropriateness, or truthfulness. It does not extend to questioning the semantic powers of one's language itself, or to challenging the boundaries of the life world which that language organizes.[36]

Thus, by ordering the speech of those who engage in it, the norms of communicative action indirectly order those individuals as well. They become, in a sense, subservient not to other individuals but to the general structures of communicative action.[37] As the slaves in an Aristotelian household were subservient not to the master but to his reason.

3. CONCLUSION

Two different philosophies run side by side through Habermas's texts. Both set forth the structures of communicative action, with its three and only three validity-claims; both set forth the move to discourse when one of those claims is challenged. But one philosophy, broadly Kantian, claims universality for those structures and that move. The other merely claims centrality.

The universalistic philosophy is the more problematical. Habermas's explicit arguments for his universality-claim are not only inadequate but, I have argued, suspiciously so; the motivation for making the claim in the first place is also obscure. It becomes comprehensible, however, as part of a tacit reinstatement of ousia on the level of the life world, a reinstatement guided by the structure of the theory of communicative action itself. This reinstatement triggers dogmatic construals of other levels of Habermasian theory —of the nature of the life world, of the communities which arise within it, and of the individuals who form such communities. The result is that one form of social integration—argumentation over validity-claims—becomes the only rational form. The aesthetic-social, to take just one example, drops from sight.

The other Habermasian philosophy, more Hegelian, is reached by recognizing that Habermas's strategies for arguing universality either actually establish centrality, rather than universality, or else aim at most at a "plausibility" which accords better with an invitation than with the statement of a truth. This Habermas, like Hegelians in general, is more modest: he need not show that the structures of communicative rationality are universal, but only that they are central to a broad variety of modern practices. But Habermas's Hegelianism is weakened and inconsistent. For if, in its Hegelian form, Habermas's thought arises (as he himself says) via the determinate negation, or *Aufhebung*, of other theories, such *Aufhebung* is not carried all the way through: the subversive, dialectical activity of Habermas's thought, unlike Hegel's, ceases when it reaches his own theory.

This limit to dialectical transformation is an effect of Habermas's residual acceptance of the traditional view of truth (or presence) as the goal of rational, "objective" inquiry. Like Rorty, Habermas accepts this for scientific discourse in general; unlike Rorty, he also accepts truth—in the form of the objectivity that comes with universality—as the paramount goal of his own discourse. This is in contrast to his view of the various discourses he appropriates. To be sure, they all make truth claims. But seen in Habermas's historical perspective, truth was not their real telos: their actual fate was to be critically taken up into his own theory of communicative action. Habermas nowhere envisages such a fate for his own theory. Nor can he: for if it is to be universal, the theory of communicative action must apply to itself. And if it is advanced in a case of communicative action, it must claim truth; it must transcend centrality in the direction of universality. From that point on, innovation can only come about via refutation.

The remedy, then, may well be to carry Habermas's Hegelianism a bit further than he does: to view the theory of communicative action, not as universal, but merely as central to an impressive variety of other discourses and important practices in the modern life world. This would open it out to transformation by other theories and events in the life world. (*Indeed: by this time sheer things concern him—and how many things!—which no longer* trouble *him!*)

Such a move would also save Habermas from reinstating ousiodic structure on the various levels of his thought. The life world, for example, would cease to be structured by the "immanent telos" of communicative understanding, and become what Habermas sometimes calls it—merely a "reservoir" of truisms and accepted practices, upon which we depend for our mutual understanding and which we can critically question at any time. When we no longer limit such critical questioning to the three claims of truth, appropriateness, and sincerity, it can include the "semantic capacities" of the life world: the structures of intelligibility with which our language at any time provides us. Such questioning would, of course, be challenging the very "limits" of the life world itself.

Freeing the concept of a communicative action community from the domination of the norms and structures of communicative action would open it out to construal as the more general phenomenon of social integration which, I suggested, was the real telos of Habermas's tale of the replacement of subject centered reason. The reciprocal transformations that occur within such a community would be brought about, not only by three types of rational critique, but in an indefinite and growing variety of ways: through the establishment of centrality, through shared laughter, through eros, through the experience of the sublime mystery of the Other. Communicative action as Habermas understands it would be one particularly "central" form of such social integration. But it would not be the only one, or even the only rational one.

The individual moral agent, finally, would be freed from the one ousiodic structure that it retained on Habermas's account: the dominance within it of Habermasian rationality as the capacity to make and argue all three validity-claims. In Habermas's view, when I abandon my "strategic" purposes to enter into a communicative action community, I do not abandon these structures of rationality: I must make and redeem validity-claims according to accepted principles of argumentation keyed to each. Freed from the dominance of those principles, the moral agent could be decisively structured, not only by argument and the capacity for it, but by such things as erotic affection, humor, and joy.

The view that the theory of communicative action could be advanced only via communicative action was just one of the two motivations my earlier discussion of the universality-claim left as plausibly attributed to Habermas. The other concerned critical purchase. For Habermas to restrict his claim to mere centrality would be, in his own view, to relativize the theory of communicative action to current cultural practice. And this, he fears, would rob his theory of its critical force. For the primary vehicle of critique for Habermas, as I noted above, is the unconditionality of validity-claims.

This fear, I think, is largely unfounded. As Habermas's own practice shows, simply bringing diverse theories into harmony with one another requires a great deal of criticism and readjustment of those theories, and thence of the life world practices which they claim to structure. But such readjustment is in the service of the Hegelian claim of harmony over diversity, rather than of universal truth.

Such readjustments do not exhaust the critical potential of such a reformed, "de-Kantianized" Habermas. I have argued elsewhere that Hegel's philosophy, with its grand goal of harmony over diversity, was called forth by a specific phenomenon of Hegel's culture—of, we might say, Hegel's life world. That phenomenon was multiple diremption—the dismembering of the private sphere into a mere battleground of subjective standpoints, and the contrast of that private agony with a public sphere which had ossified into a mere mass of habits.[38]

Habermas's theory of communicative action also arises, he writes, out of a set of disruptions in the life world, which call it forth through the deformations and threat they present (*TKH,* vol. 2, p. 593/403). These disruptions, in turn, are effects of a single basic rupture: what Habermas calls the "uncoupling" of system and life world.[39] The life world is disrupted and threatened for Habermas by two "delinguistified media," highlighted by contemporary system theory: money and power (*TKH,* vol. 2, pp. 230, 246f, 255f, 264/154, 164f, 170f, 177). Though system and life world have a common site of origin in tribal societies, in modernity they are fundamentally estranged. Neither is the ground or basis of the other (*TKH,* vol. 2, pp. 275f /185f); neither can be understood in terms appropriate for the other (*TKH,* vol. 2, pp. 232, 277f/155, 186). But neither can be understood without the other, either: their conflict is definitive for both. For the system is essentially a *de*linguistification: it exists by replacing, or "colonizing," the communicative practices of the life world. And the fact that the life world is under stress from this is essential to understanding it, as well, for it is what calls forth the theory of communicative action itself. These realms are so disparate that their conflict is unfathomable—not merely incomprehensible but invisible; it is what Habermas characterizes as a hidden violence, operating in the "pores" of the life world. This unfathomable violence is the active gap around which modernity is definitively gathered. It is, in my term, the diakenon at its heart.[40]

Habermas's theory of communicative action thus arises—though he does not put it that way—diakenically. This places him outside of Hegel, for whom the disruptions calling forth his philosophy could at least be reconciled in thought. Habermas does not seek to reconcile the life world to the systems of money and power, but to remain attentive to and articulate their disparity. His thought can thus derive critical purchase from what Hegel never managed: constant attention to a growing, shaping gap—that between system and life world. But this diakenon—unlike those of Heidegger and Derrida—is not for Habermas ultimate. For the whole intent of his thought is, like that of Rorty, to provide the concepts which will make the conflict of system and life world visible and comprehensible. Revealing the diakenic interplay of that violence is in the interest of terminating it, of rescuing the life world from the disruptions and threats of the "uncoupling" at its heart.

The activity of thought which does this, however, even if it is Habermas's own, is not a "theory" in his "objectivating" sense.[41] It is more like the articulation of a phenomenon than the statement and defense of a thesis. The issue with Habermas thus becomes one of the usefulness of his vocabulary of communicative action, understanding, and discourse, rather than the truth of his thesis that these are universal.

If the autonomous discourses of the social sciences constitute the "periphery" of Habermas's shield, and the theory of communicative action is its center, then the anguish of the life world is the dynamism of the arm which holds that shield, and which provides a critical thrust independent of those autonomous discourses themselves. Since that critical thrust is an articulation of pain here and now, it cannot claim universality. But it can, like Kantian reflective judgment, hope to find agreement among those with whom we can actually talk. We thus arrive at the picture of (dialogically) autonomous discourses finding their way to a center which is doubly heteronomous: it "takes its law" both from the discourses which converge upon it and from the stresses in the life world which it articulates. It exercises the power of inducing self- and mutual critique into other discourses. But its special critical perspective is unlocked only when it demands that those other discourses, in coming to the center, contribute to the articulation, and perhaps to the eventual healing, of the life world.[42] It is to be seen, then, in respect of the Jewish conception of the *tikkun olam,* the mending of the world.[43]

So construed, Habermas's project can be viewed as the step-by-step remodeling of existing conceptualities—a public realm of ossified theory—into a new vocabulary which can do justice to the diremption at the heart of the life world. It would, in this, treat the social theories it encounters as themselves fundamentally ambiguous: as on the one hand rationally formulated accounts of various practices within the life world and, on the other hand, as efforts to articulate the threat to the life world as a whole. It would take them as elicitors in what I call "normal poetic interaction": as words which have not fewer than one meaning (as in the "abnormal poetic interaction" of which Derrida and Rorty are variants), but more than one. And it would respond to them with its own multiply significant words. For it would reshape its inherited vocabulary into vehicles which were both conceptually and expressively adequate: not only consistent, harmonious, and diverse in ways the social theories that originally harbored them cannot be, but able to articulate the threat to the life world. Habermas's thought would thus be a developed case of what I call "nonterminating normal poetic interaction." As such, it would enter into the service of freedom as the restoration of wholeness, and into the Great Demarcation.

MICHEL FOUCAULT'S CHALLENGES TO OUSIA

. . . The free spirit approaches life again, slowly to be sure, almost recalcitrantly, almost distrustfully. It grows warmer around her, as if more yellow; feeling and sympathy gain depth, mild winds of all kinds pass over her. It seems to her almost as if her eyes, for the first time, were opening up to what is nearby. She is amazed, and sits still: where has she been, then? These near and nearest things: how they seem transformed! What fluff and magic they have acquired in the meantime! . . . How it pleases her to sit still in her affliction, to spin forth patience, to lie in the sun! Who is as expert as she at happiness in winter, in spots of sun on the wall?

Michel Foucault did not acknowledge his debt to Heidegger until near the end of his tragically short life; but when the acknowledgment came, it was intense:

> . . . Heidegger has always been for me the essential philosopher. . . . My whole philosophical development was determined by my reading of [him]. . . . I probably wouldn't have read Nietzsche if I hadn't read Heidegger. . . . Nietzsche by himself said nothing to me. Whereas Nietzsche and Heidegger—that was the philosophical shock![1]

In the eyes of this hidden Heideggerean, Heidegger's gravest sin was the undifferentiated nature of his epochal analyses. Foucault (who does not, in the passage I am about to quote, have only Heidegger in mind) calls this a "totalitarian periodizing" of history according to which

> from a certain time on everyone would think in the same way in spite of surface differences, would say that same thing via a polymorphous vocabulary, and would produce a sort of grand discourse which one could run through indifferently in all directions. (*AS*, pp. 193f/148; also see pp. 10, 226/4, 173)

Viewed as an attack on Heidegger, this is of course directed against the same dominance of Being in *Seinsgeschichte* that we saw Habermas criticize: the view that Being "*dominates [durchherrscht]* all the phenomena that distinguish the age"[2] to such an extent that other historical phenomena need not even be discussed. In opposition to this, Foucault's own project of archeology

> describes a level of enunciative homogeneity which has its own temporal *découpe,* and which does not bring with it all the other forms of identity and difference which can be identified in language. (*AS,* p. 194/148)

Unlike Derrida, for whom the main target of serious challenge is a metaphysics so overarching and unified that it can be radically contested only at the price of forsaking intelligibility itself, Foucault challenges ousiodic structure in ways that remain concrete. Unlike Rorty, whose ironist sought a wholly self-enclosed, because wholly original, vocabulary, Foucault remains directed upon other discourses—those whose "enunciative homogeneity" he seeks to "describe." Where Habermas seeks to gain a central viewpoint from which to look over a vast array of modern social theories, Foucault seeks to set us down among such discourses, to examine them from a certain sort of proximity. (. . . *The free spirit approaches life again, slowly to be sure, almost recalcitrantly, almost distrustfully.*)

As with Derrida, I will not undertake here a complete inventory of Foucauldian challenges to ousia; that task deserves a book of its own. This chapter will concentrate on six of Foucault's many challenges to ousiodic structure; for reasons to be clarified later, I take them from his *Discipline and Punish* and the first volume of *The History of Sexuality.* The next chapter will examine Foucault's own reflection on these procedures in *The Archeology of Knowledge.* I will argue that Foucault, trapped in the problematics of presence and truth typical of the Great Demarcation, also remains trapped in doubts and aporias concerning the descriptive status of his own discourse.

1. THE PANOPTICON

My first example is the prison as described in *Discipline and Punish* (*SP,* pp. 201ff/200ff). Constructed after Jeremy Bentham's "Panopticon," this prison is built so that the inmates can be observed by the authorities without being able to see each other. The cells are arranged around the inside of a hollow ring, in the center of which stands a tower. Guards positioned in the tower can look directly into any cell without being seen by the inmates. But no inmate has an unimpeded view of any other inmate: none can see at all into nearby cells, and the view of the cells opposite is blocked by the tower.

When Foucault writes, in this same section, that "we are much less Greek than we think we are," it is with heavy but unconscious irony.[3] For the prison he has described is clearly a version, pushed to modern extremes, of the House of Pansa at Pompeii which I have discussed elsewhere.[4] It is, in fact, a profound realization of the three axes of domination inherent in ousia.[5] To begin with, it possesses unbreachable boundaries—it is, after all, a prison. And it shows a similarly unbreachable disposition: not only can its inmates not relate to each other except as the authorities dictate, they cannot relate to each other at all. For it is a tacit presupposition of the Panopticon that any interaction must be first and primarily visual, and the visual field of the prisoner is completely controlled by the authorities.[6] Hence, as Gilles Deleuze has written in his remarkable book on Foucault: "The abstract formula of Panopticism is . . . no longer 'see without being seen,' but 'impose some type of behavior on some human multiplicity.'"[7] This imposition, Deleuze continues, is carried out through "partitioning in space, ordering and serializing in time, composition in space-time," etc.[8] This listing, as Deleuze notes, could be continued indefinitely; but we see clearly that what is being listed are forms of disposition. The Panopticon thus exhibits at least two of the three familiar traits of ousiodic domination. (*It grows warmer around him, as if more yellow . . .*)

The dissociation of seeing and being seen, to be sure, has no ready analog in the ancient world. As long as it remains basic to the Panopticon,[9] the Panopticon appears to be something radically new and different in history. The invisibility of the center appears as a simple expression, further unfathomable, of the fact that the prison is "modern" and the House of Pansa "ancient"; the innovation would be traceable, if to anything, to convulsions of history as unfathomable as Heidegger's "mittences of Being." Foucault's exclusive emphasis on historical discontinuity, which I will discuss later,[10] encourages such a reading. But any simple appeal to the mutual incommensurability of historical periods to explain the panoptical structure of the prison would be wrong. For when we look at the prison as the imposition of a form of conduct on multiple human material, the invisibility of its center has at least two perfectly good explanations.

One concerns the specific type of causality the institution exhibits. The ancient household was constructed so as to manifest a final causality in which the *pater* was the *telos*. The wife, children, and slaves were to look to his good as their own. But he did not, as Aristotle notes, look to them in the same way.[11] In particular, he paid attention to his servants only when they did something wrong. It was not properly his function to give them actual orders or to manage their day-to-day behavior: he did not *speak* to them. They had to know what to do, in short, without being told. And for that, the master—and his *tablinum*—had to be visible to them. The prison, by contrast, reposes on no such teleological structure, and requires no goodwill on the part of its inmates. It and they are, in Foucault's word, organized as a "machine," as a field of efficient causality. As befits mechanical parts, the inmates are hardly asked to take the good of the guards to be their own purpose; and so they need not know the guards, who can operate from concealment.

Indeed, if the prison is geared to the "good" of anyone within it, it is that of the prisoners: of its component parts, not its disposing form. For what comes from the prison, what it produces, is merely the individuals who have resided in it and who, when their sentences are done, pass through its boundaries. In what I call "initiative," it is not the parts but the unifying form of a thing that passes unchanged into the external world: as the *pater familias* alone was able to leave his house and participate in the political world outside its walls. In Foucault's "carceral" version of ousia, then, the prison's disposing form, its unified center of guardian authority, does not transgress its boundaries. The prison affects the world outside itself only negatively, by removing certain miscreants from it, and piecemeal, by returning its prisoners to society as reformed citizens.

The prison as such, therefore, exhibits no initiative: the third and most problematic of ousia's defining traits is missing. This second distinction between the House of Pansa and the modern prison, then, explains the first: because the prison does not exhibit initiative, its controlling power does not need the goodwill of the controlled, and there is no need for that power to be visible.[12]

The effects of the prison on the world outside go beyond the negative and piecemeal ones that I have mentioned, however, and when they do Foucault's account of them becomes quite traditional. For the Panopticon is not merely the model for a prison. It is also a general (parametric) structure which "should be detached from any specific use" and applied in constructing schools, hospitals, asylums, factories, and poorhouses (*SP*, p. 207/205). Because of the generality of its form, writes Foucault, "the panoptical schema is destined, without effacing itself or losing any of its properties, to diffuse itself in the social body" (*SP*, p. 209/207). The form of the prison has a paradigmatic status with respect to the rest of society:

> The theme of the Panopticon found its privileged place of realization in the prison. If it is true that panoptical procedures, as concrete forms of the exercise of power, have had a very large diffusion—at least in a dispersed state—it is in penal institutions virtually alone that Bentham's utopia has been able to take material form *d'un bloc*. (*SP*, p. 252/249)

The diffusion of the panoptical form through the "social body" comes about when other institutions—such as those listed above—take it for their model, for what they are intended to be. In this way, the Panopticon becomes the paradigm of what Foucault calls "the carceral":

> And, distancing itself ever further from penality properly so called, the carceral circles enlarge themselves, and the form of the prison attenuates itself slowly before disappearing altogether. . . . And finally this great carceral network rejoins all the disciplinary mechanisms which function as disseminated through society. (*SP*, pp. 305/298, and generally pp. 300–315/293–308)

The Aristotelian analog here is (again) not to initiative—the passage of a form from its own matter into the external world—but rather to Aristotle's hierarchy of the cosmos, whose aspiration toward the Prime Mover constitutes an order which extends downward from the sphere of the fixed stars to the chaos and muck of the human world. The panoptical prison is thus presented by Foucault as the "Prime Mover," the destiny and unchosen *telos*, of society itself.

The panoptical prison thus appears, to me if not to Foucault, to be the realization of a very traditional ousiodic community—one which is founded on coercion rather than goodwill. Insofar as Foucault's description of it strikes us as disagreeable, his account of the prison—and of the "carceral" in general—stands as a challenge to ousia. But if so, it is a challenge which not only is not but cannot be acknowledged, for Foucault's "descriptive" method, which I will discuss in the next chapter, allows him no basis for an overt negative judgment.

Foucault's description of the prison, however, challenges its ousiodic structure in another, more subtle—and more Heideggerean—respect. For it emphasizes a third and final way in which the prison differs from an Aristotelian ousia: the openness of its center. The household was a completely closed system, which no one entered except with permission of the *pater.* In the case of Bentham's Panopticon, any member of society has—in theory —the right to enter not the prison as such but its very center, the tower, to see how the dispositive power of the guards is being exercised (*SP,* pp. 208f/ 207). The same structure which enables the guards to see and control the prison, in other words, also enables outsiders to place the guards themselves under surveillance. It is as if any member of society had the right to enter, not merely the House of Pansa, but its very *tablinum,* there to oversee the actions of the *pater.*

That to which the Panopticon is so radically open is not, of course, the emptiness of Heideggerean Being, but simply the larger society which the prison serves. Society is entitled to this because it has authorized and paid for the construction of the prison. Unlike an Aristotelian form, then, the guards in the tower are not the origin of the prison itself. They order, but do not create, the prisoners. They occupy, but do not establish, the walls which surround them. There would be no prison if there were not a whole system, indeed whole constellations of systems, of ideas and practices concerning crime, punishment, law, individual rights, and so on:

> What presides over all these mechanisms is not the unitary functioning of
> an apparatus or of an institution, but the necessity of a combat and the
> rules of a strategy. (*SP,* pp. 314f/308)

Thus, the disposing form of the prison—the guards—is united with its matter—the building itself and, indeed, the inmates who inhabit it—from outside. The prison's matter, building and inmates alike, must be "designated" by external agents as fit for inclusion within the prison. For Aquinas,

I noted in the introduction, this designation of the matter of a thing was the effect of divine creation: God was the primary "designator," uniting form and matter in the *actus essendi*. Foucault calls the designator in question "power," and his conception of power therefore has something divine about it—or perhaps, since power is hardly God, "demonic." Foucault's genealogical work, aimed at revealing the nature of power, is at bottom an exercise in theodicy (or demonodicy).

It is misleading, then, to view Foucault as engaging in any sort of challenge to, let alone "critique" of, power. What he does in discussing the Panopticon cannot be reduced to a mere normatively confused attempt to show that power, even in this particular case, is illegitimate.[13] Rather, what he does is show that what seems to be a self-enclosed ousia can equally well be viewed as dependent on forces from outside. Remaining (in this aspect) within the Thomistic tradition of his upbringing, what Foucault actually carries out is not a "critique of power" but a challenge to ousia *in the name* of power.[14] (. . . *feeling and sympathy gain depth, mild winds of all kinds pass over him.*)

2. CONFESSION

Another Foucauldian challenge to ousiodic structure is provided by the discussion, in *La volonté de savoir* (the first volume of Foucault's history of sexuality), of the modern practice of sexual confession. As Foucault describes it, such confession is more than a religious ritual; it is socially constitutive of the self, which in the modern world can no longer be authenticated through its relations to others (family, status, allegiances), and must be validated from within, by speaking the truth about itself (*VS*, pp. 78f/58f). The point of thus revealing oneself is not, as in the Catholic church, to confess one's infractions; it is "to seek to make one's desire, all one's desire, into discourse" (*VS*, p. 30/21). Like the structure of the Panopticon, the global confession of desires inevitably expands to include avowals of "innumerable pleasures, sensations, [and] thoughts" (*VS*, p. 29/20). This, finally, is pushed to such an extreme that it is only by way of sex and its avowal that one can have access to the totality of one's own body; only by way of confession can one become intelligible to oneself as well as to others (*VS*, p. 205/155).

Confession not only makes one intelligible to oneself but gives one power over one's desires: once these have been converted into discourse, their power to push one into action—to seize the initiative in one's conduct—is lessened. In this way, "the avowal sets free, power reduces to silence; truth does not belong to the order of power, but is in an original kinship with freedom" (*VS*, p. 80/60). The aim of confession, in this perspective, is to establish the dominance of reason and intelligibility in the individual (*VS*, p. 81/61). The ultimate effect will be to constitute the individual as a modern "subject"—which, I have argued elsewhere, is an ousiodically structured moral agent, whose desires are at the disposition of her reason and remain confined within the bounds of her body.[15] Once again, Foucault's challenge is to show that this seeming self-control and independence are really produced from outside the individual. For they too are effects of power:

> Causality in the subject, the unconscious of the subject, the truth of the subject in the other who knows . . . all this found a way to deploy itself in the discourse on sex. Not at all, however, by virtue of some natural property inherent in sex itself, but by virtue of the tactics of power immanent to this discourse. (*VS*, p. 94/70)

We will see later what it is for tactics of power to be "immanent" to a discourse. For the moment, and without repeating Foucault's discussion in detail, we can say that it targets ousia in two ways. First, as with the prison, the descriptive or explanatory power of ousiodic structure is impeached as being inadequate to the facts: understanding the practice of confession solely in terms of the individual constituting herself as an ousia misses the subjection to power that she undergoes in such confession. Second, the parametric status of ousia to structure the human world—in this case, to be the goal of the confessing individual herself—is likewise impeached: the practices of confession will actually make her, not into an autonomous individual, but into a "subject." Confession is thus part of the

> immense labor to which the West has submitted generations, in order to produce . . . the subjection of men: I mean their constitution as "subjects" in the two senses of the word. (*VS*, p. 81/60)

One of these two senses is, of course, that of someone who is "subject" to an external sovereign; the other is the modern moral agent, the "subject" whose desires are at the disposition of her reason. The practice of confession produces someone who is both at once: like the authority of the prison guards, her autonomy, however real, is established through and depends upon "designation" from outside.

3. THE CENTER

A third, more general Foucauldian challenge of ousia emphasizes that power itself can also be conceived ousiodically, in which case it is viewed as emanating from a single center. Such a concept of power is not without descriptive efficacy, for power can actually take this sort of ousiodic form—to take one instance, in the French political order. The French monarchy arose in opposition to a pre-existing multiplicity of local (feudal) powers. The institutions of the state and the monarchy

> functioned as a principle of right transcending [these] multiple and mutually confrontational powers, with the triple character of constituting it-

self as a unitary ensemble, of identifying its will with the law, and of operating by means of mechanisms of sanction and interdiction. (*VS*, p. 115/87)

To establish itself as a unitary ensemble identified with the law was for the monarchical state to establish itself as the unifying center of its territory. Within the boundaries of that territory, the center's dispositive power was exercised through sanction and interdiction. Thus setting the individual powers that it had found confronting it and each other into a unified system of domination, the state was able to turn its inhabitants into mere "matter":

> Facing a power which is the law, the subject constituted *as* a subject—who is "subjected"—is the one who obeys. To the formal homogeneity of power through all its instance there will correspond, among those whom power constrains, the general form of submission. Legislative power on one side, and obedient subject on the other. (*VS*, p. 112/85)

The reduction of the inhabitants to obedient docility was thus their "designation" with the characteristic that would enable them to "receive" the various concrete dispositions of the ruler—the various specific sanctions and interdictions the monarch would proclaim. This general form of domination extended far beyond the purely political realm, to codify relations between father and child, censor and author, master and disciple, and so on through the human world, which thus became—as I have argued that it was for the modern philosophers generally—structured like an ousia.[16]

The flaw in this was, at the time, stated to be that the monarchy—true to Aristotle's conception of form as that in a thing which can be understood—was supposed to be not merely a unified dominion, but an intelligible and intelligent one. Its power was to be not arbitrary or despotic but lawful and therefore rational. In practice, monarchical power was neither lawful nor rational: all sorts of caprice and whim were carried out against the obedient "subjects," who eventually revolted. But for Foucault, the French Revolution basically *continued* the monarchical "juridification" of ousiodic power. It continued, that is, to see power as flowing from a rational center, and only sought to make that center *truly* rational. This concept of power as centralized had descriptive efficacy for Foucault; but only for a time. The form of power it captured was particularized and transitory. That the concept of centralized power continues to be employed in political discourse shows, for Foucault, that "we have still not cut off the head of the king."[17]

4. SEXUALITY

Similarly, in a fourth example: until the end of the eighteenth century, sexuality for Foucault was regulated in a unified way, via three major explicit codes (over and above custom and opinion): canon law, civil law, and the theory and practice of Christian pastorship. All of these concerned matrimonial relations, which they set out to govern in detail (*VS*, pp. 51f/38f). All nonmarital behavior—infidelity, homosexuality, marriage without parental consent, bestiality—was condemned equally. It was only in the eighteenth and nineteenth centuries that heterosexual monogamy lost its central place as the prime object of sexual regulation, so that sexuality itself became the object of regulation and proliferated into a network containing various kinds of "unnatural" and "debauched" practice (*VS*, pp. 52–54/38f).

Matrimony itself, of course, has traditionally had an ousiodic structure in which the husband dominates the wife. Centered on matrimony as its regulable and thus comprehensible paradigm, sexuality in the Middle Ages was structured according to an ousiodic ideal; as with political power, the modern era saw it disperse itself into "networks." But on Foucault's analysis, sexuality did not escape ousiodic structure entirely by this. Rather, various of its subspecies came to be viewed as sorts of ousia in their own right. For as the undifferentiated condemnation of earlier ages began to break up, "perversion" became distinct from "infraction": perversion was no longer a sin but a condition. Each specific perversion became knowable on its own terms, as distinct from the others: crimes against nature "assumed autonomy" over against other sexual offenses (*VS*, 54f/39f). Though the natures of these different perversions were still obscure, the view that sex was no longer a moral but a legal matter suggested that they could be understood scientifically. Such understanding was the more urgent because sexuality itself now had initiative: it had been invested with an "inexhaustible and polymorphic causal power" to disrupt society (*VS*, pp. 88f/66).

Thus provided with a knowable nature and inexhaustible causal power, each different "perversion" was fit to become a sort of ousiodic form, while those who practiced it were seen as constituting a discrete, ousiodically structured community. This happened in particular with homosexuality; homosexuals became a virtual species of their own. As Foucault presents this development, the (male) homosexual, like any Aristotelian ousia, was assigned a certain sort of past, a certain "form of life," and a certain physical morphology. His specifically homosexual form dominated him as thoroughly as, for Aristotle, only the human form itself could dominate a person:

> Nothing that he is *in toto* escapes his sexuality. It is present everywhere in him. . . . It is *consubstantial* to him. . . . [Under the earlier regime] sodomy was a relapse; the homosexual is now a species. (*VS*, p. 59/43; emphasis added)

The modern homosexual, then, is not considered to be a human being, for reason does not determine his actions. Neither does the conflicting multiplicity of desires that dominated the Aristotelian "incontinent" and "unhindered" men.[18] Rather, his sexual desire alone constitutes his dominating form.

Sexuality, in the modern era, has then not truly been decentered; it has, rather, multiplied its centers to become polycentric. Foucault portrays each such center of sexuality as functioning like an ousiodic form, so that modernity does not bring about an exclusion of aberrant sensualities, but the "specification and regional solidification of each" (*VS*, p. 60/44). All this, Foucault seeks to show, is again nothing but an effect of power—no longer centered, but polycentered. Though power in the modern world no longer flows from a single source, it has not somehow transcended ousiodic structure: "never have there existed so many centers of power" (*VS*, p. 67/49).

Foucault's descriptions of modern sexualities thus seek, as do those of the prison and confession, to show that they are neither self-constituting phenomena nor givens of nature. The notion of "sex" itself, he writes, is an artificial unity, grouping together diverse phenomena of anatomy, conduct, sensation, and pleasure (*VS*, pp. 204f/154f). It follows that there is no such thing as "a homosexual"; using the category to describe individuals as if they constituted a separate species is misleading. It also follows, though Foucault does not explicitly draw the inference, that using it to condemn them is wrong. Once again ousia is challenged along the two fronts of its legitimacy: explicitly as a concept and implicitly as a parameter.

5. HISTORY

A similarly twofold challenge to ousia can be found, in my fifth example, when Foucault criticizes what he calls "global history." This, the familiar modern model of history,

> . . . seeks to restore the overall form of a civilization, the principle—material or spiritual—of a society, the common meaning of all the phenomena of a period, the law which accounts for their cohesion. . . . [In this project] it is assumed that among all the events of a well defined spatiotemporal area, among all the phenomena of which traces have been found, one ought to be able to establish a system of homogeneous relations. . . . A global description gathers all the phenomena around a unique center—principle, meaning, spirit, worldview, overall form. (*AS*, pp. 18/9f)

For global history—among whose practitioners, clearly, was Heidegger—the facts of history come grouped in packets defined by the boundaries of a region and a period. A central "principle" gives them intelligible form and accounts for their appearance; it is the business of the historian to grasp that "form." Global history, in short, approaches its facts armed with the Aristotelian conception of a bounded and dispositive ousia.

The structures of domination ascribed to history by such an approach are hardly invisible to Foucault. When global history places its conceptual and intelligible principles in time, he writes, it sees them as developing units.

In so doing, it "submits" historical phenomena to the exemplary power of organic life (which, of course, is Aristotle's paradigm of sensible ousia). It thereby "masters" time. When global history construes its basic principles idealistically—in terms of "mentalities" or of Hegelian or quasi-Hegelian "spirit"—it appeals to the "sovereignty" of collective consciousness (*AS*, p. 32/22).

Foucault's challenge to such global history can be understood only in terms of the alternative he proposes to it, which I will discuss in the next chapter. But it is already clear that, as in the other cases I have adduced, his challenge will be a challenge to ousia. (*It seems to him almost as if his eyes, for the first time, were opening up to what is nearby.*)

6. DISCOURSE

Foucault's challenge to ousiodic structure in the case of discourse itself is the last such challenge I will discuss here. For in it, Foucault is already preparing the transition into his own attempt to give a positive view of what discourse should be—an attempt which focuses on the non-ousiodic unity he seeks to vindicate for the *énoncé*, or utterance.

By "discourse," Foucault means a set of statements (*énoncés*) produced according to a single "system of formation" and claiming (in virtue of that adherence) to be "scientific" (*AS*, p. 141/107). The second and third parts of *The Archeology of Knowledge*—about two-thirds of its entirety—address the question of the unity of a discourse: how do we know, given a mass of statements, that they in fact adhere to a single "formation system"?[19]

The four central chapters of part 2—chapters 3 through 7—hypothesize in turn that the unity of a discourse is caused by the objects it treats; the modalities of its arrangement; the concepts in which it is carried out; and the strategies which motivate it.[20] These four possible grounds of discursive unity align themselves, I suggest, with Aristotle's moving, formal, material, and final causes. When each is rejected in turn, the cumulative effect will be to "de-ousiodify" discourse. The whole of part 2 can thus be seen as a challenge to the idea that discourse can be treated as an ousia. (*He is amazed, and sits still: where has he been, then?*)

The first possibility is that a group of statements all belong to the same discursive formation if they are about the same thing. To fulfill that role, the "object" of a discourse must be external to it; itself unified; and capable of imparting unity to the discourse which mirrors it. In this way, it functions similarly to Aristotle's moving cause, which also conveys form from one thing to another. But such a cause, Foucault argues, cannot explain the unity of the discourse which treats of it for two reasons. One is that scientific discourse, at least of the kind Foucault has considered in his previous writings, transforms and indeed constitutes its objects. Mental illness, for example, only became a unitary object through the discourse that distinguished it from other things, named it, explained it, judged it, and so on.[21] Furthermore, the objects thus constituted are themselves irreducibly plural. What medical discourse in the seventeenth and eighteenth centuries meant by "mental illness," for example, was not identical with what juridical or police discourse meant by the term. Indeed, the nature of mental illness itself changed as new ways of talking about it emerged (*AS*, pp. 45f/32). In general, then, the unity of a discourse is not to be derived from the objects it treats.

Perhaps, suggests Foucault, it is the result of the general patterns according to which the multiple objects of the discourse coexist or succeed one another, so that "the unity of the discourses on madness would be the play of rules which define the transformations of these different objects" (*AS*, p. 46/33). To explain the unity of a discursive formation in terms of its object would be to

> describe the dispersion of these objects, grasp all the interstices which separate them, measure the distances which obtain between them—in other words, formulate their law of partition. (*AS* p. 47/33)

The second hypothesis is that the unity of a discourse is established not by its objects but by its modality—"the form of sequencing" (*forme d'enchaînement*) of the statements it contains. A "certain constant character" of the statements—itself, then, a sort of form—would explain their unification into a discourse (*AS*, p. 47/33). But this second analogy to Aristotle, this time to his formal cause, also fails. This is because the statements in a discourse can be of very different types: descriptive statements, of course, but also laboratory protocols, statistical and other calculations, therapeutic prescriptions, etc. (*AS*, pp. 47f/33f). Since these have no common form, unity is once again to be found by looking to the relations among these very different types of statement: to the "set of rules which made [these distinct varieties of] statement possible, either simultaneously or in succession" (*AS*, p. 48/34). For a second time, unity is to be sought in the play of rules which governs the emergence of heterogeneous entities.

The third hypothesis is that the unity of a discourse lies in the concepts which it uses and in which it "reposes," i.e., in the stability and coherence of its intellectual medium—or, in Aristotelian terms, in its conceptual "matter." Once again, the required unity is lacking in the concepts themselves, for the concepts which a given discourse uses change as they are used, and new ones emerge. Moreover, at any given moment the concepts in play in a discourse are of heterogeneous types, some even being incompatible with others. But, once again, all hope is not lost:

> Perhaps, however, one would discover a discursive unity if one looked for it not on the side of the coherence of the concepts, but on the side of their

simultaneous or successive emergence, of their distance from each other, even of their incompatibility. . . . One would attempt to analyze the play of their apparition and disparition. (*AS*, p. 49/35)

Fourth and finally, the unity of a discursive formation can perhaps be found in its strategic "theme." This is the issue or problematic to which the discourse is directed, and which in Aristotelian terms would constitute its *telos:* the problem it is to solve, the field it is to articulate. But two very different discourses can treat the same theme. Creation "science" and evolutionary theory, to use an example which is not Foucault's, are very different discourses, each seeking what it would consider an adequate treatment of the same fossil record. Similarly, one set of concepts and modalities can establish two very different themes, as in physiocratic and utilitarian approaches to economics (*AS*, pp. 50f/36). So once again, unity must be sought not in individual themes but in the patterns and rules governing the emergence of such themes: the strategic possibilities present at each stage for reawakening old themes, occasioning opposed strategies, providing place for irreconcilable interests (*AS*, pp. 51/36f).

In sum, as Foucault argues throughout the book, objects, modalities, concepts, and themes are given not as unities but as "bundles of relation," as the place of "a network of different positions," or as "a play of relations":[22]

> If unity there be, it is certainly not in the visible and horizontal coherence of the elements formed; it resides well beyond that, in the system which makes possible and directs their formation. (*AS*, p. 95/72)

A discourse is thus, as Foucault puts it, "essentially lacunary," a "partitioning of . . . emptinesses, absences, limits, divisions" (*AS*, pp. 156f/119; also cf. pp. 38f/27). Its unity is a highly contingent matter, for it comes about through the intersection of diverse sets of rules: rules for the multiplying of objects, of forms of statement, of concepts, and of strategic themes (*AS*, pp. 98f/74). The various rules of a discourse are not mutually indifferent, for in their coinciding play, they *are* the discourse in question. But their unity cannot be grounded in one of their number, or in any *thing* outside (such as a more general rule). Insofar as a Foucauldian discourse holds together at all, its unity thus fits my criteria, listed in the introduction, for a diakenic interplay. In Foucault's account, the unity of a discursive formation is not, at bottom, governed and constituted through the plenitude of a form, but through the interplay of a variety of rules of proliferation. Where we would expect to find plenitude—in the objects, forms, themes, and concepts of discourse—we find only proliferating gaps.[23]

A discursive formation for Foucault is thus, like the jug in Heidegger's essay "The Thing," a sort of "gathering" of mutually diverse components.[24] Indeed, Foucault has here, like Heidegger there, brought about a displacement of Aristotle's fourfold causal scheme. When he turns discursive objects, modalities, concepts, and themes into lacunary dispersals, Foucault rewrites Aristotle's moving, formal, material, and final causes respectively.[25] Where Heidegger called the gathering of the Fourfold a "mirror play," Foucault's gathering is what he calls, in the discussion of discursive objects quoted above, a "play of rules."

Foucault's account of the unity of discursive formations is thus not wholly unprecedented. It is not, for example, simply a capricious introduction from nowhere of the view that discourse has to be a type of what Foucault calls a "dispositive," which Gilles Deleuze has characterized as "a tangle, a multilinear ensemble" of vectors

> which do not outline or surround systems which are homogeneous in their own right . . . but trace balances which are always off balance, now drawing together and then distancing themselves from one another.[26]

Foucault's radically non-ousiodic view of discourse is, rather, a determinate, but conceptually unclarifiable (and hence diakenic) displacement of the Aristotelian four causes. Analogously for the famous Foucauldian "power" itself, which as Deleuze points out is nothing but a general name for all those tangled vectors.[27] The word *power* for Foucault thus names a general space of displacement from Aristotle. It is what Heidegger would call a "polemical" check on ousiodic discourses, and what Derrida would call a "paleonymic intervention" into them. The very word is a challenge to ousia.

CHALLENGE AND DESCRIPTION IN FOUCAULT

1. STATEMENT AND DESCRIPTION

It is a truism that Foucault's thought, in different texts and different ways, contests structures of domination. As he himself puts it, its essential task is to "free the history of thought from its transcendental subjection" (*AS*, p. 264/203; also cf. pp. 28, 209/17, 160). In the previous chapter, however, I argued that the subjection and submission brought about by prisons, confession, the monarchical state, the "scientific" study of sexuality, global history, and standard views of discourse are not in any sense "transcendental." They are empirical effects of what I call ousiodic structure. To some extent, then, Foucauldian thought can be identified as a challenge to the domination of such structure, and with a promise of liberation from it. This gives rise to a question and a hope. The question is whether, like Derrida and Rorty, Foucault carries such challenge all the way to his own discourse. The hope is that somewhere in his writings he has gone beyond merely challenging ousia to giving a reflective account of it. The question can be answered, and the hope evaluated, simultaneously if we look at Foucault's reflective account of his own endeavor. Does he provide an alternative to ousiodic views of discourse, including his own? And is his account adequate to the practice on which it reflects?

It is unpromising to seek a general account of himself from the thinker who wrote the famous words, "Do not ask me who I am, and do not tell me to remain the same; leave it to our bureaucrats and our police to see that our papers are in order" (AS, p. 28/17). But the very book in which Foucault wrote those words, *The Archeology of Knowledge,* to some extent belies them. For it is an explicit attempt to "give the theory" behind such earlier works as *The Order of Things* and *Madness and Civilization.* As such, it reflects on the writings that preceded it.[1] Similarly, though not as clearly, the book also looks forward to what will come after. At its end, for example, Foucault projects a discourse on sexuality that he calls "archeology" but which, examining discursive practices which help constitute sexuality, sounds much like the "genealogical" projects undertaken in the later *History of Sexuality* (AS, pp. 252f/193). So, with some misgivings, I will examine what light the reflections in that work can shed on Foucault's thought as a whole. These misgivings were responsible for the choice of my examples in the previous chapter. Except for the last, I took them from writings postdating *The Archeology of Knowledge,* the better to see whether Foucault's reflection on his earlier writings applies also to later ones—thus helping myself to gain some critical purchase on his whole enterprise.[2]

Why does Foucault, in an account of his own practice and of the lessons to be derived from it, pose as a central topic the unity of discourse in general? Is that not, rather, in the nature of an important but preliminary investigation? The unity of the human body, for example, is assuredly an important topic for medicine—but the investigation of it would not occupy the larger part of a discussion of medical procedures.

The answer, I take it, is that Foucault considers his own practice to be, in a sense I will discuss in more detail later, one of description. As he puts it, for a discursive formation to exist is for it to be describable (AS, p. 208/159), and in order to be the object of a description, it must have enough unity that a true proposition can be asserted of it.[3] The question of the unity of discursive formations in general thus relates to Foucault's account of his own thought via the issue of what I will call "descriptive efficacy": only if other discourses (and eventually discourses in general) have enough unity to be describable by his own can his own be efficacious.

Descriptive efficacy, in turn, becomes a problem for Foucault because of the emancipatory concern of his thought. As part of that emancipation, he wants (as will be seen) to replace the traditional kinds of historical unit —e.g., the epochs that we saw him criticize at the outset of the previous chapter—with his own different ones. Such replacement will be impossible if the standard units of history are unproblematic. Only if their unity is itself something other than a primary given can other kinds of unity be substituted for it. In fact, as I argued in that previous chapter, Foucault's view of discourse in general ultimately sees it as unified not by the plenitude of a rational form but by a diakenic interplay of diverse sets of rules—an interplay which itself arises from what Foucault calls the "archive." Thus, part of Foucault's emancipatory endeavor will be to replace the standard units of history by diakenic ones.

This invocation of diakenic interplay, however, makes the descriptive efficacy of Foucault's own discourse problematic. Foucault's general picture of discursive unity is fairly clear from the preceding chapter. Rules, independent of one another and changing over time, surge up and intersect in contingent ways. A "discourse" or "discursive formation" is produced when a number of rules come together to govern a set of utterances. But if a discourse is defined by intersecting proliferations of absences and lacunae—if it is defined diakenically—how can it be described? What in such proliferation can be the object of a true, descriptive sentence? Is it the gaps themselves? Or the rules which come together around them? If the latter, by what sort of indirection are we to get to the former? What, in short, can be "present" for Foucault?

The idea of a "play of rules" is a difficult one—rules being, in our ordinary understanding, precisely what can prevent looseness or "play." But setting that aside (for the moment), the idea seems, at least, to give Foucault what he needs: a set of objects of description. For, as we have seen, it is the job of Foucauldian analysis to state the rules in question, and so to describe the unity of discourse—and, from that, the unities of object, modality, concepts, and themes, whose existence the rules condition:

> We will call the conditions to which the elements of this partitioning (objects, modalities of statement, concepts, thematic choices) are submitted "rules of formation." Rules of formation are the conditions of existence (but also of coexistence, of maintenance, of modification, and of dispersion) in a given discursive partitioning. (*AS*, p. 53/38; also cf. p. 52/37)

We saw an example of this project of describing dispersions carried out in the late *History of Sexuality*, as it traced the dispersion of sexuality itself from the centrally structured practices of medieval times into a proliferating modern network (cf. *VS*, pp. 46f/33).

The aim of archeology—its own strategic theme—is then to describe the rules by which objects, modalities, concepts, and strategies of discourse differentiate themselves from one another and proliferate internally.[4] But this does not really answer the question of whether such description itself is possible. For unless it is explicitly written or stated, a rule cannot, of course, be directly known or described. We do not "see" Newton's laws, or he would not have been their discoverer; unless we have the appropriate rule book, it is very difficult to figure out the rules of tennis or habeas corpus. The nature and existence of a rule or law must be inferred from the behavior of what it governs: it is known from its instances. But what are the instances of a Foucauldian formation rule?

It is tempting to suggest that they are the things Foucault discusses in part 2 of *The Archeology of Knowledge,* and which I discussed in the previous chapter: objects, modalities, concepts, and themes. But these themselves are not, as we have seen, elementary or unified: they are proliferating multiplicities which can be recognized as unitary only when it is known that they accord with certain rules of formation. The existence of those rules themselves, then, must be inferred from some yet more basic given. This, Foucault now suggests, is the individual statement (*énoncé*),[5] to which part 3 of *The Archeology of Knowledge* extends its investigation.

That extension is thus motivated by the *failure* of the inquiry in part 2 of the book.[6] Part 2 showed that objects, modalities, concepts, and themes as traditionally considered cannot explain the unity of discursive formations, and that the rules of their dispersal cannot serve as objects of description. Part 3 seeks to determine whether it is individual statements which appear as governed by rules of formation. If so, those rules can be described in terms of the statements which follow them, and can in turn be shown to bring about unified discourses—which themselves, at last, would exhibit objects, modalities, concepts, and themes in Foucault's reconceived sense.

But this new investigation also fails. In order to serve as an object of description, an individual statement must have some degree of unity of its own, however minimal. And (without recapitulating Foucault's argument in all its detail), it turns out that statements have no such unity. Like the discursive formation to which it is coordinated, the individual statement is an intersection of different fields, rather than a unitary given: "[The statement] is not at all a unity in itself, but a function which intersects a domain of structures and of possible unities" (*AS,* p. 115/87). Thus,

> the least statement . . . puts into operation the whole play of the rules according to which are formed its object, its modality, the concepts which it uses and the strategy of which it is part. . . .[7]

The statement, in fact, has a structure of lacunary dispersal much like that of a discursive formation:

> The statement, far from being the principle of individuation of signifying ensembles (the signifying "atom," the minimum on the basis of which there is meaning), is [rather] what situates these signifying unities in a space where they multiply and accumulate. (*AS,* p. 131/100)

The statement, then, cannot provide the unity that Foucault is seeking. His search for what unifies a discursive formation, and thereby renders it describable, takes one more twist. Like a quantum particle, a statement has the unity both of a (repeatable) event and of a thing as well (*AS,* pp. 131–

138, 169/100–105, 128). Temporalized in this way, it has a "before" and an "after": an historical location. In particular, a statement's "before"—the constellation of historical circumstances which permit it to be made—functions as what Foucault calls an "historical a priori" (*AS*, pp. 167ff, 153/127ff, 113). Foucault's general name for this historical a priori is the "archive"; he defines it as "the general system of formation and transformation of statements" (*AS*, pp. 169, 171/128, 130). Where the intersection of sets of rules of proliferation accounted for the unity of discursive formations, then, the archive accounts for the unity of the individual statements in which those proliferations and rules manifest themselves. The archive provides at last, or so it seems, the basic explanation of discursive unity for which Foucault has been searching. For it seems to be the basic unifying factor in what might be called the "discursive cosmos" of *The Archeology of Knowledge*.

2. ARCHIVE AND DESCRIPTION

It now appears that we cannot evaluate Foucault's success with regard to either liberation or description until we have understood certain things about his account of the archive. In particular, we must understand whether and to what extent Foucault attributes ousiodic structure to the archive. If he does, then its describability will be unproblematic, and liberation from subjection will just amount to a challenge to ousiodic structure. But any attribution of ousiodic structure to the archive will be in tension with Foucault's invocations of diakenic structure on other levels of discourse. And if he accords to it diakenic structure, it is hard indeed to see how it can be described, or what sort of thing liberation from it can possibly be.

The ousiodic structure which the archive seems to exhibit becomes apparent when we compare its traits to those of *Being and Time*'s conception of world.[8] For as an "historical a priori," the archive—like Heideggerean world—belongs to the past which produces our present. Moreover, as the "law of what can be said" (*AS*, p. 170/129) it forms, like Heideggerean world, our own horizon of intelligibility. Hence, we inhere in the archive like Dasein in world: we "speak from its interior."

> ... at once near to us, but differentiated from our present actuality, it is the border of the time which surrounds our present. . . . It is that which, outside us, delimits us. (*AS*, pp. 171f/130)

Indeed, Foucault's account of the archive's relation to the discursive formations it is to contain and explain can be rather precisely aligned with *Being and Time*'s account of world. Both Foucault and Heidegger conceive this relation as a tri-level structure. On the "lowest" level, the individual statement, always obvious but always hidden (*AS*, p. 145–148 /110f), would correspond to what Heidegger calls the being which is ready to hand, or equipment. The discursive formation would be the analog of the Heideggerean context of meaning (*Bedeutungsganze*) or of involvement (*Bewandt-nisganze*). And the archive itself, as the totality of intelligibility, would correspond to Heidegger's world.

The analogy can be pursued into the three traits of ousiodic domination. Like Heidegger's world, the archive has boundaries; indeed, as "the border of the time which surrounds our present," it presents the temporal limits of intelligibility. Because it provides "the law of what can be said," it permits the appearance of individual statements at particular times within the limits of intelligibility that it sets, and differentiates the discourses into which they combine: "It is that which differentiates discourses in their multiple existence and specifies them in their own duration" (*AS*, p. 171/129).

The archive orders the discourses it makes possible, then, and orders as well the statements that occur within them. By virtue of constituting the series of discourses to which we belong, it also orders or, as we saw, "delimits" us. It thus exercises, in addition to boundary, disposition over statements, discourses, and those who make and engage in them.[9] And—again like Heideggerean world—the archive, as the largest context of intelligibility, cannot relate to anything beyond itself: it must be without initiative.

The proposed alignment of archive and world has its limitations—most signally as regards the teleological structure of the latter. World for Heidegger is organized by a series of "in order to's," in which each of its contexts of involvement points toward further contexts, through them back to Dasein and, finally, to Dasein's ownmost possibility, death. But all teleology is absent from Foucault's discussion of the archive—and together with this goes any hint that the archive itself has a unified structure. True to what we saw was Foucault's opening criticism of Heidegger, the archive is not a single unit which forms a variety of different phenomena, but a massive, lacunary ferment of heterogeneous statements which dispose other statements. It is what Gilles Deleuze calls a *murmure anonyme*,[10] which disposes of the discursive phenomena it makes possible without having a dispositive form of its own.

Foucault's search for the unified object of possible description has led him from the gaps which are constitutive of discourses to the rules which disseminate and intersect in those gaps; from those rules to the four factors of objects, modalities, concepts, and themes; thence to the *énoncé;* and finally to the archive. Here the search ends—aporetically. For the archive —again like Heideggerean world—cannot be described. No archive can be described exhaustively, because of its size and complexity (*AS*, p. 170/ 129). This is even more true for our own archive because of our very inherence in it:

> . . . It is not possible for us to describe our own archive, since it is from within these rules that we speak. . . . It emerges in fragments, regions, and levels, more fully, no doubt, and with greater sharpness the greater the time that separates us from it. . . . (*AS*, p. 171/130)

This leads Foucault into a pair of vicious circles. One concerns what may be called the "order of knowing." Statements are, we have seen, formed and transformed in the archive. Their production in this way accounts for their unity. For a statement is, as we also saw, not an atomic unit but a "function which intersects a domain of structures and of possible unities." As an intersection, it can only be understood by describing the structures and possibilities which it intersects. If it "intersects" them, they must somehow be there before it occurs, and hence must constitute part of its historical a priori— the relevant part, then, of the archive. For a statement to be describable, in short, the relevant part of the archive—the part whose "intersection" it is— needs to be describable. But we can only discriminate the "relevant" part of the archive from the rest of it if we already know the statement in question, and this means that we must already have described that statement.[11]

The other circle concerns the order of being. What makes *these* regions and levels, structures and possible unities the ones whose intersection constitutes this particular statement? It cannot be the statement itself, which is comprehensible only as emerging from that relevant portion of the archive and thus presupposes it. But the archive, as a mere "anonymous murmur," cannot provide such unities from within itself and so must presuppose a statement which somehow arose elsewhere. Foucault's account of the archive thus cannot explain either how statements are possible or how they can be described.

Foucault's view of our "delimitation" by our own archive parallels Heidegger's account, which I have discussed elsewhere, of what in the introduction I called the "unconditional inherence" of Dasein in its world. That view, I argued, was methodologically motivated. Because world could not be directly described, it could be rendered phenomenologically accessible only by describing the structures of Dasein's inherence in it. That inherence thus had to be "unconditional" in the sense that structures of world could be directly read off from structures of Dasein. Similarly for Foucault, though apparently in the reverse direction: it is because we inhere so tightly in our own archive that we cannot describe it. This reversal of direction suggests that the indescribability of the archive is not basic for Foucault, as it was for Heidegger, but follows from our inherence in the archive. The above quote from Foucault, in fact, suggests that we can describe other archives more easily than we can the one in which we ourselves inhere. Is it possible for us also to free ourselves from our own archive sufficiently to gain some sort of descriptive purchase on it? If so, what kind of purchase would this be?

3. DESCRIPTION AND LIBERATION

I will defer discussion of that issue until we have seen how the two questions with which I began this chapter—that of the descriptive efficacy of

Foucault's enterprise and that of the nature of the liberation it promises—are connected. For in order to legitimate his own discourse as descriptively efficacious, Foucault must show how we can be freed from the archive itself. But it is not as if we could first free ourselves from the archive and then describe it. For as I have noted, both liberation and description are to be performed by the same discourse: Foucault's own. This suggests that they are to be simultaneous.

We can see how Foucault undertakes both at once by considering his opposition to what he calls "global history." Global history, we have seen, is one form of the "transcendental subjection" he wishes to contest. We have also seen that it is in his view a project of domination: of seeing historical phenomena as grouped around central principles, and thus ultimately as grounded in the sovereignty of the synthesizing subject. As a project, global history allows certain things to be said, and prohibits other things from being said; as the dominant historical tradition, it is a very important part of Foucault's own archive. Hence, Foucault's challenge to global history, and his articulation of his own alternative to it, are precisely efforts at liberation from at least part of his own archive.

Foucault's own discourse, it now seems, is to have something of the power that Heidegger, in "The Origin of the Work of Art," ascribed to the work of art: simply by being something that must be perceived or felt, in a new way—indeed, for Heidegger, a *radically* new way—the work of art destroys the claim of the old ways to be the sole, inevitable possibility.[12] And this, certainly, is *part* of how Foucault says things are to work:

> in liberating [the facts of discourse] from all groupings which are given out as natural, immediate, and universal unities, one gains the possibility of describing—but this time by a set of controlled decisions—other unities. . . . It could be legitimate to constitute, *on the basis of relations correctly described,* discursive ensembles which would no longer be arbitrary, but would however have remained invisible. (*AS*, pp. 41f/29; emphasis added)

In liberating the object of his discourse from the old groupings, or categories, in terms of which it has previously been understood, Foucault frees himself from his own historical a priori: the part of his own archive that contains those very categories or groupings, and which passes itself off as natural and universal. His view of the emancipatory capacities of his own discourse is thus keyed from the start to its descriptive efficacy: his descriptions are ipso facto liberations.[13] Liberation for him is not, as it is for Habermas, a matter of discursive evaluation of validity-claims, because for Foucault what holds us captive is precisely what, for Habermas, could not be transcended: the "semantic capacities" of our language, the limits of our life world.

Crucial to the emancipatory function of such description, then, is that it be couched in new terms—terms which name, and thus allow the description of, "other unities" than those traditionally accepted. When Foucault describes a reality already understood in traditional terms (such as global history), he thus does so in new ways which immediately show that the old ways are not the only possibility. His descriptions, like Heideggerean works of art, are instances of radical newness—what Rorty would call "redescriptions." Unlike Rorty, however, Foucault does not, in transforming his own historical a priori, claim to leave it completely behind; rather, it remains as the object of his description. His discourse thus assumes the burden of describing previous discourses—even when, like global history, they are parts of his own archive—in ways which are not only new, as with Rorty, but demonstrably less arbitrary than the ways those discourses describe and understand themselves. (*These near and nearest things: how they seem transformed! What fluff and magic they have acquired in the meantime!*)

To show how Foucauldian description is intrinsically related to Foucauldian liberation is not, of course, to show how or even whether such description is possible. I will defer that issue to the next section. For the moment, no fewer than three qualifications need to be made concerning the emancipatory possibilities Foucault claims for his own discourse. First, in spite of my earlier comments about "freeing us," Foucauldian discourse is not really aimed at the liberation of human individuals. Many passages of *The Archeology of Knowledge* illustrate that, as with Derridean "epistemological liberation," it is discourse itself, together with its non-ousiodic unities and elements, which needs to be liberated from "subjection."[14]

Second, freedom in this is not instated as a universal goal, or even as necessarily good. It can be neutral: a statement, for example, can be placed in a "free state" by disregarding its discursive background.[15] Even "bad" things can be rendered free: the sovereign subject, when it exercises its dominating and founding functions unhindered, is "free."[16] Thus, freedom itself is not a goal to be pursued unreservedly, and the real aim of Foucault's discourse—if there is one—is more specific. It is, I have argued, liberation from what he calls "transcendental subjection": from what I call the ousiodic structures of the modern subject and from the discourses with which it is associated.

4. DESCRIPTION AND "POSITIVISM"

Third, and most importantly, there is one way in which Foucault's own discourse differs from a Heideggerean work of art: it is an exercise in a determinate genre, that of description. It is enough for Heidegger that a work of art be new and that it find an audience. A new kind of painting or music, for example, may not even be seen as a painting or heard as music, but as long as people look at or listen to it at all, it can teach them new ways to perceive and feel, and eventually to judge and live. Foucauldian discourse, however, is, as we saw, to be simultaneously emancipatory and descriptive: a new instance of the old genre of description. And descriptions must, of course, be accurate. Unless Foucault's new descriptions are somehow faithful to the reality of that which they describe, then, they will not count as descriptions at all—and hence will be unacceptable to anyone as alternatives to the traditional way of doing things. Whether other people take up his way of describing things will be, as it is for Rorty, at best a matter of "luck."

That is why, in the above quote, Foucault insists that his discourse "correctly describe" the relations it treats. His categories must not only be acceptable as categories of description; they must be better than the traditional categories, and in a very traditional sense: they must describe ensembles which, unlike the "old" ones, are "no longer arbitrary." It is thus a basic claim of Foucault's that his discourse is capable of showing discourses in their "true" unity, rather than in the arbitrary kind imputed to them by global history.[17] Foucault's archeology, in sum, will liberate discursive unities by describing them as they really are, rather than as global history has arbitrarily presented them. Thus coordinated to description, liberation comes to approximate "rendering visible" or "making apparent."[18]

What, then and finally, is "description" for Foucault? I have so far operated (and only implicitly at that) with a very rough view of description, according to which a description of a thing consists in a set of sentences which are true of it. Description and truth are thus coordinated, and we can see how Foucault views description by seeing that it is not lightly, or exclusively with ironic intent, that in *The Archeology of Knowledge* he calls himself a "positivist" with respect to truth (*AS*, pp. 164–167/125–127). He means by this to convey that he is describing relatively stable entities: formation rules that can give rise to the various dispersions and proliferations he discusses "without themselves having to be modified" (*AS*, pp. 60f/44). This "positivism" is further articulated here in three negative ways:

(1) Archeology does not arbitrarily invent the differences and ruptures it treats; it "only tries to take them seriously." Correspondingly, it

> does not have the project of surmounting differences, but of analyzing them, of saying in what precisely they consist, and of *differentiating* them. (*AS*, pp. 222f/170f)

(2) Archeology is not interpretive. This is why Foucault's basic units have to be *given* as unified: they cannot be simply *interpreted* as unities on the basis of some anterior theory, but must possess unity in and of themselves. For archeology is to be, on its basic level, theory-free: it does not seek a hidden meaning in the statements it describes, but simply asks how they arise and pass away (*AS*, pp. 143f/ 109). It seeks the conditions of such appearance and disappearance

in other statements which constitute the historical a priori, or field of emergence, of the statement to be described, and which can themselves be described in the same way (*AS*, p. 42/29). If, as with hermeneutics, "all is never said" (*AS*, pp. 156–159/119–121), this does not mean that we understand a statement in terms of an unspoken background of higher order or more general meanings, but in terms of other statements and the formation rules of which they are instances.

(3) The unities archeology describes are not merely "retrospective regroupings," constituted as unitary only in the eyes of later observers. They must actually have existed as unities at the time (*AS*, pp. 45, 63/31, 46). Discursive formations may have a very weak sort of unity—as the contingent intersections of various systems of formation. But they do have existence—or, as Foucault puts it (in a sense reminiscent of Aquinas's treatment of presence as a weak sense of Being), they are capable of being described.[19]

Foucault's concept of description turns out to be quite traditional, and even naïve. It is to take a difference, rupture, or unity that already exists and, without interpreting it in the light of any larger concept or theory, say precisely what it is: how, as a discursive event, it arises and passes away.

This naïveté is surprising. For one thing, the stability of the entities described via such "positivistic" truth-claims is in obvious contrast with Foucault's own view, expressed earlier in *The Archeology of Knowledge*, that discourses in general do not merely describe but actually constitute their objects. Furthermore, I have argued that Foucault's efforts in *The Archeology of Knowledge* to characterize the unity of the discourses he describes are aporetic: the object of possible description is not given as already existing, à la "positivistic" accounts of truth, but keeps dissolving into diakenic intersections of varieties of discursive fields, whose indescribable elements (statements) disseminate within the similarly indescribable matrix of the archive.

Reconciling Foucault's "positivism" with his other views is a bind which, it appears, he could escape in two ways. The first way out would be to accept a new version of Heidegger's unconditional inherence, this time of statements rather than ourselves, within the archive. A statement is an event; to describe it is therefore to describe how it appears, how it comes to be (*AS*, pp. 39, 142/27, 108). This includes a description not merely of the statement itself but of the conditions of its appearance, which can be read directly off from it. Foucault, in fact, goes even beyond this, addressing himself to the question "how does it happen that this statement should appear, and *none other in its place?*" Thus,

> one studies statements at the limit which separates them from what is not said, in the occurrence which makes them surge up to the exclusion of all the others. (*AS*, pp. 39, 156/27, 119)

This in turn amounts to locating the statement within the discursive functions which produce it:

> Description thus does not consist, with respect to a statement, in finding the unsaid of which it occupies the place . . . but on the contrary in finding the singular place it does occupy, those ramifications within the system of formations which permit us to grasp its localization, how it isolates itself in the general dispersion of statements. (*AS,* p. 157/119)

To describe a statement is then to describe, in a passage I quoted earlier, "the whole play of the rules according to which are formed its object, its modality, the concepts which it uses and the strategy of which it is part . . ." (*AS,* pp. 191f/146f). True to its status as the nexus of a field of discursive force, the statement cannot be described in isolation but only in its emergence and disappearance within a larger field—which itself, as a general dispersion of statements, turns out to be the archive. To describe a statement is thus to describe the relevant part of the archive. There is then a second simultaneity here: Foucault's enterprise is not only simultaneously emancipatory and descriptive, but simultaneously emancipatory and descriptive both of individual statements and of the relevant part of the archive. The vicious circles I located above do not arise now, because describing the relevant part of the archive is not a condition for describing a statement, or vice versa. To describe the one simply *is* to describe the other.

But a problem remains. In order for this solution to be possible, the "play" of rules must be very strict indeed: the rules of the archive must determine an individual statement so rigorously as to be virtually identical with it, so that to describe the statement is to describe the rules. And this degree of rule governance, for Foucault, is impossible:

> The homogeneity (and heterogeneity) of statements intersect with linguistic continuities (and changes), with logical identities (and differences), without any of them proceeding at the same pace or necessarily regulating each other. (*AS,* p. 191/146)

In short, for a statement to be described as part of the archive, it must be strictly determined by the formation rules which constitute the relevant part of its archive—which it cannot be. This is a conflict noticed by Manfred Frank:

> The definition . . . of discourse as a singular, systematically ungovernable and multiple connection of talk stands in extreme contrast to the method of discourse analysis as a (non-hermeneutic but strict) science. In this way, discourses can be described and analyzed, as Foucault himself does, only if they are constructed according to principles of formation, which contradicts our definition of them.[20]

The problem may be put somewhat differently. Foucault has all along been concerned with finding describable unities. He has not, we saw, explained how such unities can exist: not on the level of the discourse, or the statements that make it up, or the archive itself within which they inhere. Now we see, instead of an answer, the postulation of yet another unity: that of the individual statement with the set of archival structures and possibilities that constitutes it. But if neither of these has unity on its own level, how can they be united with each other?

The view that archive and statement stand in such tight unity that to describe the one is to describe part of the other thus breaks down. The other way for Foucault to escape from his bind and reconcile his "positivism" with his other views takes the opposite tack: it begins not from the unity of the statement with the archive but with "how [the statement] isolates itself in the general dispersion of statements." What constitutes the process by which a statement (or a discourse) does this?

According to Foucault's account of the objects of discourse, which I discussed earlier, the "isolation" which constitutes a discursive object comes about, at least in part, through the discourse which treats of it—for his general contention was that discourses constitute their objects. It now appears that they do so, at least in part, by separating them out from the "general dispersion." And they must separate out as well, from the anonymous murmur of the archive, various functions which they constitute as the relevant part of the archive: that part which conditions the particular statement described.

5. DESCRIPTION AS TRANSFORMATION

It follows, however, that the descriptions such discourse contains are not faithful to what they describe. And this, if true of discourse in general, must also apply to Foucault's own. This is presumably why he says, for example, that archeology seeks not to "describe" defining lacunae or ruptures but to "multiply" them.[21] Archeology, in fact, is to *introduce* rupture, or isolation, into the proliferating networks of discursive formation and reformation. Thus it is, for another example, that discontinuity for Foucault is not merely the object of archeological description but its result: it is the "operation" of the historian and something which the historian, in and through her work, constantly redefines and transforms (*AS*, pp. 16f/8f). And so, as Foucault recognizes, his "descriptions" are in fact "regulated transformations" of the previous discourses they treat (*AS*, p. 183/140). Archeology does not report discontinuities but "has to *make* differences: to constitute them as objects" (*AS*, p. 268/205).

Thus there comes to be what might be called a "dialectic" of description and object described: the notion of discontinuity is both instrument and object of the investigation, and as such "delimits the field of which it is the effect" (*AS*, p. 17/9). This leads in turn to another dialectic, for the field from which the description of a statement isolates that statement continues to affect the statement which has been isolated from it, and vice versa. As Foucault puts it, grasping discursive formations reveals the level of the statement, while the manner in which statements are organized conduces to the individualization of discursive formations: "The two procedures are equally justifiable and reversible. The analysis of the statement and that of the formation are established correlatively" (*AS*, p. 152/116; cf. *VS* p. 130/98).

This dialectical turn, if I may call it that, seems to have landed Foucault in proximity to Hegel. What I earlier called the "simultaneity" in which statement and field were given now becomes not the identity presupposed by unconditional inherence but a movement from each to the other and back. Indeed, Foucault comes very close to identifying his type of history not only as "dialectical" but as—in spite of himself—a variety of traditional hermeneutics: one which approaches its objects not with a pre-established and provisional conception of meaning (a type of hermeneutics which we have seen him criticize) but with a pre-established and provisional concept of rupture.[22] In this he goes well beyond anything that could conventionally be called "description"—and surpasses as well his own claims to be "positivistic" and true to the phenomena he treats.

The fundamental problem remains. In order for a hermeneutic or dialectical enterprise to succeed, its two sides—here, statement and field—must to some degree be given independently of one another; they, and our understanding of them, are then enriched by their interplay. Providing such initial independence is the role of what Hegel calls "immediacy." Such a path is not open to Foucault, because his thought makes overt use *only* of the concept of discontinuity or rupture. This is why he could not explain the unity of the objects of his own "descriptions." The finally aporetic nature of Foucault's views on the applicability of truth to his own discourse, and hence his equally ambivalent stance as regards the descriptive efficacy of his own thought, is baldly expressed in one of his interviews:

> I am fully aware that I have never written anything other than fictions. For all that, I would not want to say that they were outside the truth. It seems plausible to me to make fictions work within truth, to introduce truth-effects within a fictional discourse, and in some way to make discourse arouse, "fabricate," something which does not yet exist, thus to fiction something.[23]

(*How it pleases him to sit still in his affliction, to spin forth patience, to lie in the sun!*)

6. CONCLUSION

Foucault's effort to undo the indiscriminate generality of Heidegger's *Seinsgeschichte* thus runs up against a problem that Heidegger himself encountered: it cannot achieve its goals while retaining claims to be descriptive. As long as Foucault considers the aim of archeology to be to show the "real" natures of discourses, he must instate those discourses as objects that can be described in such a way that those "real" natures become evident. But the diakenic unity he wants to ascribe to those objects forbids anything to have a "real" nature; it requires that everything be seen to exist only in and through a play of emptinesses. The successive replacement, in *The Archeology of Knowledge,* of objects (as well as modalities, concepts, and themes) with rules in play, of rules in play with individual statements, and of statements with the archive, testifies to this on every level.

The solution, from Heidegger's point of view, would be to abandon the fiction that diakenic emptinesses—the generative activities of the archive, or of power—exist wholly independently of the discourse which accords them validity. The aim of Foucauldian archeology (or genealogy) as the "regulated transformation" of previous discourses would be to set those diakena into play. On this view, which abandons Foucault's claims of "positivism," Foucault would take a discourse that was trying (as the monarchical state tried) to constitute itself as an ousia, and allow it to turn into a diakenic play.

Foucault's account of the prison, with which I opened the preceding chapter, can be construed in such terms. For in itself, the prison is neither ousiodic nor non-ousiodic. Its governing center, the observation tower, is, we saw, open to externality in that any citizen has the right to enter it and observe the activities of the guards. But whether the prison is in fact opened up in this way depends on whether the citizens actually exercise that right. Only to the extent that they do so does the tower lose its capacity to govern the prison entirely from within. And the only way to get citizens to exercise the right in question is to inform them of it. This may, to be sure, be accomplished by a discourse that looks like a description. Such would be Foucault's own discourse (or even Bentham's), if it were disseminated widely enough in society. Unlike the description of, say, an eclipse, the "description" of the prison would then have a capacity to alter that which it describes: when citizens learn of their right to observe—certainly not before —they may undertake to make that right real by exercising it. What such a "descriptive" discourse will do to the citizens who read it, then, is similar to what Heidegger's "description" of the jug does to the readers of his essay "The Thing." It makes them aware of, brings them before, an active nothing which cannot itself be in play until they are aware of it.

So construed, Foucauldian discourse would provide accounts of other discourses (or social practices) which awaken in the readers of those accounts awareness of a diakenon, and thus put that diakenon into play. Such treatment provides an alternative to traditional ways of understanding the discourses it treats: it would show that those discourses need not be understood only in terms of the traditional unities. It would no longer be necessary, for example, to construe a discourse as valid only if it could be assigned a set of external objects which it mirrored; a stable character to its own statements; a clear and efficient conceptual medium for its articulation; and a set of specifiable goals and themes. The status of such ousiodic structures as the only way to understand discourse would be impeached. So, on a more general level, would be their parametric capacity to structure discourse itself. And Foucault's challenges to ousiodic structure would begin to find an adequate reflective account of themselves.

In contrast to the "abstract negations" of Derrida and Rorty, and to the universalistic overview offered by Habermas, Foucault thus contests ousia by offering concrete accounts of individual discourses. But why is it so important that he call those accounts "descriptions"? Is his embrace of "positivism" merely the desperate act of a thinker driven into a corner by his own conceptual confusions? Or does his concern with description reveal something important about his discourse, something which he perhaps does not understand but cannot dispense with?

In his treatments of various discourses, early and late, Foucault always brings them into a certain proximity to his own; he refuses to interpret them, for example, through the lens of any other discourse, which could furnish hermeneutic clues to their meaning.[24] Rather, he attempts a direct confrontation with each: a treatment from up close, from proximity. In this, however, two sets of categories always remain in play: those of ousiodic structure and those of its undoing. Because of Foucault's demand for proximity, however, those categories cannot be viewed as structures which exist, say, in his own mind, as a hermeneutical base in terms of which objects then get interpreted. Rather, they are taken by him to be directly manifested by the phenomena he is treating. And this, I take it, is the inescapable core of "description" for Foucault. His claim of positivism is the claim that he is not merely interpreting other discourses in terms of categories he himself brings to them. But he is also not describing them as they exist "independently" of his own—for his claim to positivism is, taken at face value, false. Rather, he is describing diakenic unifications which, though his own description puts them in play, are nonetheless—once they are in play—to be taken as directly manifested by the discourses described.

At this point, my reading of Foucault passes over into emendation. As I am putting it, the phenomena Foucault "describes" are to be taken as at once ousiodic and non-ousiodic: his "descriptivism" means that both aspects are equally attributable to the phenomena in question. Hence, they are to be seen as trying simultaneously to establish and to abolish their own ousiodic structure. So the prison exhibits ousiodic structure in its very floor plan, while contesting it through the openness at its center. The confessing individual constitutes herself as a "subject" in two senses, not one: as an autonomous (ousiodic) subject which could, nonetheless, be such only through the designating force of "power." State power emanates from a central government which is at once rational and arbitrary, accepted and contested from below. The various sexual codes Foucault discusses regulate sexuality in ousiodic terms which are nonetheless oppressive to those they regulate. And so on.

But Foucault always privileges the non-ousiodic categories. François Russo had noted this shortly after the appearance of *L'archéologie du savoir,* when he criticized Foucault's

> refusal to see that unities of different types coexist in the history of thought. ... By isolating within the history of thought an "archeology of knowledge" which only takes account of a single type of unity, the discursive formation, one imposes on oneself a categorial scheme which cannot recognize the close relation between this [type of] unity and other forms of unity.[25]

Falling with equal validity under two sets of categories, such an object for Foucault has what we may call (in spite of his own strictures) two "meanings": it can be described in two ways. Thus, it functions for him as did modern social theories for Habermas—as what I call a "normal poetic elicitor," a statement that has more than one meaning. Unlike Habermas, however, Foucault does not seek to respond with a discourse that is similarly double. Rather, he seeks to eliminate the ambiguity by adhering strictly to his own non-ousiodic categories. It is because of this that he sees his thought as in the unambiguous service of presence: as substituting "truer" categories for false ones.

In this respect, he fails to see that his work has two, possibly harmonious, sides—challenge and description—and attempts to see it as merely descriptive. Were he clearly to distinguish these two sides, he could see that the object of his challenge—ousiodic structure—is not the same as the object of his description—the ambiguity of the phenomena described. He could see his thought as a paradigm of what I have called "terminating normal poetic interaction." And he could see the diakenic interplay which his own discourse is not merely to describe but to set into play and therefore liberate, entering into the service of freedom and into the Great Demarcation. (*Who is as expert as he at happiness in winter, in spots of sun on the wall?*)

9

THE GREAT DEMARCATION
AND THE SITUATION OF FREEDOM

*How wonderful that he did not remain, like a loving, stolid
loafer, always "in my house," always "self-contained." For
that he was beside himself, there is no doubt. Only now does
he see himself, and what surprises he finds! What unsuspected
shudders! What happiness still lies in fatigue, in the old illness,
in the relapses of recovery! Convalescent!*

Greeks point out on many occasions that we understand nothing, at least
not in its basic nature, until it is over with. It is perhaps appropriate, then,
to begin concluding this investigation of the Great Demarcation by asking
what it is.

It is first of all, of course, a story: the linking of four contemporary thinkers into a sequence first traversed, imaginatively, by Nietzsche. From most
points of view, the story is a notably bad one. Philosophically speaking, it is
quite implausible. Who can seriously accept that such complex and subtle
philosophers could be bound together by a few pages from a thinker who
died a generation before they were born? And how could any such linking
be made plausible by my tactics here: with no argument or explanation, but
merely the lighthearted juxtaposition of a few selected quotes?

Matters are not helped by the recurrent rapprochements I have effected
between the thinkers of the Great Demarcation and Hegel and Heidegger.
Not that these rapprochements are surprising; on my reading of the history
of ousia, Hegel and Heidegger were, after all, the first to challenge it within
the confines of its final modern redoubt, philosophy itself. But *these* rap-

prochements are themselves too sporadic and random to offer much beyond the hope that increased attention to Hegel and Heidegger might help us move from mere challenges to ousia toward a more lucid and consistent approach.

Apparently too willful to capture the thinkers it treats, the story of the Great Demarcation cannot tell us what they really are, or how they really relate to one another. Unable to capture them, it also cannot explain itself. For capturing them was its function, its proper work; not having accomplished it, it really is nothing. It cannot tell us what it itself really is, or how it really relates to us. At most, perhaps, it can serve to nudge us into a trajectory that points beyond itself, and back to the thinkers it connects. This makes of it what I have elsewhere called a "demarcative" narrative, one which undercuts itself as it is told, by showing the inability of its overall linking narrative to capture the complexities of what it purports to link.[1]

Accepting it as such, we can still ask whether there is more. Is there not something to the Great Demarcation beyond its own willfulness? If it does not fully capture the thought of Derrida, Rorty, Habermas, and Foucault, might it not at least tell us *something* useful about them? Does it not articulate something genuinely common to their pursuits?

As I noted in the introduction, Nietzsche claims that his Great Getting-Loose, which I have modulated here into the Great Demarcation, has not only an intelligible narrative structure but one which can and must be generalized: "How it went with me is how it must go for everyone."[2] He might be charitable enough to see the present volume as attempting just such a "generalization." But he would demand to know what exactly was getting generalized. What, in other words, is the theme or idea that links the four thinkers of the Great Demarcation, not only with each other but with Nietzsche's original story?

As Nietzsche himself presents it, the Great Getting-Loose is the genesis of a "free spirit," and so portrays a process of emancipation. Similarly, as has been seen for the Great Demarcation: its thinkers all propose, sometimes in spite of themselves, emancipatory roles for philosophy. They seek to undo its exclusive dependence on truth by placing it in the service of freedom as well. Nietzsche and the four thinkers of that Demarcation can all be viewed as setting forth ways—*philosophical* ways—of becoming free. In so doing, they show us what freedom is for us, here, now: they help us begin writing the *situation* of freedom.

1. THE GREAT DEMARCATION AND POETIC INTERACTION

The Great Demarcation overtly aims its challenges at philosophy, which appears in different guises along its course: as the rationalizing foundation of metaphysical binaries for Derrida, as the (A)analytical pursuit of truth for

Rorty, as substantive theories of subjectivity for Habermas, and as the most global kind of global thinking for Foucault. Aiming, if darkly, to change the nature of philosophy itself, the Great Demarcation presents itself first of all as a phenomenon of cognition, one which contests traditional views of what philosophical knowing is all about. My presentation suggested this dimension, for it argued that the Great Demarcation could be captured, not only by Nietzsche's story of liberation, but by the basic categorical scheme of my own account of poetic interaction. The alignment, I suggested, was as follows

Derrida—nonterminating abnormal poetic interaction

Rorty—terminating abnormal poetic interaction

Habermas—nonterminating normal poetic interaction

Foucault—terminating normal poetic interaction

To summarize these again: In abnormal poetic interaction, an utterance is made which has, rather than a single clear (or not so clear) meaning, none whatever: it is up to the hearer to create a meaning for it. In nonterminating poetic interaction, the response to such an utterance continues the "poetic," or creative, nature of the encounter. Thus, I argued, Derrida locates moments within philosophical texts which, by the lights of those texts themselves, are meaningless. He does not seek to generate a meaning for them but to destabilize them around his own kind of diakenic binary: hence the "abnormal nonterminating" character of his thought.

When Rorty's philosophical practice is theorized more concretely than he himself does, I suggested at the end of chapter 2, it also begins from a lack of meaning: from what I characterized as a "lack of fit between a vocabulary and the realities of the situation." Rorty's ironist does not, like Derrida, remain in the uncertain creativity of this situation, but restores "normalcy" by inventing new words to do the new jobs that need doing. Hence the "abnormal terminating" side of Rorty's thought.

An utterance may also be unintelligible not because it lacks meaning but because it has too many meanings. In such normal poetic interaction, the nonterminating response retains the ambiguity of the original utterance. Habermas's thought, I argued in chapter 6, reworks previous social theories which themselves arose doubly: as articulations of social practices within the life world, and as responses to the threat which power and money pose to the life world. Habermas's own vocabulary, that of the theory of communicative action, is supposed to carry forward both challenges: to show how earlier social theories converge upon it, and in so doing to articulate the threat to the life world which calls the theory forth. In this way, his thought stands as an example of "normal nonterminating" poetic interaction.

Finally, the thought of Foucault operates in what I called a "descriptive proximity" to phenomena. Such proximity shows them to have more than one meaning in that they are both constituting and subverting their own ousiodic structure. His thought seeks to understand the phenomena it describes in terms of just one of these two meanings: the subversive one. In this way, it operates as a case of normal terminating poetic interaction.

If my argumentation here is correct, each of these thinkers provides an example of a normed version of one of the four types of poetic interaction. The *epistemological* narrative link which joins them would then be the development of situating reason itself, moving through normed versions of the four types of poetic interaction. On this narrative, the thinkers of the Great Demarcation would show us what poetic interaction looks like when raised to a philosophical level of normativity, which I call "situating reason." They show us what reason is like when freed from its "transcendental subjection" to truth.

But this alignment with McCumber, alas, may be no more promising than the original alignment with Nietzsche. It is certainly no better when it comes to capturing the complexities of the four thinkers themselves, or conveying the richness of their insights. In any case, detailed discussion of this cognitive implication of the Great Demarcation requires a separate treatment.

2. SITUATING FREEDOM IN THE GREAT DEMARCATION

Situated reason is not free, for it is bound to the cultural, social, and linguistic peculiarities of its time and place. Universal reason is not free either, because it is bound to universal truth: its subjection, to use again a phrase of Foucault's, has merely become "transcendental." Only reason which is situating—which is not trapped in the peculiarities of its situation but actively constructs them, and in doing this over and over approaches the universal—can be free.

The most basic concept of poetic interaction, and perhaps of all philosophy after Heidegger, is therefore that of the "situation," which I will define quickly as an interplay of parameters. Some parameters, and some situations, are as fleeting and unique as the play of light in the branches of a maple tree in a June breeze. Others, those with which philosophers ought to be concerning themselves, are more lasting and widespread. The philosophical freedom brought about by the thinkers of the Great Demarcation comes about as an interplay of four different parameters of freedom, an interplay which I call the "situation of freedom." These parameters can be characterized as follows:

(1) *Displacement:* A being is free to the extent that it exhibits a structure not of domination, but of the displacement of domination. It exists because, and insofar as, it has thrown something off without itself assuming the kind of domination it has suspended.

(2) *Incommensuration:* A being is free to the extent that it becomes opaque to other beings.

(3) *Centration:* A being is free to the extent that it establishes relations with other beings.

(4) *Rupturing.* A being is free to the extent that the centers it establishes together with other beings lead to a descriptive proximity which in turn produces further ruptures.

Each of these, I will now argue, is inspired by a stage in the Great Demarcation.

2.1. Displacement

Derrida's thought achieved its characteristic "epistemic liberation" not with the overthrow of metaphysical binaries but with deconstruction's next step: the displacing of them. Hence, this first parameter of freedom's situation is derived from Derrida—but not from the Derrida who challenges presence and who, I argued, is as a result either unintelligible or banal: unintelligible if the "presence" contested is merely the kind of ordinary givenness on which truth and reference depend, and banal if it is the "full presence" which only a few foundationalist philosophers ever advocated in the first place.

On the view I advocated in chapters 1 and 2, Derrida should not be seen as challenging presence as such but rather its status as the ordering goal —the dispositive form—of philosophical investigation. From this perspective, he is free to retain what I will call a "weak presence," one which is not an absolute but a complex and relative matter. The greenness of a patch of grass is "weakly present" if the grass is sufficiently similar in color to other things that I have been taught to call "green"—that to say "that grass is green" has a good chance to inform those who hear it, rather than misinforming them. It need not be the case for this that the grass is fully present in greenness: its greenness need not be an object which "refers only to itself," and is in need of nothing else to be experienced. Nor need it be the case that the distinction between "informing" and "misinforming" is somehow noncontextual and absolute: most sentences, as Plato realized in his accounts of *logos* as *pharmakon,* both inform and misinform us.[3]

Presence of this sort is a matter of more and less, of preponderance, of taking *as*. In the view advocated here, deconstruction leaves such "weak presence," and an appropriately thin variety of truth, intact. But this does not deprive deconstruction of critical or subversive potential. That potential is directed not against presence itself but against its status as the dispositive and bounding concept of philosophy: against its dominance. Allowing Derrida to contest the ousiodic role of presence while accepting "weak presence" would leave his truly emancipatory gestures and insights basically intact, while cutting away his banality and appeals to unintelligibility. His thought would then be seen as disrupting the unities established in and for philosophical texts by that dominating concept of presence. It would provide a rich set of gestures directed against the ousiodic structures of those texts, and of philosophical inquiry itself.

For a philosophical text to enter the labyrinth of Derrida's discursive space is thus for its basic philosophical structure—comprising the assertions and concepts which bound and unify it, and those of its aspects which are subordinated to that end—to be overturned and situated without new relations of dominance, or a new unity, being established. We do not discover, as with Freud, that a repressed erotic theme was "unconsciously" unifying the text. We do not learn, as with Marx, that class struggle was being "ideologically" suppressed by it. Rather, the different components of the text remain together, but in a state of displacement: their unity becomes what I have called "diakenic."

Examples of such "displacing freedom" offer themselves far beyond the domain of strictly philosophical texts. Kolonus, the region on the borders of Athens where Oedipus completes his life's drama, is for example an area of such displacing freedom: everybody there is addressed as *"xeinos,"* foreigner. Outside literature altogether, a woman may exist "displacingly" because she has thrown off male dominance without assuming a dominance of her own. No longer reduced to the obscurity of matter, she is free to renounce the transparency of form as well, so as to become something indescribably new. So also, possibly, for a man: he displaces himself in our situation to the extent that he throws off his own male dominance, without reducing himself to mere matter. Displacing freedom comes about only insofar as one engages in a Derridean displacement—not a mere inversion—of traditional patterns of domination which previously defined them.

As a single, emphatic example of the kinds of freedom propounded by the situating ontology of the Great Demarcation, I will consider, rather than a god or a great man, a couple: a man and a woman—indeed (*ma foi qu'il est louche!*), "A Man and a Woman."

> They meet on New Year's Day, in the town where his son and her daughter, each from a previous marriage, attend boarding school. They have spent the day with their respective children, each undreaming of the other's existence. But in the course of that day the customary child-parent relationships have been inverted. The young girl has dictated to her mother a story for her mother to tell her; the son has driven his father around in the father's car. These inversions of the parent-child binary do not lead either to their own prolongation or to the reinstatement of traditional parental dominance. For the parents, unable to care for their children, return them to the school. They are thus displaced from their parenthood: they have thrown it off, but without subjecting themselves in turn.
>
> The woman misses her train, and the headmistress prevails upon the man to drive her back to the city. And now they are driving, listening to the car radio. A sen-

timental song "of pre–World War One vintage" comes on, and the woman begins to chuckle. The man, driving, looks at her and says, "You mustn't laugh. . . . Songs like that made people cry in 1914."

"Oh," she responds with mock seriousness. ". . . Did they . . ."[4]

With that, the man and the woman join in a space where the dominance not only of familial tradition but of the past in general is suspended. Anything is possible: their displacing freedom, their progress from binary through binary to binary, is released.

2.2. Incommensuration

The second parameter of situating ontology is derived from Rorty. But not from the Rorty who, as I argued in chapter 2, mistakes opacity for disconnection and thereby reinstates ousiodic structure for the disconnected discourses with which he is left.

Rorty's renunciation of truth, together with his refusal to put anything else in its place, ties him to the view that language is basically a truth-telling device, so that the paramount connection between one discourse and another resides in such truth. It also leads him to the view that there can be no argument about vocabularies as wholes. The overall result, I argued, is a radically disconnected and impotent discourse, disconnected by its rejection of truth from the realities of history and text, unable to see its own derivation from its precursors, able to consider its future only in terms of luck.

The first step out of Rorty's disconnection of discourse is—as it was with Derrida—to give up the impossible task of trying to get beyond truth and argument altogether. This means reinstating sentential truth—but as merely one moment of the undertaking: not as constituting our goal, but as regulating our means. This in turn allows us to take a stand different from Rorty's as regards incommensuration and its result, mutual opacity.

Rorty, along with thinkers such as Kuhn,[5] Foucault, and Derrida, has shown that incommensurability is indeed an historical fact. But it is not a condition of all history, if only because history has no universal conditions. It follows that there are other ways to move forward than the ironic invention of new vocabularies wholly *de novo*.

In geometry, for example, we learn that any set of points on a plane can be connected by a line whose formula can be given in an equation. Similarly, I suggest, for vocabularies and discourses: No matter how incommensurable two of them might seem, we can take it that there is some set of larger or mediating words or practices in terms of which both can be understood. Or rather (and this is the whole point): there will be such a set if we are sufficiently industrious and imaginative to produce it. For the reason that Kuhn, Foucault, Derrida, and Rorty do not discover such middle, or "linking," terms is *precisely that they are looking for them*. If they wanted them they could, often quite easily, invent them.[6] Of course, such terms would never be per-

fect: they would never capture all aspects of the vocabularies they are trying to harmonize. But that is in keeping with the nature of language generally as a matter of weak presence or *taking as* rather than of capturing fully.

The "opacity" of one discourse with respect to others is, then, just this:
that a vocabulary linking them remains to be invented. Such a state of affairs, considered in terms of the Great Demarcation, is not simply given: it
comes from something and leads to something. What it comes from is Derridean displacement, now taken as a concretization of Rortyan irony. For
what Derrida displaces is, precisely, the authority of the ancient meanings
codified in philosophical texts over our readings of those texts. And opacity leads to something: to a vocabulary which, in some sense and to some
degree, is "adequate" to mutual comprehension.

Rorty's views on opacity thus yield the second parameter of the situation
of freedom: freedom as incommensuration. A being becomes "opaque" to
other beings to the extent that it assumes a diakenic distance from those
other beings. Kierkegaard's Abraham, riding silently toward Mount Moriah
with the son he loves and yet intends to kill, exemplifies such freedom for
the individual.[7] Emil Fackenheim's account of Jewish existence after the
Holocaust shows it in the case of a group. For just as Kierkegaard's Abraham could hardly explain himself to Isaac, so Jews, on Fackenheim's understanding, cannot bridge or even comprehend the gap between themselves
—uniquely victimized in the Holocaust Kingdom—and those who either
remained outside that Kingdom or entered it for reasons other than the
religion of their grandparents. Hence, even the "fraternal reading" of their
shared sacred text with Christians can only, for Fackenheim, "set [the two
groups] starkly apart,"[8] into the freedom of their mutual opacity.

Incommensuration is thus the defining rejection with which people em-
bark on their own adventures, refusing even to be understood by outsiders.
It is a type of freedom which induces anguish, for to refuse to be understood
is not to break off relations altogether. It is, rather, to remove them to a
nonlinguistic plane, and is thus a form of emancipatory repression, however
odd that sounds. We may say that in the human universe, individuals and
groups exist incommensurately insofar as they undertake such rejection,
which in spite of its anguish is not to be deplored but accepted parametrically—i.e., as something which can change.

> *The man's profession is to skirt death in a race car. He drives alone, or with a single
> companion—the road (chemin).[9] It is a solitary profession, "difficult to talk about
> . . . all I could tell you are anecdotes."[10]*

> *Thus enclosed within his vocational opacity, he is without even the memory of how
> he became solitary (the death of his wife is not remembered but is told in flashback).
> He finds that the woman becomes opaque to him as well: driving to join her after a
> long race, he finds it impossible to imagine their meeting. He cannot conceive what*

he should say: "No, that's a stupid idea. Anyway, fortunately I've . . . I've got quite
a long way to go, plenty of time to think of something."[11]

When he reaches her apartment, at 6 a.m., she is not there.

2.3. Centration

This third parameter of freedom's situation addresses in general terms
the issue of how a new vocabulary linking mutually opaque ones can arise
and in what its "adequacy" might consist. As the third stage of the Great
Demarcation, it is inspired by Habermas—but not by the Habermas who
belies his own attempts to establish the centrality of the theory of communicative action by making a suspicious and unnecessary claim of universality
on its behalf.

Once we abandon the idea that the structures and norms of communicative action apply universally to all "rational" discourse, two further things
happen. First, as Habermas does, we avoid any temptation to accord our
own discourse a privileged status as stating truths to which all other discourses must conform; it becomes merely one of the rest, and must adjust
itself to them as well as vice versa. Second, we see, as Habermas does not, the
establishment of centrality as more than the theoretical adjustment of truth-
claims. It can become, in particular, the invention of words or concepts
which are justified to the extent that they can be seen, and agreed, to capture the underlying dynamics of a variety of seemingly opaque discourses,
making them comprehensible to each other.

The motor of this invention is anguish, which can be conceived as a more
emotionally honest version of Rortyan hope. Rorty's reading of the American soul (in *L'espoir au lieu du savoir,* for example) is relentlessly optimistic.[12]
But most Americans know that to place one's hope in the future is to recognize the horrors of the present. And most of them know that the strict-
est anguish for a human being, the narrowest angle into which she can be
forced, is to share space with someone she cannot understand or communicate with. At the end of *The Theory of Communicative Action,* Habermas
introduces the concept of the "anguish of the life world": the stresses and
disruptions brought about in the life world by the "colonizing" systems of
money and power. The activity of thought which articulates that anguish is
carried out by Habermas, I argued, in numerous ways. But such articulation
is not a "theory" in Habermas's "objectivating" sense. It is the invention of
linking words which can connect disparate discourses.

If the autonomous discourses of various social sciences constitute the
"periphery" of Habermas's shield, and the theory of communicative action
its center, then the anguish of the life world could be the dynamism of the
arm which holds that shield, and which can provide a critical thrust independent of those autonomous discourses themselves. Habermas fails to see

this, and seeks to obtain critical thrust from his universality claim instead. This failure of vision occurs, I argued, because he does not see that his account of the life world does not merely describe it truly, but arises out of it—from a set of specific disruptions in it, which call it forth through the anguish they present.

Centrality, we saw, can only be established by saying true things about other discourses and then showing how those discourses converge on one's own. This requires viewing them not as static theories but as "learning processes" developing in their own right, via rational self-critique. We thus arrive at the general picture of (dialogically) autonomous discourses centering themselves upon a center which is doubly heteronomous: it "takes its law" both from the discourses which converge upon it and from the stresses in the life world which it articulates. With respect to those converging discourses, it exercises the power of inducing self- and mutual critique in them. But its own special critical perspective is unlocked only when it demands that those other discourses, in coming to the center, contribute to the articulation and, perhaps, to the eventual healing of the life world. In this demand, it can be critical, both of other discourses and of the realities to which they are "internally connected," without needing to be universally true.

Such centration inevitably leads to words—for if there are no absolutes, incommensurability is not an absolute, and linking words can always be invented. But they will not capture the realities of either side fully; no words ever do that. The center thus established is empty, or partially empty; the new words will never fully overcome the opacity which calls them up—will never be what Rorty calls a "final vocabulary." This guarantees an endless proliferation of centers: centration leads, in the first instance, to further centration, producing new and newer words around which new lives can gather.

The formation of new, larger, or different human centers may result in communities whose binding center and purpose is clearly formulated. To the extent that such a codified center is allowed to decide who can join the community and what roles they will play—in a traditional marriage contract, for example—the community becomes ousiodic in character. But to the extent that the center remains Habermasian—i.e., shadowed and defined by the opacity from which it comes—it simultaneously ruptures ousiodic structure. Another way to put this is that a specific diakenon gathers specific beings to each other through the anguish of their pasts. But as an emptiness, a diakenon cannot be distinguished from other gathering emptinesses; to relate diakenically to one's own past is thus to relate with equal diakenicity to everything past. The process of centration could stop only if all diakena were eliminated—an ancient fantasy of the West.

Habermas's philosophical practice thus furnishes the third parameter of situating ontology. So viewed, centration (like incommensuration) is not a simple given but comes from something and leads to something. It comes from mutual opacity when that is viewed not merely as a present given but as something that has arisen from a unified past; and it will lead, in Foucault, to a proliferation of ruptures.

> *The man does not remain in his solitary anguish, but—through a ruse—finds out where the woman is and pursues her there. He does this because he and she have begun a common history, comprising not only their common displacement and the ensuing opacities but dinner, on an intervening Sunday, with their children—as well as a telegram which she sent him after his race, containing the words "I love you." Their mutual opacity was only possible, in other words, because they were centrating as well: engaging in a learning process which will only bring them together because in it they learn about each other.*

> *Her inner dynamic has led her to the seashore, with both their children, whom she has taken from the school for the day. There—where earth, water, and air come rhythmically together—the centration is brought about by fire: by the rhythmic flashing of the headlights of the man's car, signaling his arrival to the other three. The definition their common situation now achieves is expressed by the children, each of whom addresses him as "daddy" and her as "mom." The words, of course, are only partially correct.*[13]

2.4. Rupturing

This fourth parameter of the situating of freedom is inspired by Foucault—but not the Foucault who proclaims his positivism, insisting that he is merely describing unities as they have "truly" established themselves. Nor by the Foucault who says he has never written anything but "fictions." Rather, it is the Foucault who neither seeks nor abjures truth, but rather puts diakena into play by bringing the objects of his discourse into a proximity which shows them to be primally ambiguous: both seeking and fleeing ousiodic structure, establishing and abolishing their own status as ousiai. It is, in short, not simply a "descriptive" proximity but an "active" one.

When Foucault is read in this way, we can resolve the tortured aporetic of discursive unity I explored in chapter 8. A discursive formation is unified, and describable, to the extent that it seeks to establish itself as having an ousiodic structure, exhibiting the ousiodic traits of boundary, disposition, and initiative. It is ruptured when the counter currents to this are recognized, and the precariousness of its ousiodic structure is revealed. The revelation is necessary to the rupture, for a rupture of this sort is not complete until it is recognized. Nor is it complete before one of the open pathways—in Foucault's case, that of his own post-ousiodic vocabulary—is chosen. Without such a choice, the revelation takes the form of the mere trembling or instability of a structure which remains whole—as in the banal Derrida.

This yields freedom as rupturing. Seen in terms of the Great Demarcation, such rupturing takes its start from centration. For the kind of center with which Habermas deals is always inexhaustibly less than what it relates. It can never completely capture what it started from. Indeed, centration itself requires turning away from part of the past: from those aspects of its opacity which will not be captured by the new, provisional center. The formation of such a center is thus in part the exclusion of other beings with which centers could have been formed; it is inevitably the proliferation not only of new centers but of new ruptures. Rupturing thus brings centers into the double proximity which I argued to be proper to Foucauldian "description": it shows both the establishment and the abolition of ousiodic structure.

> *The incommensuration which has led to centration did not all come from the man and his profession. There is part of the woman's life into which he can never enter, which remains opaque to him: her relationship to her dead husband—a relationship so unfathomable to the man that he is recurrently unclear as to whether the husband is dead or not:*

>> *"I'm very sorry. You talked about him so lightheartedly that I never imagined he was dead."*[14]

>> *". . . Why did you tell me your husband was dead?"*

>> *"He is dead—but he still lives for me."*[15]

> *The man and the woman drop the children off at school, excluding them from their adult community. Then they try to make love. But their attempt at definitive proximity becomes—in her case—coldly descriptive: she cannot help comparing the man's embraces with those of her dead husband. The session becomes visual: instead of caressing one another, the man and the woman end up staring mutely at one another, subverting the union they seek. And this leads to a new rupture. They part, she to take the train back to the city, and he—to drive.*

> *This rupture is resolved only later that evening. The woman sees the man, whom she had thought to leave behind, on the station platform when she disembarks in the city. They stand and face one another, trapped for a last moment in the epistemology of presence which they, like we, have inherited from Descartes. And then they embrace, while the background turns into the pure white of a future in which they will not stay together.*

2.5. The Freedom of the Great Demarcation

Strung together in the narrative of the Great Demarcation, the four parameters of situating freedom belong loosely together. Displacement ends in incommensuration, which refers back in anguish to what was displaced. Articulating that relation yields new centering words. Shadowed by the opacity which drives them, these lead in turn to the proliferation of ruptures. Together, the four parameters sketch a multiple conception, or "situation," of freedom: to be free must be to be suspensive, incommensurating, centrating, and rupturing.

The "must" above is not logical or empirical, or even moral, but historical in character: this is how things "must" be *if* we are to come after Derrida,

Rorty, Habermas, and Foucault. Its strength thus seems to be no more than the force with which these thinkers impose themselves on us here and now. But in fact it is not merely a question of these four thinkers—as if they came from nowhere and spoke only for themselves. If my sketch elsewhere of the history of ousia has merit, it is also a question of Heidegger and Hegel and Kant and Locke and Hobbes and Aquinas and Aristotle and many others, not all of them "philosophers." If this view of our philosophical history is right, the traits I have listed are derived from more ancient ones by a process that has become inescapable. The "must," though uncompelling, is therefore not without all sway; for the cumulative might of comprehended history can bind many things.

If so, then we (as individuals and groups) are historically called to join that comprehended history. We are called, that is, to respond to these four parameters: to get clear on each of them as it shapes itself and us, and thereby to situate ourselves. The call is a call to clarity and hence begins not with a set of answers but with a set of questions. The philosophical situation I have sketched says that, in order to understand how we are situated, we must ask ourselves:

(1) What and whom are we throwing off?

(2) What and whom will we not permit to understand us?

(3) Toward what and whom are we ineluctably under way?

(4) What and whom are we rupturing?

My claim is that these four questions constitute basic items which must always, today, be interrogated if we are to situate ourselves as individuals and communities. Only when they have been thought through can we understand ourselves as situated, and only then can ethics in any more traditional sense gain purchase in our lives.

P.S.

One more thing, curtly. Nature, too, exists displacively, to the extent that it suspends human domination over it without returning to dominate humans. Nature can organize itself into an opaque company of black holes, from which no information escapes. Nature can be viewed as centrating itself: when planets are viewed as "forming" a solar system, for example, they relate to one another through the manifold opacities of their atmospheres. Each such system in turn is taken up into a galaxy, and thence into a cluster of galaxies, and so on. Or when animals couple. Finally, nature exhibits ruptures and catastrophes. When a part of a population ceases to interbreed with the rest of it, it centrates itself as a new "species." In so doing, it shows that the new species, too, is mortal and will be ruptured in turn. The sit-

153

uation of freedom is thus also, though I cannot discuss this here, nothing
less than the basis for a post-ousiodic ontology comprising the human and
natural worlds. As Catullus told us long ago:[16]

> That boat you see there, guys—
> The little one, shaped, see, like a kidney bean—
> She isn't just what you see. She tells you things.
> She says . . .
> She was once the fastest of ships,
> No swiftness of swimming timber that she couldn't scoot past
> Whether the job was to fly with oars or canvas.

> —The shore of the boisterous Adriatic joins her in this statement, she says, and

> The Cyclades, and noble Rhodes, and savage Propontis Thraciae.
> As well as the harsh gulf of Pontis
> Where she who After was a little bean-ship
> Before was a whole leafy, voluble forest.
> Certainly on the high reaches of Cytoris she often
> Spoke with the rustling leaves.

> —Pontic Amastris, Cytoris green with boxwood,
> These things were and are well known to you!

> The little bean-boat says, Cytoris, that:
> She stood on your summit from her oldest origin
> Dipped her blades in your water,
> And from there, through riotous straits,
> She carried her master well
> Whether the wind came from left or right
> Or Jupiter cut down from behind
> On both sheets at once.

> No vows to the shore gods
> Were made on her behalf, when she came
> From the furthest sea
> To this limpid lake.

> But those things were earlier. Now laid by,
> She grows old and dedicates herself to you,
> Twin Castor,
> Twin of Castor.

NOTES

INTRODUCTION

1. Friedrich Nietzsche, *Menschliches allzu Menschliches: Ein Buch für freie Geiste* (*Sämtliche Werke*, vol. 3) (Stuttgart: Kroner, 1964), pp. 5–10. An English translation, differing from my own, can be found in Nietzsche, *Human, All Too Human: A Book for Free Spirits*, trans. R. J. Hollingdale (Cambridge: Cambridge University Press, 1986), pp. 6–9.

2. Martin Heidegger, "Der Ursprung des Kunstwerkes," in Heidegger, *Holzwege*, 4th ed. (Frankfurt: Klostermann, 1963), pp. 7–68, pp. 54, 62; English translation, Martin Heidegger, "The Origin of the Work of Art," in Heidegger, *Poetry, Language, Thought*, trans. Albert Hofstadter (New York: Harper and Row, 1971), pp. 15–88, pp. 66, 75. For a discussion of such aesthetic liberation in Heidegger, see my *Poetic Interaction* (Chicago: University of Chicago Press, 1989), pp. 136–142.

3. See my *Poetic Interaction,* pp. 16–19.

4. Nietzsche, *Menschliches allzu Menschliches*, pp. 10f/9.

5. Nietzsche, *Menschliches allzu Menschliches,* p. 11/10.

6. Heidegger, "Über Nietzsches Wort: Gott ist Tod," in Heidegger, *Holzwege*, 4th ed. (Frankfurt: Klostermann, 1963), p. 221. My translation.

7. See the general introduction to my *Poetic Interaction.*

8. Jacques Derrida, *Limited Inc.*, ed. Gerald Graff (Evanston, Ill.: Northwestern University Press, 1988), p. 156 n. 9.

9. John McCumber, *Metaphysics and Oppression: Heidegger's Challenge to Western Philosophy* (Bloomington: Indiana University Press, 1999).

10. Aristotle, *Politics* I.4 1254a28–32.

11. This definition of "presence" is found in Jacques Derrida, "Force et signification," in *ED*, p. 26/14.

12. David Hume, *A Treatise of Human Nature*, ed. L. A. Selby-Bigge (Oxford: Clarendon, 1896), p. 415.

13. See my *Metaphysics and Oppression: Heidegger's Challenge to Western Philosophy* (Bloomington: Indiana University Press, 1999), chapters 5–8.

14. Heidegger, "Das Ding," in Heidegger, *Vorträge und Aufsätze,* 3 vols. (Pfullingen: Neske, 1967), vol. II, pp. 37–59; English translation, "The Thing," in Heidegger, *Poetry, Language, Thought,* trans. Albert Hofstadter (New York: Harper & Row, 1971), pp. 163–186.

15. See my *Metaphysics and Oppression,* chapter 11.

16. See Jürgen Habermas, "Work and Weltanschauung: the Heidegger Controversy from a German Perspective," trans. John McCumber, in *Critical Inquiry* 15 (1989), pp. 431–456.

17. So that, as Roger Scruton has written, "in philosophy . . . truth is all-important, and determines the structure of the discipline"; Scruton, *Modern Philosophy* (Allen Lane, UK: Penguin, 1994), p. 5.

18. See my *Poetic Interaction,* passim.

1. CHALLENGES TO OUSIA IN
THE WORK OF JACQUES DERRIDA

1. Heidegger, Martin *Sein und Zeit,* 11th ed. (Tübingen: Niemeyer, 1967), pp. 166–180; page numbers to this edition are given marginally in Heidegger, *Being and Time,* trans. John MacQuarrie and Edward Robinson (New York: Harper and Row, 1962).

2. Jacques Derrida, "Les fins de l'homme," in *Marges,* p. 130/130; emphasis added. Though I will cite English translations, all translations here are my own. Also see *Marges,* pp. 147–153 generally, and pp. 154 n. 16, 158 n. 19/123–128, 129 n. 25, 131 n. 35.

3. Rodolphe Gasché, *The Tain of the Mirror* (Cambridge, Mass.: Harvard University Press, 1986), p. 4. For excellent introductory accounts of Derrida, see John D. Caputo, *Deconstruction in a Nutshell* (New York: Fordham University Press, 1997), and Christopher Norris, *Derrida* (Cambridge, Mass.: Harvard University Press, 1987).

4. Jacques Derrida, "La pharmacie de Platon," in *Diss.,* p. 79/70.

5. *Gramm.,* p. 124/83. For a discussion of "logocentric repression," cf. Jacques Derrida, "Freud et la scène de l'écriture," in *ED,* p. 294/197. Among the ways out of domesticity, for Derrida, are such "estrangements" as the *pharmakon,* which in Plato's *Phaedrus* entices Socrates away from his "natural and habitual pathways and laws," taking him out of the hominess of Athens onto little traveled country paths.

6. For a discussion of challenges to the "imperialism of the logos" see *Gramm.,* p. 12/3.

7. Jacques Derrida, "Signature, événement, contexte," in *Marges,* pp. 392f/329.

8. Cf. the predictable hostilities of Thomas McCarthy, "The Politics of the Ineffable: Derrida's Deconstructionism" in McCarthy, *Ideals and Illusions* (Cambridge, Mass.: MIT Press, 1991), pp. 97–119. For a more sympathetic formulation of the problem, see Peter Dews, *Logics of Disintegration* (London: Verso, 1987), pp. 35–37; and for a positive recuperation of Derrida for Marxist critique see Bill Martin, *Humanism and its Aftermath* (Atlantic Highlands, N.J.: Humanities Press, 1995), pp. 36–46.

9. Jacques Derrida, "La différance," in *Marges,* p. 18/17.

10. Derrida, *Gramm.,* p. 381/270; also cf. Jacques Derrida, "Violence et métaphysique," in *ED,* p. 151/102.

11. The insight is also one of his most difficult. Peter Dews points to the problem:

"Derrida has not been noticeably successful in articulating the relationship between 'deconstruction' in its initial discursive sense . . . and his more concrete political concerns"; Dews, *Logics of Disintegration,* pp. 36f. As I will argue in the next chapter, when the object of Derrida's challenges is conceived as presence—as Dews takes it here—it yields too global a notion to ground an effective critique: one cannot criticize everything, and "presence" covers everything we can talk about in all. The problem can be solved by taking ousia, not presence, as the object of challenge.

12. Derrida, "La différance," in *Marges*, p. 17/16; "Violence et métaphysique," in *ED*, p. 136/91.

13. See Jacques Derrida, *La vérité en peinture* (Paris: Flammarion, 1978), pp. 23f; English translation, Derrida, *The Truth in Painting*, trans. Geoff Bennington and Ian McLeod (Chicago: University of Chicago Press, 1987), pp. 19f.

14. Jacques Derrida, "La structure, le signe, et le jeu dans le discours des sciences humaines," in *ED*, p. 414/282; also cf. the discussion of Levi-Strauss in *Gramm.*, pp. 149–202/101–140.

15. Derrida, *Gramm.*, p. 187/128; for examples of the ways in which scientific practice challenges this, see *Gramm.*, p. 12/3, and *Pos.*, p. 47/34.

16. Derrida, *Pos.*, pp. 30f/20.

17. Derrida, *Gramm.*, p. 68/46; also see Jacques Derrida, "Violence et métaphysique," in *ED*, p. 166/113, and "Les fins de l'homme, in *Marges*, p. 162/134.

18. Derrida, "La différance," in *Marges*, p. 22/22.

19. Jacques Derrida, "Signature, événement, contexte," in *Marges*, pp. 392f/329f, and *Pos.*, pp. 57–59/41–43; Jacques Derrida, "L'exorbitant," in *Gramm.*, pp. 226–234/157–164. On what I am calling "deconstructive procedure," cf. Rodolphe Gasché, *The Tain of the Mirror*, pp. 171–174, and Irene Harvey, *Derrida and the Economy of Différance* (Bloomington: Indiana University Press, 1986), p. 83.

20. Derrida, "Signature, événement, contexte," in *Marges*, pp. 392f/329f, and *Pos.*, pp. 56–59/41–43; Derrida, "L'exorbitant," in *Gramm.*, pp. 226–234/157–164.

21. Jacques Derrida, "Hors-livre," in *Diss.*, pp. 9–11/4–6; *Gramm.*, pp. 102f/70; also cf. Gasché, *The Tain of the Mirror,* pp. 166f.

22. "One of the two terms commands the other"; *Pos.*, p. 57/41.

23. Derrida, "La pharmacie de Platon," in *Diss.*, p. 144/125f.

24. Though secondary writers on Derrida do not put matters as I do, some of them have come very close to seeing them this way. Thus, Irene Harvey phrases deconstruction's concern with boundary as follows: "The *reason* for the 'limits' being in precisely *where* they are and therein excluding or including precisely what they do is clearly the concern for deconstruction." She puts its concern with philosophy's epistemological disposition as follows: "Thus the hierarchy of concepts can be revealed as a system of constraints of genres/species in which all forms of knowledge, of science, have a place. . . . Philosophy, of course, forms and performs the foundation for all such systems"; Harvey, *Derrida and the Economy of Différance*, pp. 40, 114. John D. Caputo discusses boundary in *Deconstruction in a Nutshell,* p. 81, and as a political phenomenon on, pp. 106–108; his account of textual disposition is on p. 83, and of domestic disposition on p. 110. Also cf. Christopher Johnson, *System and Writing in the Philosophy of Jacques Derrida* (Cambridge: Cambridge University Press, 1993), pp. 49f, 154f, 161.

25. This is part of recalling that for Heidegger Being is not an *archê*, is not the source from which a being is primordially constituted. Derrida, "Violence et méta-

physique," in *ED, pp.* 203, 208/136f, 141; "La différance," in *Marges,* p. 6/6; "Ousia et grammé," in *Marges,* p. 74/64.

26. "Logocentric teleology," Derrida tells us, is pleonastic; Derrida, *Gramm.,* p. 123/82; also *VP,* pp. 8, 38f, 109/9, 36, 97; "Violence et métaphysique,"in *ED,* pp. 172/116f; "La mythologie blanche," in *Marges* 295/247f; "Les fins de l'homme," in *Marges,* p. 144/121.

27. *VP,* p. 69/62; also cf. the treatment of centers in general in "La structure, le signe, et le jeu dans le discours des sciences humaines," in *ED,* pp. 409f/278ff.

28. Derrida, "Violence et métaphysique," in *ED,* p. 132/88. The deconstruction with respect to Hegel is in "Hors-livre," in *Diss.,* pp. 22f/16f; with respect to Heidegger and Kant in *La vérité en peinture,* pp. 53/43f (cf. the general treatment in that work of the "frame"); to Husserl in *VP,* p. 96/86; to Levinas in "Violence et métaphysique," in *ED, pp.* 131f, 165f/88f, 112f.

29. Derrida, "La structure, le signe, et le jeu dans le discours des sciences humaines," in *ED,* pp. 409/278f.

30. Derrida, "La structure, le signe, et le jeu dans le discours des sciences humaines," in *ED,* p. 411/280.

31. E.g. in Jacques Derrida, "La double séance"in *Diss.,* pp. 244, 300 n. 56/215, 268 n. 67; "Violence et métaphysique," in *ED,* pp. 127–134/85–90; "Hors-livre," in *Marges,* pp. 52f, 56/44f, 48; *Pos.,* pp. 112, 120/84, 86.

32. Derrida, "Violence et métaphysique," in *ED,* pp. 131–133/88f.

33. Derrida, "Hors-livre," in *Diss.,* pp. 50f/43f.

34. Derrida, "Hors-livre," in *Diss.,* p. 43/36; "Force et signification," in *ED,* p. 30/17.

35. Derrida, "L'exorbitant," in Derrida, *Gramm.,* p. 227/158.

36. Derrida, "Hors-livre," in *Diss.,* p. 42/35; also see "La pharmacie de Platon," in *Diss.,* pp. 118/103; *Gramm.,* pp. 52, 65ff/35, 44ff.

37. Jacques Derrida, "De l'économie restreinte à l'économie générale," in *ED,* p. 404 n. 2/338 n. 42.

38. Derrida, "De l'économie restreinte à l'économie générale," in *ED,* pp. 381f/260. I have argued elsewhere against the view that Hegel's System is "brittle" in this way. Though Derrida is surely correct in saying that it can be interpreted differently from each of its own immanent moments, this is not damaging to Hegel's conception of it. See my *The Company of Words,* especially part 2.

39. The pedagogical intention which Derrida, for example, ascribes to Hegel's *Encyclopedia;* Derrida, "Hors-livre," in *Diss.,* pp. 54/46f.

40. Derrida, *Pos.,* pp. 14f/6f; "L'exorbitant," in *Gramm.,* pp. 226–228/157–159.

41. Derrida, "L'exorbitant," in *Gramm.,* p. 227/158.

42. Derrida, "La pharmacie de Platon," in *Diss.,* p. 72/64.

43. *Gramm.,* p. 229/160; also cf. "Hors-livre," in *Diss.,* p. 53/45.

44. Jacques Derrida, "La double séance," in *Diss.,* pp. 282–294/251–262; also p. 383/345.

45. Derrida, "La pharmacie de Platon," in *Diss.,* pp. 193f/167f.

46. For an excellent and entertaining treatment of such critics—though not directly from my point of view—cf. the running battle in Caputo, *Deconstruction in a Nutshell.*

47. *VP,* p. 111/99; *Diss.,* pp. 349f/246; *Gramm.,* p. 25/13f. On closure cf. Johnson, *System and Writing in the Philosophy of Jacques Derrida,* pp. 50, 151f.

48. See respectively *VP,* p. 111/99; *Diss.,* pp. 218f/192f; *Gramm.,* pp. 24f, 31, 41, 164 n. 8, 401,. 405f/13, 18f, 26, 337 n. 8, 283, 286f; "Signature, événement, contexte," in *Marges,* p. 370/311.

49. *Gramm.,* p. 349/246; cf. Harvey, *Derrida and the Economy of Différance,* pp. 96–102.

50. For general points about this, cf. Derrida, "La différance," in *Marges,* pp. 10, 22/10, 21f; "Ousia et grammé," in *Marges,* pp. 34, 36/32, 34; "Violence et métaphysique," pp. 197/134f; *Gramm.,* pp. 23f, 145f/12f, 97f, and pp. 208/144f for a valuable illustration.

51. *VP,* pp. 8, 38f, 70, 109, 111/9, 36, 63, 97, 99; "Violence et métaphysique," in *ED,* p. 172/117; *Diss.,* p. 217/191; "Ousia et grammé," in *Marges,* p. 58/51.

52. See Rodolphe Gasché, "Deconstruction as Criticism," in Gasché, *Inventions of Difference* (Cambridge, Mass.: Harvard University Press, 1994), pp. 1–21.

53. Hilary Putnam, "Between the New Left and Judaism: Interview with Giovanna Borradori," in Borradori, *The American Philosopher,* trans. Rosanna Crocetto (Chicago: University of Chicago Press, 1994), p. 60.

2. THE PRIVILEGE OF PRESENCE
AND THE DERRIDEAN KNOT

1. Jacques Derrida, "Force et signification," in *ED,* p. 26/14.

2. *VP,* p. 70/63; *Gramm.,* pp. 60, 146/40, 97; for a discussion of clearness and distinctness in Descartes, see my *The Company of Words,* pp. 100–102. For a discussion of actuality in Aristotle, see the first two chapters of my *Metaphysics and Oppression.*

3. Derrida, "La structure, le signe, et le jeu dans le discours des sciences humaines," in *ED,* p. 410/279.

4. *VP,* pp. 66f, 69/58–61, 62; *Pos.,* p. 37/26; "La structure, le signe, et le jeu dans le discours des sciences humaines," in *ED,* p. 426/291; *Diss.,* p. 336/302; "Ousia et grammé," in *Marges,* p. 75/64f; *Gramm.,* pp. 97, 236f/66f, 166.

5. Distinguishing presence from its privileging in this way separates the issue of what I call the "descriptive capacity" of the concept of presence from that of its "parametric validity." The question of descriptive capacity is the question of whether and to what extent a concept actually applies to things: whether it can be truly asserted of anything, and if so of what. This, clearly, is an important issue as regards any concept; but it is not the only one. For we are always free—as Aristotle's own deployment of ousia has shown us—to go ahead and apply concepts and categories which do not actually fit the realities to which we apply them. The question of whether and when we should do so for a particular concept is the question of its parametric validity. In particular, the parametric use of the concept of presence, within metaphysics, would for Derrida be its privileging: the instatement of presence as the bounding and disposing norm for all discourse.

6. Martin Heidegger, "Die Onto-theologische Verfassung der Metaphysik," in Heidegger, *Identität und Differenz* (Pfullingen: Neske, 1957), pp. 51–67.

7. As generations of analytical philosophy have taught us. Hence, for example, the plausibility to so many of Donald Davidson's reduction of meaning itself to truth conditions. See Davidson, *Inquiries into Truth and Interpretation* (Oxford: Clarendon, 1984).

8. Derrida, "La différance," in *Marges,* p.10/10. But even here the situation is

equivocal: absence conceived as a "simple symmetrical opposite" is presumably absence conceived as given all in once, as present.

9. See Barbara Johnson's "Translator's Introduction" to *Diss.*, p. xv.

10. *Pos.*, p. 37/26; see generally pp. 28–41/18–29, and "La différance," passim.

11. Examples of this relentless conflation can be found in Derrida, "La différance," in *Marges*, pp. 10/9, 13/13; "Ousia et grammé," in *Marges*, pp. 35, 44, 75/32, 40, 64; "La structure, le signe, et le jeu dans le discours des sciences humaines," in *ED*, p. 411/279; "Violence et métaphysique," in *ED*, p. 149/101; *Gramm.*, pp. 41, 209/26, 145 (where the conflation is with "essence").

12. Derrida, "La pharmacie de Platon," in *Diss.*, p. 144/125.

13. Jacques Derrida, "La forme et le vouloir-dire," in *Marges*, p. 188/158; *Diss.*, p. 390/351; also "La pharmacie de Platon," in *Diss.*, p. 130/114; *VP*, p. 5/6.

14. On these two senses cf. Irwin, *Aristotle's First Principles* (Oxford: Clarendon Press, 1988), pp. 225, 588 n 13.

15. Like Heidegger, then, Derrida fails to notice the crucial transformation in the status of form that took place when Aristotle rethought Plato. Further evidence of Derrida's inattention to Aristotle in his discussions of form is, perhaps, his occasional use of the phrase *la forme matricielle*, the "maternal" form—a locution which would be extremely perplexing, if not a sheer *contradictio in adjecto*, to any Aristotelian; see Derrida, "La différance," in *Marges*, p. 17/16 (where the phrase is translated as "the absolutely central form"); "La structure, le signe, et le jeu dans le discours des sciences humaines," in *ED*, p. 411/279 (where the rendering is simply "matrix"); *Diss.*, p. 217/191 (where it is more accurately rendered "matrix-form"), and p. 238/210.

16. Derrida, "La différance," in *Marges* p. 11/11.

17. Derrida, "La différance," in *Marges*, p. 28/26; "Ousia et grammé," in *Marges*, p. 77/66; *VP*, p. 86/77; "Violence et métaphysique," in *ED*, pp. 219/147f.

18. Derrida, "Violence et métaphysique," in *ED*, p. 102/131; *Diss.*, p. 390/351; see also *Pos.*, p. 109/82.

19. *Diss.*, p. 391/352. Heidegger's alternative "as" is left unmentioned.

20. *Gramm.*, p. 68/46; "Ousia et grammé," in *Marges*, p. 78/67.

21. Derrida, "La structure, le signe, et le jeu dans le discours des sciences humaines," in *ED*, p. 412/280; also cf. *Gramm.*, p. 24/13, and Derrida, "Violence et métaphysique," in *ED*, p. 166/113.

22. Derrida, "Force et signification," in *ED*, p. 46/28.

23. *Pos.*, p. 35/24; also p. 27/17; "Hors-livre," in *Diss.*, p. 10/4; *Diss.*, pp. 105, 204f/93, 178f; "La structure, le signe, et le jeu dans le discours des sciences humaines," in *ED*, pp. 427f/292f; *Gramm.*, p. 58, 103/39, 70; "De l'économie restreinte à l'économie générale," in *ED*, pp. 406f/276f.

24. *Gramm.*, pp. 58, 103/39, 70; "L'exorbitant," in *Gramm.*, p. 229/159f; Derrida, "Force et signification," in *ED*, pp. 13f/6.

25. *Gramm.*, p. 136/89; see also the references to "pure" presence, suggesting that there is some other kind, in Derrida, "Signature, événement contexte," in *Marges*, p. 378/318, and in *Diss.*, p. 336/302, as well as to "full presence" in Husserl in *VP*, p. 109/97.

26. *Diss.*, p. 368/331; Derrida, "La forme et le vouloir-dire," in *Marges*, p. 206 n.14/172 n. 16; *Gramm.*, p. 345/243.

27. Derrida, "Signature-événement-contexte," in *Marges*, p. 392/329.

28. *Diss.*, p. 220/193; *Gramm.*, p. 376/266; "Violence et métaphysique," in *ED*, p. 163/111.

29. Jacques Derrida, *Limited Inc.*, ed. Gerald Graff (Evanston, Ill.: Northwestern University Press, 1988), p. 147.

30. See on this Richard Rorty, "Two Meanings of Logocentrism," in Rorty, *Essays on Heidegger and Others* (Cambridge: Cambridge University Press, 1991), pp. 107–118.

31. Derrida, "Violence et métaphysique," in *ED*, p. 226/152; "L'exorbitant," in *Gramm.*, p. 232/162; "La structure, le signe, et le jeu dans le discours des sciences humaines," in *ED*, p. 421/288. Derrida's complaint about coherence is warranted by my own account of the empiricists as given in the introduction, for their entire endeavor rests upon the idea that one can "innocently" separate the critique of ousia in nature from the way ousia functions parametrically in structuring the human world.

32. These are mentioned respectively in "La différance," in *Marges*, pp. 8f/8f; *Pos.* pp. 17f/9; "La différance," pp. 17/16f; also cf. *Gramm.*, pp. 92, 206, 236f/63, 143, 166; *Diss.*, pp. 368/330f; "La différance," in *Marges*, pp. 6, 25f/6, 24ff; "Ousia et grammé," in *Marges*, pp. 76f/65f; "La forme et le vouloir-dire," in *Marges*, p. 206 n. 14/172 n. 16; "Violence et métaphysique," in *ED*, p. 160/108; *VP*, p. 95/85; *Diss.*, pp. 337f/304.

33. Derrida, "La pharmacie de Platon," in *Diss.*, pp. 144/125f.

34. As Rodolphe Gasché has noted, "The infrastructural process of accounting is distinguished from the speculative mode of resolving contradictions insofar as it maintains contradiction and resists its sublation into a higher unity"; the maintenance of such contradiction is the result of the "undecidability" of the third term; Gasché, *The Tain of the Mirror* (Cambridge, Mass.: Harvard University Press, 1986), pp. 151, 242; also cf. pp. 205 and especially 220. The most thorough exploration of this proximity between Derrida and Hegel is in Gasché, pp. 23–105. Also cf. Deborah Chaffin, "Hegel, Derrida, and the Sign," in *Derrida and Deconstruction*, ed. Hugh Silverman (New York: Routledge, 1989), pp. 77–91.

35. Hegel's Logic of Essence treats pairs of terms in which one term is valorized at the expense of the other: Being/Essence, Cause/Effect, Substance/Accident, and so on. For an extended comparison of Derrida and Hegel on this issue, which I am generally following here, see Gasché, *The Tain of the Mirror*. Gasché's main problem is that he stops with the Logic of Essence, failing to see how for Hegel it leads to the Logic of the Notion.

36. For an account of this, see the introduction.

37. Heidegger, "Das Ding," in Heidegger, *Vorträge und Aufsätze*, 3 vols. (Pfullingen: Neske, 1967), vol. 2, p. 42; English translation, "The Thing," in Heidegger, *Poetry, Language, Thought*, trans. Albert Hofstadter (New York: Harper and Row, 1971), p. 170.

38. Derrida, *Spectres de Marx* (Paris: Galilée, 1993), p. 57; English translation, Derrida, *Specters of Marx*, trans. Peggy Kamuf (New York: Routledge, 1994), p. 28.

39. *Spectres de Marx* thus undertakes an important critique of Heideggerean "gathering" (Derrida, *Spectres de Marx*, pp. 49–57/2–29). Derrida claims that in his essay "The Anaximander Fragment," Heidegger interprets justice as "joining, adjustment, articulation of accord or harmony," while injustice is left, in classic metaphysical fashion, to be merely the reverse of these things (Derrida, *Spectres de Marx*,

p. 49/23). True enough; but insofar as the gathering of justice is for Heidegger a diakenic one, it will continue to manifest blockages, derangements, and disadjustments. Justice and injustice—gathering and dispersal—are thus, for Heidegger as for Hegel, ingredients in one another. Gathering remains privileged for Heidegger in one way, and I think it is an important one: it is what allows us to see that criterion A of diakenicity is met, that the sides of a diakenon are not merely indifferent to one another but belong together in spite of the lack of a clear relation among them. In other words, gathering remains for Heidegger privileged "epistemically," but not "ontologically." If Derrida is going to reject this "epistemic" privilege, he will have to replace it with something; for unless criterion A is met, we cannot distinguish between encountering a diakenon and simply fooling around, even in the case of Derrida's own "overthrows and displacements." That Derrida has no account of unity other than the traditional, metaphysical kind is manifest here.

40. Heidegger, "Das Ding," p. 52/179.

41. Hence, the inaccuracy of some of Derrida's portrayals of figures from the history of philosophy; for examples from his reading of Husserl, pursued relentlessly, see J. Claude Evans, *Strategies of Deconstruction* (Minneapolis: University of Minnesota Press, 1991).

42. Ludwig Wittgenstein, *Philosophical Investigations*, 3rd. ed., trans. G. E. M. Anscombe (New York: Macmillan, 1958), ¶ 124.

3. OUSIODIC STRUCTURE VS. THE SPEECH COMMUNITY IN RICHARD RORTY

1. Richard Rorty, "Pragmatism without Method," in Rorty, *Objectivity, Relativism, and Truth* (Cambridge: Cambridge University Press, 1991), p. 74.

2. Martin Heidegger, "Dichterisch Wohnet der Mensch," in Heidegger, *Vorträge und Aufsätze,* 4th ed. (Pfullingen: Neske, 1978), p. 190; English translation, Martin Heidegger, *Poetry, Language, Thought,* trans. Albert Hofstadter (New York: Harper and Row, 1971), pp. 215–216; quoted in Richard Rorty, "Wittgenstein, Heidegger, and the Reification of Language," in Rorty, *Essays on Heidegger and Others* (Cambridge: Cambridge University Press, 1991), p. 64.

3. Martin Heidegger, *Die Selbstbehauptung der deutschen Universität und das Rektorat: 1933/34* (Frankfurt: Klostermann, 1983).

4. For an assessment of this dialogue see my "Language and Appropriation: The Nature of Heideggerean Dialogue," in *The Personalist* 60 (1979), pp. 384–396

5. See Martin Heidegger, "Andenken," in Heidegger, *Erläuterungen zu Hölderlins Dichtung,* 1st ed. (Frankfurt: Klostermann, 1951), pp. 75–143.

6. Richard Rorty, "Keeping Philosophy Pure," in *CP,* p. 19.

7. This is argued most forcefully in Richard Rorty, "Philosophy in America Today," in *CP,* pp. 211–230.

8. Rorty, "Philosophy in America Today," in *CP,* pp. 216–218.

9. Rorty, "Philosophy in America Today," in *CP,* p. 221.

10. Rorty, "Philosophy in America Today," in *CP,* p. 221.

11. Giovanna Borradori, *The American Philosopher,* trans. Rosanna Crocetto (Chicago: University of Chicago Press, 1994), pp. 103f.

12. Rorty, "Philosophy in America Today," in *CP,* p. 221.

13. Richard Rorty, "Philosophy as Science, Metaphor, Politics" in Rorty, *Essays on Heidegger and Others*, pp.19–21.

14. Rorty, "Philosophy in America Today," in *CP,* p. 217

15. Rorty, "Philosophy in America Today," in *CP,* pp. 224f.

16. Rorty, "Philosophy in America Today," in *CP,* pp. 228f.

17. Cf. Rorty, "Philosophy in America Today," in *CP,* p. 225.

18. Rorty, "Wittgenstein, Heidegger, and the Reification of Language," in Rorty, *Essays on Heidegger and Others*, p. 64.

19. Arthur Fine, *The Shaky Game* (Chicago: University of Chicago Press, 1986), pp. 137–142.

20. For further treatment of this conjunction, which I call "assertionism," see my *The Company of Words* (Evanston, Ill.: Northwestern University Press, 1993), pp. 70–90.

21. Gottlob Frege, "Thoughts," in Frege, *Philosophical Investigations,* ed. P. T. Geach and R. H. Stoothof (New Haven: Yale University Press, 1977), pp. 2ff. The article dates from 1918, which means that it only took about thirty years for Analytical Philosophy to exhibit clearly its own founding gesture. Most philosophical schools never achieve this at all. The traditionally crucial distinction between sentences and propositions, by the way, is irrelevant to my purposes; I include both kinds of entity under "assertion."

22. For such elevation cf. W. V. O. Quine, *Pursuit of Truth* (Cambridge, Mass.: Harvard University Press, 1990), p. 77, and Gerold Prauss, "Zum Wahrheitsproblem bei Kant," in *Kant-Studien* 60 (1969), pp. 166–182, p. 171 n. 28.

23. Roger Scruton, *Modern Philosophy* (Allen Lane, UK: Penguin, 1994), p. 5.

24. *CIS*, pp. 5, 9f.

25. This, presumably, is why Rorty accepts some of Analytical Philosophy's characteristic views. Freedom, for example, tends to be allocated to the isolated human individual. That individual's mind is basically a basket of beliefs, i.e., of events or attitudes that claim to be true or false. Though the beliefs are webbed together and complemented by desires (the basket shakes, in other words), there is no hint that the mind could contain anything like, for instance, Husserlian essences, Heideggerean *Verstehen,* or Hegelian negativity. Similarly, the "canonical sequence" of philosophers—Plato to Kant—is seen as founding vocabularies based on the "appearance-reality distinction": where Heidegger sees philosophy as the forgetting of Being, and Derrida as the project of presence, Rorty, like Quine, sees it as the pursuit of truth. See *CIS,* pp. 28ff (but also 68), 88, 76.

26. For an account of such Hegelian showing—and of its contrast with saying and arguing—see my *The Company of Words*, pp. 130–148.

27. For an account of such Heideggerean putting into play—and of its contrast with saying and arguing—see my *Metaphysics and Oppression,* chapter 11.

28. Whereas for an Hegelian it would merely provide grist for dialectical refutation and consequent enhancement of the structured polysemy of the words it contains.

29. Whether the truth in question be the external world or the "higher truth" of the self: *CIS,* pp. 4f.

30. *CIS,* pp. 197, 48; also cf. p. 75, where the ironist is said to feel that her inherited vocabulary is wrong but is unable to give a criterion of wrongness.

31. *CIS*, pp. 13, 19, 21, 29, 55. When Rorty refers to general goals which any linguistic behavior as such must aim in achieving—and in spite of his "contextualism" he does do this—it is under the very traditional (and, for a free spirit like Rorty, rather disconcerting) rubric of "prediction and control"; *CIS*, pp. 4, 6, 14, 15, 67.

32. As do many analytical philosophers: cf. Saul Kripke, "Naming and Necessity," in *Semantics of Natural Language*, ed. Donald Davidson and Gilbert Harmon (Dordrecht: Reidel, 1972), pp. 260f.

33. Richard Rorty, "Solidarity or Objectivity?" in *Post-Analytical Philosophy*, ed. John Rajchman and Cornel West (New York: Columbia University Press, 1985), p. 13.

34. Thomas McCarthy, "Philosophy and Social Practice: Avoiding the Ethnocentric Predicament," in *Zwischenbetrachtungen im Prozeß der Aufklärung*, ed. Axel Honneth et al. (Frankfurt: Suhrkamp, 1989), pp. 190–209.

35. Hilary Putnam, "Why Reason Can't be Naturalized," in Putnam, *Realism and Reason* (Cambridge: Cambridge University Press, 1988), pp. 235–238.

36. The "institutional tail" *should* wag the "pseudoscientific dog," for example: Rorty, "Philosophy in America Today," p. 218.

4. IRONY AND REDESCRIPTION
AS CHALLENGES TO OUSIA

1. Richard Rorty, "On Ethnocentrism: A Reply to Clifford Geertz," *Michigan Quarterly Review* 25 (1986), pp. 525–534.

2. *CIS*, p. 96. Michael Williams has aptly entitled this motivation for irony a *nostalgie de la vérité:* what for Rorty bothers the ironist can only, on a general level, be the fact that final vocabularies are taken for true when they are not. Michael Williams, *Unnatural Doubts: Epistemological Realism and the Basis of Scepticism* (Princeton, N.J.: Princeton University Press, 1996), pp. 364f n. 51.

3. Richard Rorty, *Philosophy and the Mirror of Nature* (Princeton, N.J.: Princeton University Press, 1979), pp. 42–45.

4. Rorty, *Philosophy and the Mirror of Nature*, pp. 107f.

5. This is the side of metaphor emphasized by Donald Davidson's two articles, "What Metaphors Mean," in Davidson, *Essays on Truth and Interpretation* (Oxford: Oxford University Press, 1984), pp. 245–264, and "A Nice Derangement of Epitaphs," in *Truth and Interpretation: Perspectives on the Philosophy of Donald Davidson*, ed. Ernest LePore (New York: Blackwell, 1986), pp. 433–446.

6. This is part of what Davidson is trying to capture when he claims that the only "meaning" metaphors have is that traditionally derived from their component words: Donald Davidson, "What Metaphors Mean," in Davidson, *Inquiries into Truth and Interpretation* (Oxford: Oxford University Press, 1984), pp. 245–264. I will admit, but not apologize for, the low quality of this metaphor, which is my own.

7. See Richard Rorty, *L'espoir au lieu du savoir* (Paris: Albin Michel, 1995), p. 23.

8. Characterized in *CIS*, pp. 9, 44.

9. See G. F. W. Hegel, *Werke*, 20 vols., ed. Eva Moldenhauer and Karl Markus Michel (Frankfurt: Suhrkamp, 1970–71), vol. 7 (*Philosophie des Rechts*), p. 28; vol. 17 (*Philosophie der Religion*), pp. 340–344.

10. Martin Heidegger, "Letter on Humanism," in Heidegger, *Basic Writings,* ed. David Krell (San Francisco: Harper and Row, 1977), p. 193.

11. Derrida, "Envois," in Derrida, *The Post Card,* trans. Alan Bass (Chicago: University of Chicago Press, 1987), p. 185.

12. Thomas McCarthy, *Ideals and Illusions: On Reconstruction and Deconstruction in Contemporary Critical Theory* (Cambridge, Mass.: MIT Press, 1991), p. 219 n. 8.

13. G. W. F. Hegel, *Science of Logic,* trans. A. V. Miller (New York: Humanities Press, 1976), pp. 73, 78.

14. Speaking roughly, the public domain for Heidegger is "metaphysical," and as Rorty notes—without connecting it to his own problematic—Heidegger wanted to "leave metaphysics to itself" (*CIS,* p. 97 n. 1). But Heidegger recognized that setting out to inhabit a purely private domain is itself a political act. The public and the private compete, if not for our identity (*CIS,* pp. xiiif, 198), then for our time and resources: Any victory for either is a defeat for the other. That is why, for Heidegger, leaving metaphysics alone can overcome it. For an interesting critique of Rorty's absolutizing of the public/private dichotomy and of his views on irony see Dianne Rothleder, *The Work of Friendship* (Albany, N.Y.: SUNY Press, 1999).

15. See my *Metaphysics, and Oppression,* chapter 10.

16. Richard Rorty, "Unger, Castoriadis, and the Romance of a National Future" in Rorty, *Essays on Heidegger and Others* (Cambridge: Cambridge University Press, 1991), p. 191.

17. Rorty's aversion to political reality is not a mere lack of interest or attention. Philosophy, for Rorty, *should* be wholly apolitical. This is because political rhetoric, for him, remains inherently metaphysical. The political vocabularies people use are considered, by those who use them, to be final, not in Rorty's sense that it is with them that argument stops, but in that they are assumed to be ultimate and unchallengeable. Bringing political terms into radical doubt either undercuts them to no purpose or is done with the political intent of establishing a new vocabulary as similarly ultimate. This is a violation of the basic nature of "irony," for the true ironist can propose new vocabularies but no new ultimate ones. Political significance, the enhancement of solidarity, is for Rorty best left to those whose work is inescapably personal: novelists such as Nabokov, or writers like Orwell, who do not engage in wholesale redescription but who also do not arrogate to themselves any special status in the end of any global development: *CIS,* pp. 87f, 96–108.

18. *CIS,* pp. 7, 79. For Rorty's doubts about his own understanding of Hegel, see *CIS,* p. 104; for Heidegger and Nietzsche as continuations of the ironist tradition Hegel founded, see *CIS,* p. 108. I place Rorty in proximity to Hegel despite his overt interest in Heidegger, evident in many essays and in what Rorty calls his "abortive, abandoned attempt to write a book on" Heidegger: Rorty, *Essays on Heidegger and Others,* p. 1. The estrangement of Rorty's thought from Heidegger's can be gauged from that fact that, as I began this chapter by noting, Rorty overlooks cases of diakenic unity when Heidegger advances them. The concept of diakenic unity is not only unrecognized by Rorty, but unexploited. The discourses whose mutual estrangement Rorty celebrates, for example, are indeed related by "nothing," but, as I have noted, they are not gathered together around this nothing but float free.

19. Rorty, "Philosophy in America Today," in *CP,* p. 218; also cf. *CIS,* p. 56, where

the vocabulary of a speech community gets more distinctive as the community develops.

20. Cf. Hegel, *Phänomenologie des Geistes,* in Hegel, *Werke,* vol. 3, p. 74; English translation, Hegel, *Phenomenology of Spirit,* trans. A. V. Miller (Oxford: Oxford University Press, 1979), p. 52; *Wissenschaft der Logik,* in Hegel, *Werke,* vol. 5, p. 49; English translation, Hegel, *Science of Logic,* trans. A. V. Miller (New York: Humanities Press, 1976), p. 54.

21. Cf. *CIS,* p. xvi, for freedom as in such "endless proliferation"; also *CIS,* pp. 76f.

22. For a discussion of Aristotle and Hegel on truth see my *The Company of Words,* pp. 112–118.

23. Hence, Rorty's claim that "it took Hegel a lot of work to manage the dialectical inversions he then pretended to have observed rather than produced" is not as accurate as he takes it to be, and fails utterly as a *criticism* of Hegel; *CIS,* p. 134.

24. As Hegel's does not: see my *The Company of Words,* pp. 64f.

25. For which cf. *CIS,* p. 9: "Conforming to my own precepts, I am not going to offer arguments against the vocabulary I want to replace. Instead, I am going to try to make the vocabulary I favor look attractive by showing how it may be used to describe a variety of topics."

26. See Richard Rorty, "Pragmatism, Davidson, and Truth," in Rorty, *Objectivity, Relativism, and Truth* (Cambridge: Cambridge University Press, 1991), p. 126. True, the "truth" Rorty claims for such redescriptions is, in Donald Davidson's term, "unassuming"; it cannot be defined and no general criteria can be given for attaining it. But, thin as it is, it provides, as I have argued, the only standard of evaluation Rorty is ready to recognize in the case of final vocabularies.

27. If this is the only content of Rorty's pragmatic hope in the future, it is small wonder that he pronounces himself "tired": Richard Rorty, "Unger, Castoriadis, and the Romance of a National Future," pp. 178f.

28. For a description of this see *CIS,* p. 73.

5. CENTRALITY AS A CHALLENGE TO OUSIA
IN JÜRGEN HABERMAS

1. This situation is sketched in *PDM,* pp. 169–171/141–143. For a reliable account of Habermas's recent philosophy on its own terms, see Jane Braaten, *Habermas's Critical Theory of Society* (Albany, N.Y.: SUNY Press, 1991). A good general account of Habermas's critique of Heidegger can be found in David Rasmussen, *Reading Habermas* (Oxford: Blackwell, 1990), p. 102.

2. Cf. the introduction to my *Metaphysics and Oppression: Heidegger's Challenge to Western Philosophy.*

3. Martin Heidegger, "Die Zeit des Weltbildes," in Heidegger, *Holzwege,* 4th ed. (Frankfurt: Klostermann, 1963), p. 6; English translation in Heidegger, "The Age of the World Picture," in Heidegger, *The Question Concerning Technology and Other Essays,* trans. William Lovitt (New York: Harper and Row, 1977), pp. 115–154, p. 115. Emphasis added.

4. Jürgen Habermas, "Die Philosophie als Platzhalter und Interpret," in Habermas, *Moralbewußtsein und kommunikatives Handeln* (Frankfurt: Suhrkamp, 1983), pp. 9–28.

5. An instance is Mead's view that *all* human social identity is constructed through role-playing. Cf. Habermas, "Die Philosophie als Platzhalter und Interpret," pp. 22–24.

6. Habermas, "Die Philosophie als Platzhalter und Interpret," pp. 25–27.

7. Habermas, "Die Philosophie als Platzhalter und Interpret," pp. 22–26. Also cf. *TKH*, vol. 1, pp. 15–24/1–7.

8. Oedipus, for example, blinded himself with a pair of *kentra;* Sophocles, *Oedipus the King,* 1318.

9. The radius of a circle, for example, was *ta ek tou kentrou.* For the center as "source" of the circle, see Plato, *Parmenides* 137e; Aristotle, *Rhetoric* III.b 1407b27. It is noteworthy that Euclid, in definition 15 of the *Elements,* avoids such locutions.

10. The *sumphyton pneuma* to be found, he thought, in their hearts; Aristotle, *de Motu Animalium* 698a–b, 703a.

11. Plotinus, *Ennead* IV.1.24ff.

12. The ego thus becomes a mathematical center when man, as Heidegger argues, becomes ground; see Heidegger, "Die Zeit des Weltbildes," passim.

13. Immanuel Kant, "Was Heißt: sich im Denken Orientieren?" in Kant: *Werkausgabe,* ed. Wilhelm Weischiedl (Frankfurt: Suhrkamp 1958), pp. 267–283.

14. Hugh Silverman, "Re-reading Merleau-Ponty," *Telos* 39 (1979), p. 113.

15. Jacques Derrida, "Structure, Sign and Play in the Discourse of the Human Sciences," in *ED*, pp. 278–280. For Habermas's version of this, cf. *PDM*, pp. 200f.

16. For a description of such shields, see Anthony M. Snodgrass, *Early Greek Armour and Weapons* (Edinburgh: University Press, 1964), pp. 37–51; see esp. plate 37, which very clearly illustrates the "offensive" use of the shield.

17. G. F. W. Hegel, *Wissenschaft der Logik,* 2 vols., ed. Georg Lasson (Hamburg: Felix Meiner, 1934), vol. 2, pp. 371–374; English translation, Hegel, *Science of Logic,* trans. A. V. Miller (New York: Humanities Press, 1976), pp. 721–724.

18. G. F. W Hegel, *Werke,* 20 vols., ed. Eva Moldenhauer and Karl Markus Michel (Frankfurt: Suhrkamp, 1970–71), vol. 7, p. 28; English translation, Hegel, *Philosophy of Right,* trans. T. M. Knox (Oxford: Oxford University Press, 1967), pp. 12f.

19. Such as Austinian speech act theory or Gadamerian hermeneutics. Speech act theory, I take it, is "defensive" insofar as the examples it analyzes are "institutionally bound," for which cf. Jürgen Habermas, "What Is Universal Pragmatics?" in Habermas, *Communication and the Evolution of Society,* trans. Thomas McCarthy (Boston: Beacon Press, 1979), pp. 38f. For Habermas's critique of Gadamer's view that "on-going tradition and hermeneutic inquiry merge to a single point," cf. Jürgen Habermas, "A Review of Gadamer's *Truth and Method,*" in Fred R. Dallmayr and Thomas McCarthy, eds., *Understanding and Social Inquiry* (Notre Dame, Ind.: University of Notre Dame Press, 1977), pp. 356–361.

20. *TKH,* vol. 1, pp. 201, 336f/140, 247; Jürgen Habermas, "Wozu noch Philosophie," in Habermas, *Philosophisch-politische Profile* (Frankfurt: Suhrkamp, 1981), pp. 36f.

21. Diogenes Laertius, *Lives of Eminent Philosophers* III.5–6; *Iliad* XVIII 392f; *TKH,* vol. 1, pp. 19–22/4–7.

22. Habermas's most vigorous defense of modernity is perhaps his "Modernity: An Incomplete Project," in Hal Foster, ed., *The Anti-Aesthetic: Essays on Postmodern Culture* (Port Townsend, Wash.: Bay Press, 1983), pp. 3–15.

23. *TKH*, vol. 1, pp. 39–44, 71, 141–155, 410–415/19–22, 42, 94–101, 305–310.

24. Cf. *TKH*, vol. 1, pp. 456–458/340–342; *PDM*, pp. 242f.

25. If the last of these is in fact captured by Habermasian "truthfulness," an issue which I will not discuss here.

26. *TKH*, vol. 2, pp. 586–588/398–400; also cf. Jürgen Habermas, "A Reply to My Critics," in John B. Thompson and David Held, *Habermas: Critical Debates* (Cambridge, Mass.: MIT Press, 1982), pp. 239f; "Die Philosophie als Platzhalter und Interpret," pp. 25f.

27. *TKH*, vol. 1, pp. 16, 38f, 327/2, 18f, 239; vol. 2, pp. 550, 562/375, 383.

28. As in his claim that post-Hegelian philosophy, from logic to aesthetics, exhibits a convergence upon the theory of the formal conditions of rationality, or as shown by his claim that the mutual differentiation of validity-spheres in modernity has now "meta-differentiated" itself into various centripetal moments of culture, all reconverging upon the theory of communicative action; cf. *TKH*, vol. 1, pp. 16, 504/2, 376f; vol. 2, pp. 15f, 86, 586/5f, 53f, 398.

29. As is the case with system theory and action theory: see *TKH*, vol. 1, pp. 460/343f; vol. 2, pp., 303, 550/202f, 375.

30. Habermas, "Wozu noch Philosophie," pp. 34ff.

31. Cf. *TKH*, vol. 1, pp. 17, 198–203/2f, 138–141; vol. 2, pp. 550, 562–583/375, 383–396.

32. It is even possible, in the case of theories whose terms are rigorously inter-defined and whose entailment relations are sufficiently strict, to imagine someone making the required changes without knowing what either theory is "about."

33. Cf. my *The Company of Words* (Evanston, Ill.: Northwestern University Press, 1993), pp. 33–90, 123–178, where such thought is distinguished from propositional varieties.

34. The universality "claim" I will be dealing with should be distinguished from the "principle" of universality perspicuously discussed by Stephen K. White. The *claim* is that all rational human beings will accept the *principle*, which in turn states that "the consequences and side-effects for the satisfaction of the interests of *every* individual, which are expected to result from a *general* conformance to [that] norm, can be accepted without compulsion by *all*": Habermas, *Moralbewußtsein und kommunikatives Handeln*, p. 103, quoted in Stephen K. White, *The Recent Philosophy of Jürgen Habermas* (Cambridge: Cambridge University Press, 1988), p. 49.

35. Jürgen Habermas, "What Is Universal Pragmatics?" passim.

36. I will not rehearse this gigantic literature in detail here. Among the works in English concerned with the general issue, cf. Richard J. Bernstein, *Beyond Objectivism and Relativism* (Philadelphia: University of Pennsylvania Press, 1983), pp. 182–197; Raymond Geuss, *The Idea of a Critical Theory* (Cambridge: Cambridge University Press, 1981); Thomas McCarthy, *The Critical Theory of Jürgen Habermas* (Cambridge, Mass.: MIT Press, 1978), pp. 126–271; John McCumber, "Reflection and Emancipation in Habermas," *Southern Journal of Philosophy* 22 (1984), pp. 71–81; and the essays in Thompson and Held, *Habermas: Critical Debates*, especially those by McCarthy, Mary Hesse, John B. Thompson, and Steven Lukes, together with Habermas's responses. For a brief account of the central developments in the field, see Braaten, *Habermas's Critical Theory of Society*, pp. 19–74. In general, I agree with Stephen K. White's conclusion: ". . . it seems clear that such arguments are not likely to elicit

mass conversions among contextualists and relativists, any more than the reverse is likely to occur"; White, *The Recent Work of Jürgen Habermas*, p. 154.

6. UNIVERSALITY, CENTRALITY, AND
THE THEORY OF COMMUNICATIVE ACTION

1. *TKH*, vol. 1, pp. 197–203/137–141; also cf. Jürgen Habermas, "Moralbewußtsein und kommunikatives Handeln," in Habermas, *Moralbewußtsein und kommunikatives Handeln*, pp. 127ff.

2. Habermas, *Justification and Application*, ed. Ciaran Cronin (Cambridge, Mass.: MIT Press, 1993).

3. See Jürgen Habermas, *Erkenntnis und Interesse* (Frankfurt: Suhrkamp, 1968); English translation, *Knowledge and Human Interests*, trans. Jeremy Shapiro (Boston: Beacon Press, 1971). Also Habermas, *Zur Logik der Sozialwissenschaften* (Frankfurt: Suhrkamp, 1982); English translation, *On the Logic of the Social Sciences*, trans. Shierry Weber Nicholson and Jerry Stark (Cambridge, Mass.: MIT Press, 1988). Given recent work on truth in science, which undermines such strong validity-claims, making them at all could be merely a passing, post-theological phase of our own scientific culture. Habermas's very need to show that his theory is not culture-bound would then be evidence of its culture-boundness. Cf. on this the work in Arthur Fine, *The Shaky Game* (Chicago: University of Chicago Press, 1986), and David Hull, *Science as a Process* (Chicago: University of Chicago Press, 1988).

4. Cf. *PDM*, pp. 163, 182, 192, 299/136, 154, 162, 255 (against Heidegger); pp. 197, 222/166f, 188 (against Derrida); pp. 317, 328/270, 279 (against Foucault); and the discussion of Richard Rorty in Habermas, *Postmetaphysical Thinking*, trans. William Mark Hohengarten (Cambridge, Mass.: MIT Press, 1992), p. 135.

5. Habermas, "A Return to Metaphysics?" in Habermas, *Postmetaphysical Thinking*, p. 50.

6. *PDM*, pp. 363f/311f.

7. Hence, the bonds of cultural and historical perspectives are broken for him not merely by truth but by *any* of the three validity-claims; see, e.g., *TKH*, vol. 2, pp. 586f/399; *PDM*, p. 375/322; *Postmetaphysical Thinking*, p. 224.

8. Cf. Immanuel Kant, *Kritik der Urteilskraft*, Academy Edition, pp. 212f; page numbers to this edition are given marginally in *Kant's Critique of Judgment*, trans. James Creed Meredith (Oxford: Clarendon Press, 1952); *TKH*, vol. 2, pp. 586ff/399f; *PDM*, pp. 374f/322f.

9. J. L. Austin, *How to Do Things with Words*, ed. J. O. Urmson (New York: Oxford University Press, 1965), pp. 99–101. For a reading of Habermas along these lines, see David Couzens Hoy and Thomas McCarthy, *Critical Theory* (Oxford: Blackwell, 1994), p. 77.

10. For this kind of reinstatement, see my *Metaphysics and Oppression*, part 2.

11. In the case of the modern cultural subsystems, these are the ideas of Truth, Goodness, and Beauty. Cf. *TKH*, vol. 1, pp. 300, 302, 320, 365/217, 218, 233, 270.

12. *TKH*, vol. 1, pp. 384f/285f; also cf. Jürgen Habermas, "What Is Universal Pragmatics?" p. 3.

13. The modification consists in specifying that in strategic action the achievement of an agent's purpose requires certain actions on the part of another person

or other persons: *TKH*, vol. 1, pp. 126f/85. Teleological actions which do not require the actions of other people for the realization of their purposes are called "instrumental" actions: see *TKH*, vol. 1, p. 383/285.

14. In a good person or *phronimos*, for Aristotle, actions are produced by reason: they are cases of the initiative that the person's form, or soul, has upon the outside world: cf. Aristotle, *Nicomachean Ethics* VII.1 passim and my *Metaphysics and Oppression*, chapter 2.

15. Jürgen Habermas, "Moral Development and Ego Identity," in Habermas, *Communication and the Evolution of Society*, pp. 69–94.

16. Habermas, "Moral Development and Ego Identity," pp. 90ff.

17. Habermas, "Moral Development and Ego Identity," pp. 93f.

18. Habermas, "What Is Universal Pragmatics?" pp. 2f.

19. See on this symmetry Jürgen Habermas, "Some Distinctions in Universal Pragmatics," in *Theory and Society* 3 (1976), pp. 155–167, and Habermas, "Towards a Theory of Communicative Competence," in *Inquiry* 13 (1970), pp. 360–375.

20. *TKH*, vol. 1, p. 387/287. Fred Dallmayr suggests that this reference to teleology in connection with communicative action is inconsistent with Habermas's contrast between "teleological" and "communicative" action: Dallmayr, *Polis and Praxis* (Cambridge, Mass.: MIT Press, 1984), pp. 240f. But the telos, I take it, is different in each case. In teleological action it is a conscious purpose (of one or more of the interlocutors), while the telos assigned to communicative action is the immanent telos of language as such.

21. Cf. Joseph Owens, *The Doctrine of Being in the Aristotelian Metaphysics*, 2nd ed. rev. (Toronto: Pontifical Institute of Medieval Studies, 1963), pp. 375ff.

22. For language as a "medium," see *TKH*, vol. 1, pp. 141, 150/94, 101.

23. For Habermas's attempt to show how a wide variety of types of social action are "implicitly" structured by the norms of communicative action and understanding, see *TKH*, vol. 1, pp. 114–151.

24. For the unacknowledged dependence of Habermas's account of the life world on Heidegger's, see Robert C. Scharff, "Habermas on Heidegger's *Being and Time*," in *International Philosophical Quarterly* 31 (1991), pp. 189–201, esp. p. 196. As David Rasmussen puts it, "Habermas chooses to critique Heidegger on grounds that were established only on the basis of Heideggerean thought": Rasmussen, *Reading Habermas* (Oxford: Blackwell, 1990), p. 102. The main contrast between the two conceptions, as David Kolb notes, is that Habermas's life world is propositionally structured: Kolb, "Heidegger and Habermas on Criticism and Totality," in *Philosophy and Phenomenological Research* 52 (1992), pp. 683–693.

25. Cf. Gilles Deleuze, *La philosophie critique de Kant* (Paris: Presses Universitaires de France, 1963), pp. 39f.

26. This is because a number of individual subjects can achieve such agreement without sacrificing their own subjectivity; otherwise modern philosophy would have been impossible, for its whole aim was to achieve the agreement of thinkers it regarded as ousiodically structured subjects. Habermas recognizes this implicitly when he associates truth-claims with strategic rationality and subject centered reason: I can agree about truth with others without sacrificing my own purposes, or accepting any goal of interaction other than achieving them; *PDM*, pp. 361, 362, 392/310, 311, 337.

27. E.g., in *TKH*, vol. 1, pp. 29–34/10–15.

28. Cf. *PDM*, p. 363/312, and the discussion of the rationalization of the life world that I gave earlier in this chapter. Also see my *Poetic Interaction*, pp. 333f, 339–344, for a critical treatment of Habermas's claim.

29. I take it that Hegel's remark, in the preface to the *Phenomenology*, that "the feet of those who will carry [me] out are already in the door," refers to something he believed was essential to philosophy. For the quote, see Hegel, *Phänomenologie des Geistes*, 6th ed., ed. Johannes Hoffmeister (Hamburg: Meiner, 1952), p. 58; English translation, Hegel, *Phenomenology of Spirit*, trans. A. V. Miller (Oxford: Oxford University Press, 1979), p. 45.

30. *TKH*, vol. 1, pp. 229–231, 326f/160f, 238; Thomas McCarthy, "Reflections on Rationalization in *Theorie des kommunikativen Handelns*," in Bernstein, *Habermas and Modernity*, pp. 176–191.

31. Thomas McCarthy, "Reflections on Rationalization in *Theorie des kommunikativen Handelns*," pp. 187–189; Jürgen Habermas, "Walter Benjamin: bewußtmachende oder rettende Kritik," in Habermas, *Philosophisch-politische Profile*, pp. 336–376.

32. See Aristotle, *Politics* I.13 1260a13–15.

33. See the introduction to my *Metaphysics and Oppression: Heidegger's Challenge to Western Philosophy*.

34. *TKH*, vol. 2, p. 204/134. Dallmayr has pointed out that *Theorie des kommunikativen Handelns* "oscillates" between viewing language as structuring our thought from "behind" and as a dependable medium for conveying it: Dallmayr, *Polis and Praxis*, p. 239.

35. *Anthropos*, for example, is merely a biological term and does not convey any notion of being the bearer of rights; slaves and barbarians had none, and as Plato's *Euthyphro* shows, it was not possible to wrong a slave.

36. This is a modification, if I am correct a fateful one, of Habermas's earlier theory, in which an utterance in communicative action claimed, in addition to truth, appropriateness, and sincerity, intelligibility—a claim which could, then, be evaluated in discourse. The modification is first advanced in Habermas, "Wahrheitstheorien," in *Wirklichkeit und Reflexion. Walter Schulz zum 60e Gebürtstag* (Pfullingen: Neske, 1973), pp. 211–265.

37. For an account of such "subservience" see my "Reflection and Emancipation in Habermas," in *Southern Journal of Philosophy* 22 (1984), pp. 71–81.

38. See my "Hegel on Habit," in *Owl of Minerva* 21 (1990), pp. 155–165.

39. This is treated generally in *TKH*, vol. 2, pp. 229–294/153–197.

40. *TKH*, vol. 2, p. 278/187. David Ingram points to such diakenicity when he argues that within a Habermasian perspective, debates about the proper balance between system and life world cannot be adjudicated: "There are no criteria of rational argumentation to which we can appeal"; David Ingram, *Habermas and the Dialectic of Reason* (New Haven, Conn.: Yale University Press, 1987), pp. 178f. Axel Honneth and Jonathan Culler launch trenchant critiques of two of Habermas's attempts to avoid recognizing such diakenicity. Honneth argues against Habermas's tendency to separate life world and system into two separate (and possibly mutually indifferent) spheres, showing that the interplay of the two can be found in all types of interaction: Honneth, *Critique of Power*, trans. Kenneth Baynes (Cambridge, Mass.: MIT Press, 1991), pp. 298–303. Culler criticizes Habermas's attempts to construe strategic action—that proper to the system—as parasitic upon communicative

action, which is proper to the life world. Anticipating Ingram (but arguing from earlier texts of Habermas), Culler concludes that Habermas is "left with two sorts of linguistic communication, that which presupposes these norms [of communicative action] and that which works differently . . . appeal to the norms that subtend consensual speech situations would just be a case of choosing values that are preferred rather than relying on values inevitably implied by linguistic communities"; Culler, "Communicative Competence and Normative Force," in *New German Critique* 35 (1985), pp. 133–147, p. 137.

41. For which cf. McCarthy, "Reflections on Rationalization in *Theorie des kommunikativen Handelns*," pp. 181f.

42. Habermas, "Die Philosophie als Platzhalter und Interpret," pp. 26f.

43. See on this Emil Fackenheim, *To Mend the World* (New York: Schocken Books, 1982).

7. MICHEL FOUCAULT'S CHALLENGES TO OUSIA

1. Foucault, "The Return of Morality," interview with Gilles Barbadette and André Serla, in Michel Foucault, *Foucault Live (Interviews, 1966–1984)*, trans. John Johnston (New York: Semiotext(e), 1989), p. 326.

2. Martin Heidegger, "Die Zeit des Weltbildes," in Heidegger, *Holzwege*, 4th ed. (Frankfurt: Klostermann, 1963), p. 6; English translation, Heidegger, "The Age of the World Picture," in Heidegger, *The Question Concerning Technology and Other Essays*, trans. William Lovitt (New York: Harper and Row, 1977), pp. 115–154, p. 115. Emphasis added.

3. *SP*, p. 219/217. The irony is compounded, of course, by Foucault's own later turn to the Greeks, for which see Mark Poster, "Foucault and the Tyranny of Greece," in Poster, *Critical Theory and Poststructuralism* (Ithaca, N.Y.: Cornell University Press, 1989), pp. 87–103.

4. The tower corresponds to the *tablinum*, the central office from which the *pater familias* could observe his household; the cells are the various *cubicula*. See chapter 4 of my *Metaphysics and Oppression*.

5. For the three traits I am about to discuss, see *SP*, pp. 238/235f.

6. Foucault notes that Bentham first designed the panopticon to incorporate control of the auditory field as well. He abandoned the attempt when hearing proved hard to control; *SP*, p. 203 n. 2/317 n. 3.

7. Gilles Deleuze, *Foucault* (Paris: Editions de Minuit, 1986), p. 41.

8. Ibid.; Deleuze's entire discussion of Foucault's treatment of the prison is, appropriately, keyed to the ancient opposition of form and matter.

9. A view encouraged by Foucault himself: "The Panopticon is a machine for dissociating the couple see/be seen: in the peripheral ring, one is seen in totality but never sees; in the central tower, one sees everything, without ever being seen": *SP*, pp. 203/201f). The inmate is thus unable to observe the guards, or their observation of her. Only the effects of that observation on her can become known to her—when she is seen to commit an infraction, for example, and is punished.

10. And for which François Russo was already criticizing Foucault in 1970: Russo, "L'archéologie du savoir de Michel Foucault," in *Archives de philosophie* 36 (1973), pp. 69–105.

11. Cf. Aristotle, *Politics* I.7, 1255b18f; 11273a36f, 1334a18ff, 1337b30f; *Nicomachean Ethics* 1177b4ff.

12. If the prison's lack of initiative shows why it is possible for the disposing power to remain invisible, yet another (a fourth) difference between the ancient household and the panoptical prison shows why it is necessary. This resides in the prison's "modern" relation to the cosmic order—or to the modern lack of a cosmic order. The Greeks placed their acropoleis, as the medievals did their castles, on the open tops of hills. This requires explanation, for common sense tells us that a defensive position is stronger the less it is seen. The reason, presumably, is a very specific desire to impress or intimidate. The acropolis, like the castle, was located on a naturally conspicuous site because it was intended, in part, to display visibly its relation to the order of things—and in particular to suggest the divine support to which its builders were entitled. In the modern world, of course, social favors such as wealth and power have no such metaphysical or cosmic sanction. Possession of them is not grounded in the order of things; it testifies not to divine favor but (merely) to the skill and energy of the individual who possesses them. Hence, it is wiser for such possession to remain unseen. Modern centers therefore dissociate seeing and being seen because the individuals who occupy those centers are metaphysically vulnerable. Again, however, this is not the result of some incomprehensible convulsion in history—or of Being, or of power. It comes about through what I call the "eviction" of ousia from nature and from the divine realm. This leaves ousia's role in structuring the human world unsupported—as are the individuals who just happen to occupy favored positions within that world.

13. In a paradigmatic work, Nancy Fraser has located the fundamentality of Foucauldian power, though not its divine antecedents. She then assumes that he is a political philosopher and faults him for having inadequate grounds for his critique: Nancy Fraser, "Foucault on Power: Empirical Insights and Normative Confusions," in Fraser, *Unruly Practices* (Minneapolis: University of Minnesota Press, 1989), pp. 17–34. Also cf. the following from Axel Honneth: "[Foucault] was not able to provide the basis for a reflexive understanding of his critical claims, however, since [power] is conceived apart from all normative agreement and moral incentives . . ."; Axel Honneth, *The Critique of Power,* trans. Kenneth Baynes (Cambridge, Mass.: MIT Press, 1991), p. xxvii. But so it should be, if power is not the object but the *fundamental* value of Foucault's "critique."

14. This does not mean that Foucault thinks that power is good; rather, power is what he aims to vindicate as being implicated, for good *or* evil, in all human relations. Cf. Barry Allen, "Government in Foucault," in *Canadian Journal of Philosophy* 21 (1991), pp. 421–439.

15. See my *Metaphysics and Oppression: Heidegger's Challenge to Western Philosophy,* part 2.

16. *VS,* p. 112/85; see my *Metaphysics and Oppression: Heidegger's Challenge to Western Philosophy,* part 3.

17. *VS,* p. 115–117/87–89. On the modern proliferation of centers of power, see Barry Allen, "Government in Foucault," pp. 425–430.

18. Cf. Aristotle, *Nicomachean Ethics* VII.1 1145a–b.

19. It is perhaps surprising that this issue should be given so much space, and I will discuss that in the next chapter.

20. For an account of these without reference to Aristotle, see James Bernauer, *Michel Foucault's Force of Flight: Toward an Ethics for Thought* (Atlantic Highlands, N.J.: Humanities Press, 1990), pp. 107–111.

21. *AS*, p. 45/32. As Jeffrey Minson puts it: "The idea is to treat discursive materials less as representing the things on which they bear, than as means of attempting to *organize* them"; Minson, *Genealogy of Morals: Nietzsche, Foucault, Donzelot, and the Eccentricities of Ethics* (New York: St. Martin's Press, 1985), p. 124.

22. *AS*, pp. 61, 80; 74; 91/45, 60; 54; 68, where *jeu de relations* is translated as "set," rather than "play," of relations.

23. The gaps themselves, of course, are not diakenic, for their dispersal is patterned and hence *is* reducible to a higher principle: the rule itself. It is their interplay which is diakenic.

24. Heidegger, "Das Ding," in Heidegger, *Vorträge und Aufsätze*, 3 vols. (Pfullingen: Neske, 1967), vol. 2, pp. 37–55; English translation, "The Thing," in Heidegger, *Poetry, Language, Thought*, trans. Albert Hofstadter (New York: Harper and Row, 1971), pp. 163–182.

25. There is room here for a detailed examination, which I will not pursue, of the relation of Foucauldian modalities to Heideggerean sky, of Foucauldian concepts to Heideggerean earth, and of Foucauldian objects and themes to Heideggerean mortals and immortals. For the present, I will just note that Foucault's rewriting of Aristotle is more faithful than Heidegger's, for it does not omit the moving cause.

26. Gilles Deleuze, "What Is a *Dispositif*?" in Timothy J, Armstrong, trans., *Michel Foucault Philosopher* (New York: Routledge, 1992), p. 159.

27. Cf. Deleuze, *Foucault*, p. 80.

8. CHALLENGE AND DESCRIPTION IN FOUCAULT

1. The earlier concept of "episteme," for example, is said to include what *The Archeology of Knowledge*'s concept of "discursive formation" covers: *AS*, pp. 249f/191.

2. Cf. on this the observation by Gary Gutting that the analysis of the prison in *Discipline and Punish*, which I discuss above, embodies the main traits of discursive formations advanced in *The Archeology of Knowledge*: Gary Gutting, *Michel Foucault's Archeology of Scientific Knowledge* (Cambridge: Cambridge University Press, 1989), p. 270. In general I would agree with Charles Lemert and Garth Gillian that, on the one hand, *The Archeology of Knowledge* is not a summary of anything like a Foucauldian "method," since many of its basic concepts—including "archive" and "statement"— do not occur in Foucault's earlier or later works. On the other, however, it remains true that the book is ". . . a gathering up of what has gone before, and a suggestion of what [is] to come thereafter"; Lemert and Gillian, *Michel Foucault: Social Theory and Transgression* (New York: Columbia University Press, 1982), p. 48.

3. It must have the weak sense of Being that I have mentioned in the introduction in connection with Aquinas and which in connection with Derrida I identified with "presence."

4. Cf. *AS*, pp. 53/37f, and the detailed account on pp. 209f/160.

5. *AS*, p. 39/27; also cf. Jeffrey Minson, *Genealogy of Morals: Nietzsche, Foucault, Donzelot, and the Eccentricities of Ethics* (New York: St. Martin's Press, 1985), p. 130.

6. This fact is obscured if, like James Bernauer, we begin with the statement and work back to the "four causes," thus obliterating half of the circle Foucault finds

himself in: Foucault is driven to consider the statement because the "causes," as I have shown, fail. His inability to account for the unity of the statement then leads him back in the other direction. James Bernauer, *Michel Foucault's Force of Flight: Toward an Ethics for Thought* (Atlantic Highlands, N.J.: Humanities Press, 1990), pp. 104–111.

7. *AS*, pp. 191f/146f. For a helpful account of the statement's inherence on the archive, see Karlis Rascevskis, *Michel Foucault and the Subversion of Intellect* (Ithaca, N.Y.: Cornell University Press, 1983), pp. 71–73.

8. For Heidegger's account of world see Heidegger, *Sein und Zeit,* 11th ed. (Tübingen: Niemeyer, 1967), pp. 63–88; page numbers are given marginally in Heidegger, *Being and Time,* trans. John MacQuarrie and Edward Robinson (New York: Harper and Row, 1962).

9. In its complex disunity, its omnipresence, and its capacity to determine what can and cannot be said, the archive has clear affinities not only to Heideggerean world but to what Foucault will subsequently call "power." We may style "power" the analog, with reference to practices of bodily subjection, to the archive in discursive practices. Cf. *VS,* pp. 20, 122–124/11, 93f; *SP,* pp. 30–33/25–28.

10. Deleuze, *Foucault,* pp. 26, 62.

11. The problems with this are evident from the multiple evasions in Jeffrey Minson's "definition" of the related notion of "context" as ". . . the bounded group of relations which enable borrowings, exchanges, cross-references, substitutions, and complementarities. . . . Contextuality is thus pluralized and made conditional on a heterogeneous and shifting set of interdependencies." Minson, *Genealogy of Morals: Nietzsche, Foucault, Donzelot, and the Eccentricities of Ethics,* p. 133.

12. Heidegger, "Der Ursprung des Kunstwerkes," in Heidegger, *Holzwege,* 4th ed. (Frankfurt: Klostermann, 1963), pp. 7–68; English translation, Heidegger, "The Origin of the Work of Art," in Heidegger, *Poetry, Language, Thought,* trans. Albert Hofstadter (New York: Harper and Row, 1971), pp. 15–88.

13. Rascevskis puts the connection as follows: "By denying the subject his status as unifying consciousness, archeology provides access to a different reality of discourse"; Rascevskis, *Michel Foucault and the Subversion of Intellect,* pp. 79f.

14. Cf. *AS,* p. 38, 41, 65, 88, 105, 148, 150, 161, 171, 197, 209, 218, 265/26, 29, 47, 67, 79, 113, 114, 123, 130, 151, 160, 168, 203. As Alessandro Pizzorno has put it with respect to Foucault's later writings—which are concerned less with discourses than with bodies—"what stands opposed to power and ends up either free or subjected (normalized) are acts, gestures, states of mind and of body": Alessandro Pizzorno, "Foucault and the Liberal View of the Individual," in *Michel Foucault Philosopher,* trans. Timothy J. Armstrong (New York: Routledge, 1992), p. 207.

15. *AS,* p. 128/97, where *l'état libre* is translated as "in isolation"; AS, 130/99. Cf. Barry Allen, "Government in Foucault," in *Canadian Journal of Philosophy* 21 (1991), p. 439.

16. *AS,* p. 159, 161, 170, 252, 271f, 273/121, 122, 129, 193, 208f, 218.

17. Similar appeal to descriptive efficacy is found as well in the introductory volume to *The History of Sexuality,* which aims "to show how the deployments of power are directly connected to the body," and which proposes its new concept of power "not out of a speculative choice or theoretical preference, but because *in fact* it is one of the essential traits of Western societies . . ."; *VS,* pp. 135, 200/102, 151, emphasis added.

18. On Foucault's acceptance of truth for discourse, which is often overlooked or distorted by his critics, see Gary Gutting, *Michel Foucault's Archeology of Scientific Knowledge.*

19. *AS*, p. 208/159; for Aquinas, see my *Metaphysics and Oppression*, chapter 3.

20. Manfred Frank, "On Foucault's Concept of Discourse," in *Michel Foucault Philosopher*, trans. Michael J. Armstrong, pp. 112f; as Frank notes there, Foucault never resolves this contradiction. Also see Minson, *Genealogy of Morals: Nietzsche, Foucault, Donzelot, and the Eccentricities of Ethics*, pp. 130f.

21. *AS*, pp. 13, 15, 221/6 (where *multiplie* is translated as "seeking and discovering"), 7, 170.

22. As Jean-Paul Margot puts it, Foucault resolves the tension between the description which he would like to undertake and his inherited view that interpretation is infinite by interpreting, but not with a presupposition of the "surplus" of the signified over the signifier. Rather, he interprets from a standpoint of exteriority which imposes so little as to come very close to being a pure description: Margot, "Herméneutique et fiction chez M. Foucault," in *Dialogue* 23 (1984), pp. 635–648, esp. p. 641.

23. Michel Foucault, "Interview with Lucette Finas," in Foucault, *Power, Truth, and Strategies*, ed. M. Morris and P. Patton (Sydney, Australia: Feral Publications, 1979), p. 75. Fiction is both the goal ("something which does not yet exist") and the means ("all I write," to paraphrase) of Foucault's discourse. Deborah Cook sees the former but not the latter in "History as Fiction: Foucault's Politics of Truth," in *Journal of the British Society for Phenomenology* 22 (1971), pp. 139–147.

24. Thus, he does not read Greek thought about sexuality through the lens of later thought—as we today read Plato knowing that Aristotle had abolished the *chorismos* between Forms and things in time.

25. François Russo, "L'archéologie du savoir de Michel Foucault," in *Archives de philosophie* 36 (1973), pp. 69–105; the quote is from p. 100. My translation.

9. THE GREAT DEMARCATION
AND THE SITUATION OF FREEDOM

1. See the General Introduction to my *Poetic Interaction* (Chicago: University of Chicago Press, 1989).

2. Friedrich Nietzsche, *Menschliches allzu Menschliches: Ein Buch für freie Geister* (*Sämtliche Werke*, vol. 3) (Stuttgart: Kroner, 1964), p. 11; English translation, Nietzsche, *Human, All Too Human: A Book for Free Spirits*, trans. R. J. Hollingdale (Cambridge: Cambridge University Press, 1986), p. 10.

3. This view would put Derrida into proximity to Heidegger's account of the assertion in *Being and Time*, which I have discussed in my *Metaphysics and Oppression: Heidegger's Challenge to Western Philosophy*, chapter 9.

4. Claude Lelouch, *A Man and a Woman*, trans. Nicholas Fry (London: Lorimer, 1971), p. 24.

5. Thomas S. Kuhn, *The Structure of Scientific Revolutions*, 2nd. ed., rev. and enlarged (Chicago: University of Chicago Press, 1970).

6. That Rorty thinks narrative links can be created rather than found is clear from his discussion of the Proustian "contingent" association of texts, as contrasted

with the Nietzschean "dialectical" (found) association (*CIS*, p. 100). The problem is that, as a species of redescription (*CIS*, p. 101), such narrative creation is not open to argument.

7. Søren Kierkegaard, "Fear and Trembling," in Kierkegaard, *Fear and Trembling* and *the Sickness unto Death,* trans. Walter Lowrie (Garden City, N.Y.: Doubleday, 1964), pp. 26–37.

8. Emil Fackenheim, *The Jewish Bible after the Holocaust* (Bloomington: Indiana University Press, 1990), p. 73.

9. In fact, this part was played by Henri Chemin, at the time competitions director for Ford-France; Lelouch, *A Man and a Woman,* p. 88n.

10. Lelouch, *A Man and a Woman,* p. 52.

11. Lelouch, *A Man and a Woman,* p. 100.

12. Richard Rorty, *L'espoir au lieu du savoir* (Paris: Albin Michel, 1995). The optimism, together with a remarkably un-Rortyan willingness to speak for an entire country, are evident in such quotes as "L'Amérique a toujours été un pays orienté vers le futur, un pays qui se réjouit toujours de s'être inventé lui-même dans un passé relativement récent" (p. 13). Tell it to Mario Savio.

13. Lelouch, *A Man and a Woman,* p. 104.

14. Lelouch, *A Man and a Woman,* p. 35.

15. Lelouch, *A Man and a Woman,* p. 112.

16. Gaius Valerius Catullus, *Poems* IV, my translation. The Latin text, and a much more standard translation, by F. M. Cornish, can be found in *Catullus Tibullus and Pervigilium Veneris,* Loeb Classical Library (Cambridge, Mass.: Harvard University Press, 1919), pp. 4–7.

BIBLIOGRAPHY

Allen, Barry. "Government in Foucault." *Canadian Journal of Philosophy* 21 (1991): 421–439.

Aristotle. *Complete Works.* Ed. Jonathan Barnes. 2 vols. Princeton: Princeton University Press, 1984. The Bekker pagination, to which I refer throughout, is given marginally in this edition.

Armstrong, Timothy J., trans. *Michel Foucault Philosopher.* New York: Routledge, 1992.

Austin, J. L. *How to Do Things with Words.* Ed. J. O. Urmson. New York: Oxford University Press, 1965.

Bernauer, James. *Michel Foucault's Force of Flight: Toward an Ethics for Thought.* Atlantic Highlands, N.J.: Humanities Press, 1990.

Bernstein, Richard J. *Beyond Objectivism and Relativism.* Philadelphia: University of Pennsylvania Press, 1983.

Borradori, Giovanna. *The American Philosopher.* Trans. Rosanna Crocetto. Chicago: University of Chicago Press, 1994.

Braaten, Jane. *Habermas's Critical Theory of Society.* Albany, N.Y.: SUNY Press, 1991.

Caputo, John D. *Deconstruction in a Nutshell.* New York: Fordham University Press, 1997.

Catullus, Gaius Valerius. *Poems.* In *Catullus Tibullus and Pervigilium Veneris.* Loeb Classical Library. Cambridge, Mass.: Harvard University Press, 1919.

Cook, Deborah. "History as Fiction: Foucault's Politics of Truth." *Journal of the British Society for Phenomenology* 22 (1971): 139–147.

Culler, Jonathan. "Communicative Competence and Normative Force." *New German Critique* 35 (1985): 133–147.

Dallmayr, Fred. *Polis and Praxis.* Cambridge, Mass.: MIT Press, 1984.

Dallmayr, Fred R., and Thomas McCarthy, eds. *Understanding and Social Inquiry.* Notre Dame, Ind.: University of Notre Dame Press, 1977.

Davidson, Donald. "A Nice Derangement of Epitaphs." In *Truth and Interpretation: Perspectives on the Philosophy of Donald Davidson.* Ed. Ernest LePore. 433–446. New York: Blackwell, 1986.

———. *Inquiries into Truth and Interpretation.* Oxford: Clarendon, 1984.

Davidson, Donald, and Gilbert Harmon, eds. *Semantics of Natural Language*. Dordrecht: Reidel, 1972.

Deleuze, Gilles. *Foucault*. Paris: Editions de Minuit, 1986.

———. *La philosophie critique de Kant*. Paris: Presses Universitaires de France, 1963.

———. "What Is a *Dispositif*?" In *Michel Foucault Philosopher*. Trans. Timothy J. Armstrong. 159–166. New York: Routledge, 1992.

Derrida, Jacques. *La carte postale*. Paris: Flammarion, 1980; English translation, *The Post Card*. Trans. Alan Bass. Chicago: University of Chicago Press, 1987.

———. *La dissémination*. Paris: Éditions du Seuil, 1972; English translation, *Dissemination*. Trans. Barbara Johnson. Chicago: University of Chicago Press, 1981.

———. *L'écriture et la différence*. Paris: Éditions du Seuil, 1967; English translation, *Writing and Difference*. Trans. Alan Bass. Chicago: University of Chicago Press, 1978.

———. *De la grammatologie*. Paris: Minuit, 1967; English translation, *Of Grammatology*. Trans. Gayatri Chakravorty Spivak. Baltimore: Johns Hopkins Press, 1974.

———. *Limited Inc*. Ed. Gerald Graff. Evanston, Ill.: Northwestern University Press, 1988.

———. *Marges de la philosophie*. Paris: Minuit, 1972; English translation, *Margins of Philosophy*. Trans. Alan Bass. Chicago: University of Chicago Press, 1982.

———. *Positions*. Paris: Minuit, 1972; English translation, *Positions*. Trans. Alan Bass. Chicago: University of Chicago Press, 1981.

———. *Spectres de Marx*. Paris: Galilée, 1993; English translation, *Specters of Marx*. Trans. Peggy Kamuf. New York: Routledge, 1994.

———. *La vérité en peinture*. Paris: Flammarion, 1978; English translation, *The Truth in Painting*. Trans. Geoff Bennington and Ian McLeod. Chicago: University of Chicago Press, 1987.

———. *La voix et le phénomène*. Paris: Presses Universitaires de France, 1967. English translation, Derrida, *Speech and Phenomena* (David B. Allison, trans.). Evanston: Northwestern University Press, 1973.

Dews, Peter. *Logics of Disintegration*. London: Verso, 1987.

Evans, J. Claude. *Strategies of Deconstruction*. Minneapolis: University of Minnesota Press, 1991.

Fackenheim, Emil. *The Jewish Bible after the Holocaust*. Bloomington: Indiana University Press, 1990.

———. *To Mend the World*. New York: Schocken Books, 1982.

Fine, Arthur. *The Shaky Game*. Chicago: University of Chicago Press, 1986.

Foster Hal, ed. *The Anti-Aesthetic: Essays on Postmodern Culture*. Port Townsend, Wash.: Bay Press, 1983.

Foucault, Michel. *L'archéologie du savoir*. Paris: Gallimard, 1969; English translation, *The Archeology of Knowledge*. Trans. A. M. Sheridan Smith. New York: Pantheon, 1972.

———. *Foucault Live (Interviews, 1966–1984)*. Trans. John Johnston. New York: Semiotext(e), 1989.

———. *Power, Truth, and Strategies*. Ed. M. Morris and P. Patton. Sydney, Australia: Feral Publications, 1979.

———. "The Return of Morality" (interview with Gilles Barbadette and André Serla). In *Foucault Live (Interviews, 1966–1984)*, 317–331.

———. *Surveiller et punir.* Paris: Gallimard, 1975; English translation, *Discipline and Punish.* Trans. Alan Sheridan. New York: Vintage, 1979.

———. *La volonté de savoir.* Vol. 1, *Histoire de la sexualité.* Paris: Gallimard, 1976; English translation, *The History of Sexuality.* Vol. 1. Trans. Robert Hurley. New York: Vintage, 1990.

Frank, Manfred. "On Foucault's Concept of Discourse." In *Michel Foucault Philosopher.* Trans. Michael J. Armstrong. 99–116. New York: Routledge, 1992.

Fraser, Nancy. *Unruly Practices.* Minneapolis: University of Minnesota Press, 1989.

Frege, Gottlob. *Philosophical Investigations.* Ed. P. T. Geach and R. H. Stoothof. New Haven, Conn.: Yale University Press, 1977.

Gasché, Rodolphe. "Deconstruction as Criticism." In Gasché, *Inventions of Difference.* 1–21. Cambridge, Mass.: Harvard University Press, 1994.

———. *The Tain of the Mirror.* Cambridge, Mass.: Harvard University Press, 1986.

Geuss, Raymond. *The Idea of a Critical Theory.* Cambridge: Cambridge University Press, 1981.

Gutting, Gary. *Michel Foucault's Archeology of Scientific Knowledge.* Cambridge: Cambridge University Press, 1989.

Habermas, Jürgen. *Communication and the Evolution of Society.* Trans. Thomas McCarthy. Boston: Beacon Press, 1979.

———. *Erkenntnis und Interesse.* Frankfurt: Suhrkamp, 1968; English translation, *Knowledge and Human Interests.* Trans. Jeremy Shapiro. Boston: Beacon Press, 1971.

———. *Justification and Application.* Trans. Ciaran Cronin. Cambridge, Mass.: MIT Press, 1993.

———. "Modernity: An Incomplete Project." In *The Anti-Aesthetic: Essays on Postmodern Culture.* Ed. Hal Foster. 3–15. Port Townsend, Wash.: Bay Press, 1983.

———. *Moralbewußtsein und kommunikatives Handeln.* Frankfurt: Suhrkamp, 1983.

———. *Philosophisch-politische Profile.* Frankfurt: Suhrkamp, 1981.

———. *Der philosophische Diskurs der Moderne.* 2nd ed. Frankfurt: Suhrkamp, 1985; English translation, *The Philosophical Discourse of Modernity.* Trans. Frederick Lawrence. Cambridge, Mass.: MIT Press, 1987.

———. *Postmetaphysical Thinking.* Trans. William Mark Hohengarten. Cambridge, Mass.: MIT Press, 1992.

———. "A Reply to My Critics." In John B. Thompson and David Held, *Habermas: Critical Debates.* 219–283. Cambridge, Mass.: MIT Press, 1982.

———. "A Review of Gadamer's *Truth and Method.*" In *Understanding and Social Inquiry.* Ed. Fred R. Dallmayr and Thomas McCarthy. 356–361. Notre Dame, Ind.: University of Notre Dame Press, 1977.

———. "Some Distinctions in Universal Pragmatics." *Theory and Society* 3 (1976): 155–167.

———. *Theorie des kommunikativen Handelns.* 2 vols. Frankfurt/Main: Suhrkamp, 1981; English translation, *The Theory of Communicative Action* (Thomas McCarthy, trans.). Boston: Beacon Press, 1984–87.

———. "Towards a Theory of Communicative Competence." *Inquiry* 13 (1970): 360–375.

———. "Wahrheitstheorien." In *Wirklichkeit und Reflexion. Walter Schulz zum 60e Gebürtstag.* Pfullingen: Neske, 1973. 211–265.

———. "Walter Benjamin: bewußtmachende oder rettende Kritik." In Habermas, *Philosophisch-politische Profile*. 336–376. Frankfurt: Suhrkamp, 1981.

———. "Work and Weltanschauung: The Heidegger Controversy from a German Perspective." Trans. John McCumber. *Critical Inquiry* 15 (1989): 431–456.

———. *Zur Logik der Sozialwissenschaften*. Frankfurt: Suhrkamp, 1982; English translation, *On the Logic of the Social Sciences*. Trans. Shierry Weber Nicholson and Jerry Stark. Cambridge, Mass.: MIT Press, 1988.

Harvey, Irene. *Derrida and the Economy of Différance*. Bloomington: Indiana University Press, 1986.

Hegel, G. F. W. *Werke*. 20 vols. Ed. Eva Moldenhauer and Karl Markus Michel. Frankfurt: Suhrkamp, 1970–71.

———. *Phenomenology of Spirit*. (Vol. 3 of the Suhrkamp *Werke*.) Trans. A. V. Miller. Oxford: Oxford University Press, 1979.

———. *Science of Logic* (Vols. 4 and 5 of the Suhrkamp *Werke*.) Trans. A. V. Miller. New York: Humanities Press, 1976.

Heidegger, Martin. *Basic Writings*. Ed. David Krell. San Francisco: Harper and Row. 1977.

———. *Die Selbstbehauptung der deutschen Universität and Das Rektorat: 1933/34*. Frankfurt: Klostermann, 1983.

———. *Erläuterungen zu Hölderlins Dichtung*. 1st ed. Frankfurt: Klostermann, 1951.

———. *Identität und Differenz*. Pfullingen: Neske, 1957.

———. *Poetry, Language, Thought*. Trans. Albert Hofstadter. New York: Harper and Row, 1971.

———. *Sein und Zeit*. 11th ed. Tübingen: Niemeyer, 1967; English translation, *Being and Time*. Trans. John MacQuarrie and Edward Robinson. New York: Harper and Row, 1962.

———. "Der Ursprung des Kunstwerkes." In Heidegger, *Holzwege*. 4th ed. Frankfurt: Klostermann, 1963. 7–68; English translation, "The Origin of the Work of Art." In Martin Heidegger. *Poetry, Language, Thought*. Trans. Albert Hofstadter. 15–88. New York: Harper and Row, 1971.

———. *Vorträge und Aufsätze*. 3 vols. Pfullingen: Neske, 1967.

Honneth, Axel. *Critique of Power*. Trans. Kenneth Baynes. Cambridge, Mass.: MIT Press, 1991.

Honneth, Axel, et al., eds. *Zwischenbetrachtungen im Prozeß der Aufklärung*. Frankfurt: Suhrkamp, 1989.

Hoy, David Couzens, and Thomas McCarthy. *Critical Theory*. Oxford: Blackwell, 1994.

Hull, David. *Science as a Process*. Chicago: University of Chicago Press, 1988.

Hume, David. *A Treatise of Human Nature*. Ed. L. A. Selby-Bigge. Oxford: Clarendon, 1896.

Ingram, David. *Habermas and the Dialectic of Reason*. New Haven, Conn.: Yale University Press, 1987.

Irwin, Terence. *Aristotle's First Principles*. Oxford: Clarendon Press, 1988.

Johnson, Christopher. *System and Writing in the Philosophy of Jacques Derrida*. Cambridge: Cambridge University Press, 1993.

Kant, Immanuel. *Werkausgabe*. 10 vols. Ed. Wilhelm Weischiedl. Frankfurt: Suhrkamp, 1958.

Kierkegaard, Søren. *Fear and Trembling* and *The Sickness unto Death*. Trans. Walter Lowrie. Garden City, N.Y.: Doubleday, 1964.

Kolb, David. "Heidegger and Habermas on Criticism and Totality." *Philosophy and Phenomenological Research* 52 (1992): 683–693.

Kripke, Saul. "Naming and Necessity." In *Semantics of Natural Language*. Ed. Donald Davidson and Gilbert Harmon. 253–355. Dordrecht: Reidel, 1972.

Kuhn, Thomas S. *The Structure of Scientific Revolutions*. 2nd ed. rev. and enlarged. Chicago: University of Chicago Press, 1970.

Lelouch, Claude. *A Man and a Woman*. Trans. Nicholas Fry. London: Lorimer, 1971.

Lemert, Charles, and Garth Gillian. *Michel Foucault: Social Theory and Transgression*. New York: Columbia University Press, 1982.

LePore, Ernest, ed. *Truth and Interpretation: Perspectives on the Philosophy of Donald Davidson*. New York: Blackwell, 1986.

Margot, Jean-Paul. "Herméneutique et fiction chez M. Foucault." *Dialogue* 23 (1984): 635–648.

Martin, Bill. *Humanism and Its Aftermath*. Atlantic Highlands, N.J.: Humanities Press, 1995.

McCarthy, Thomas. *Ideals and Illusions: On Reconstruction and Deconstruction in Contemporary Critical Theory*. Cambridge, Mass.: MIT Press, 1991.

McCarthy, Thomas. "Philosophy and Social Practice: Avoiding the Ethnocentric Predicament." In *Zwischenbetrachtungen im Prozeß der Aufklärung*. Ed. Axel Honneth et al. 190–209. Frankfurt: Suhrkamp, 1989.

McCarthy, Thomas. *The Critical Theory of Jürgen Habermas*. Cambridge, Mass.: MIT Press, 1978.

McCumber, John. *The Company of Words*. Evanston, Ill.: Northwestern University Press, 1993.

———. "Hegel on Habit." *Owl of Minerva* 21 (1990): 155–165.

———. "Language and Appropriation: The Nature of Heideggerean Dialogue." *The Personalist* 60 (1979): 384–396.

———. *Metaphysics and Oppression: Heidegger's Challenge to Western Philosophy*. Bloomington: Indiana University Press, 1999.

———. *Poetic Interaction*. Chicago: University of Chicago Press, 1989.

———. "Reflection and Emancipation in Habermas." *Southern Journal of Philosophy* 22 (1984): 71–81.

Minson, Jeffrey. *Genealogy of Morals: Nietzsche, Foucault, Donzelot, and the Eccentricities of Ethics*. New York: St. Martin's Press, 1985.

Nietzsche, Friedrich. *Sämtliche Werke*. 12 vols. Stuttgart: Kroner, 1964.

Norris, Christopher. *Derrida*. Cambridge, Mass.: Harvard University Press, 1987.

Owens, Joseph. *The Doctrine of Being in the Aristotelian Metaphysics*. 2nd ed. rev. Toronto: Pontifical Institute of Medieval Studies, 1963.

Pizzorno, Alessandro. "Foucault and the Liberal View of the Individual." In *Michel Foucault Philosopher*. Trans. Timothy J. Armstrong. 204–211. New York: Routledge, 1992.

Poster, Mark. "Foucault and the Tyranny of Greece." In Mark Poster, *Critical Theory and Poststructuralism*. Ithaca, N.Y.: Cornell University Press, 1989. 87–103.

Prauss, Gerold. "Zum Wahrheitsproblem bei Kant." *Kant-Studien* 60 (1969): 166–182.

Putnam, Hilary. "Between the New Left and Judaism: Interview with Giovanna Borradori." In Giovanna Borradori, *The American Philosopher.* Trans. Rosanna Crocetto. 55–69. Chicago: University of Chicago Press, 1994.

———. "Why Reason Can't Be Naturalized." In Hilary Putnam, *Realism and Reason.* 235–238. Cambridge: Cambridge University Press, 1988.

Quine, W. V. O. *Pursuit of Truth.* Cambridge, Mass.: Harvard University Press, 1990.

Rajchman, John, and Cornel West, eds. *Post-Analytical Philosophy.* New York: Columbia University Press, 1985.

Rascevskis, Karlis. *Michel Foucault and the Subversion of Intellect.* Ithaca, N.Y.: Cornell University Press, 1983.

Rasmussen, David. *Reading Habermas.* Oxford: Blackwell, 1990.

Rorty, Richard. *Consequences of Pragmatism.* Minneapolis: University of Minnesota Press, 1982.

———. *Contingency, Irony, and Solidarity.* Cambridge: Cambridge University Press, 1989.

———. *L'espoir au lieu du savoir.* Paris: Albin Michel, 1995.

———. *Essays on Heidegger and Others.* Cambridge: Cambridge University Press, 1991.

———. "On Ethnocentrism: A Reply to Clifford Geertz." *Michigan Quarterly Review* 25 (1986): 525–534.

———. *Objectivity, Relativism, and Truth.* Cambridge: Cambridge University Press, 1991.

———. *Philosophy and the Mirror of Nature.* Princeton, N.J.: Princeton University Press, 1979.

Russo, François. "L'archéologie du savoir de Michel Foucault." *Archives de philosophie* 36 (1973): 69–105.

Scharff, Robert C. "Habermas on Heidegger's *Being and Time.*" *International Philosophical Quarterly* 31 (1991): 189–201.

Scruton, Roger. *Modern Philosophy.* Allen Lane: Penguin, 1994.

Silverman Hugh, ed. *Derrida and Deconstruction.* New York: Routledge, 1989.

Snodgrass, Anthony M. *Early Greek Armour and Weapons.* Edinburgh: University Press, 1964.

Thompson, John B., and David Held. *Habermas: Critical Debates.* Cambridge, Mass.: MIT Press, 1982.

White, Stephen K. *The Recent Philosophy of Jürgen Habermas.* Cambridge: Cambridge University Press, 1988.

Williams, Michael. *Unnatural Doubts: Epistemological Realism and the Basis of Scepticism.* Princeton: Princeton University Press, 1996.

Wittgenstein, Ludwig. *Philosophical Investigations.* 3rd ed. Trans. G. E. M. Ancsombe. New York: Macmillan, 1958.

INDEX

"Andenken," 45–46, 50, 76
appropriateness, 85, 94, 102, 104, 106
Aquinas, Thomas, 11, 31, 115, 134, 174*n3*
The Archeology of Knowledge, 111, 120–23,
    125–40, 174*n2*
argumentation, 16, 18, 47, 105, 106, 147; in
    analytical philosophy, 52, 53, 55; and
    reason, 52, 53, 55, 57, 58, 74, 85, 86–87;
    and Rorty, 57, 58, 68, 72, 73, 74
Aristotle, 35, 48, 71, 80, 103; compared to
    Nietzsche, 5; on form, 10, 47, 114, 117,
    118, 121, 160*n15,* 170*n14;* on four
    causes, 120, 122–23, 174*n25;* on moral
    agents, 97, 98; on ousia, 9, 10–11, 12, 13,
    14, 16, 26, 27, 112, 113–14, 118, 119–20,
    159*n5;* on *telos,* 5, 112, 113–14, 122
artificial intelligence, 55
Aufhebung, 27, 44, 72, 82, 83, 86, 89, 97–99,
    101–102, 105. *See also* Dialectic
Augustine, 80
authenticity, 20–21, 23

Being, 76–77, 110–11, 112, 114, 137–38
Being and Time, 15, 20–21, 76–77, 128–29,
    176*n3. See also* Heidegger, Martin
Benjamin, Walter, 103
Bentham, Jeremy, 111, 113, 138
Berkeley, George, 12
Bestimmung, 5
Bloom, Harold, 63
Borradori, Giovanna, 52
boundary: of analytical philosophy, 51, 52,

54, 55; of communicative action com-
    munities, 99; of Foucault's archive of
    discourse, 129; of Heideggerean world,
    77; of ironist's self, 63–64; of life world,
    100; of modern subsystems, 83–84; of
    speech communities, 58, 59; of texts,
    28–29; as trait of ousia, 8–9, 10, 12, 13,
    14, 15, 26–27, 32, 47, 51–52, 88, 99, 100,
    103, 112, 119, 129, 145–46, 151. *See also*
    ousia

Categories, 12
Catullus, 154
centrality, 151–52; and language, 81; as
    non-ousiodic, 79, 81–82, 87–88; role in
    philosophy, 80–81; of theory of commu-
    nicative action, 79, 82–83, 84–90, 96,
    104–106, 107–109, 149–51; vs. truth, 88–
    90; vs. universality, 89–90, 92–93, 95,
    106–107, 108
communicative action, theory of, 7; central-
    ity of, 79, 81–82, 84–90, 96, 104–106,
    107–109, 149–51; ousiodic structure in,
    76, 96–97, 99, 101–104, 106; relation-
    ship of reason to, 82–83, 84, 86, 89, 92,
    94, 96, 101–102; relationship to other
    social theories, 82–85, 96, 143; universal-
    ity of, 79, 83, 89–90, 91–96, 104–105,
    149–50; validity-claims in, 85–86, 89, 92,
    94–96, 97, 98, 99, 102, 103, 104, 105,
    106, 131, 169*nn3,7. See also* Habermas,
    Jürgen

JOHN McCUMBER is Professor of German at North-western University. He is author of *Poetic Interaction; The Company of Words;* and *Metaphysics and Oppression.*

Lightning Source UK Ltd.
Milton Keynes UK
UKHW021205091019

351201UK00016B/284/P